Praise for *Articulatory Phonetics*

"Life has just become less lonely for Acoustic and Auditory Phonetics. Gick, Wilson, and Derrick have given us a marvelous addition to the classroom, providing an authoritative description of speech articulation, an insightful and balanced guide to the theory of cognitive control of speech, and a highly readable introduction to the methods used in articulatory phonetics. All students of phonetics should study this book!"

Keith Johnson, University of California, Berkeley

"Gick, Wilson, and Derrick offer an engaging, comprehensive introduction to how articulation works and how it is investigated in the laboratory. This textbook fills an important gap in our training of phoneticians and speech scientists."

Patrice Beddor, University of Michigan

"A rich yet approachable source of phonetic information, this new text is well structured, well designed, and full of original diagrams."

James Scobbie, Queen Margaret University

D1263179

ARTICULATORY PHONETICS

Bryan Gick, Ian Wilson,
and Donald Derrick

⊛WILEY-BLACKWELL

A John Wiley & Sons, Ltd., Publication

This edition first published 2013
© 2013 Bryan Gick, Ian Wilson, and Donald Derrick

Blackwell Publishing was acquired by John Wiley & Sons in February 2007. Blackwell's publishing program has been merged with Wiley's global Scientific, Technical, and Medical business to form Wiley-Blackwell.

Registered Office
John Wiley & Sons Ltd, The Atrium, Southern Gate, Chichester, West Sussex, PO19 8SQ, UK

Editorial Offices
350 Main Street, Malden, MA 02148-5020, USA
9600 Garsington Road, Oxford, OX4 2DQ, UK
The Atrium, Southern Gate, Chichester, West Sussex, PO19 8SQ, UK

For details of our global editorial offices, for customer services, and for information about how to apply for permission to reuse the copyright material in this book please see our website at www.wiley.com/wiley-blackwell.

The right of Bryan Gick, Ian Wilson, and Donald Derrick to be identified as the authors of this work has been asserted in accordance with the UK Copyright, Designs and Patents Act 1988.

Library of Congress Cataloging-in-Publication Data

Gick, Bryan.
  Articulatory phonetics / Bryan Gick, Ian Wilson, and Donald Derrick.
    p. cm.
  Includes index.
  ISBN 978-1-4051-9321-4 (cloth) – ISBN 978-1-4051-9320-7 (pbk.)   1. Phonetics.   2. Speech–Physiological aspects.   3. Speech processing systems.   I. Wilson, Ian, 1966–   II. Derrick, Donald.
  P221.G48 2013
  414'.8–dc23

                    2012031381

A catalogue record for this book is available from the British Library.

Cover image: Brain scan © Photodisc. Graphic of a digital sound on black bottom. © iDesign/ Shutterstock. Active nerve cell © Sebastian Kaulitzki/Shutterstock.
Cover design by Nicki Averill Design

Set in 10.5/13 pt Palatino by Toppan Best-set Premedia Limited
Printed in Singapore by C.O.S. Printers Pte Ltd

4   2015

Table of Contents

List of Figures

Acknowledgments

We owe thanks to many people without whom this book might not exist.

For the beautiful images, thanks to Chenhao Chiu, Anna Klenin, Ekaterina Komova, Naomi Francis, Andrea Yeung, and especially to Winifred Murphey. Thanks to J. W. Rohen, C. Yokochi, and E. Lütjen-Drecoll for their *Color Atlas of Anatomy*, the photographs from which inspired us, and to W. R. Zemlin for his excellent work, *Speech and Hearing Science*. A special thanks to the countless authors and creators who produced the publicly available articles and videos that have inspired us. These resources and the detailed sourcing they provided saved countless hours of effort on our part, and made this textbook better than it would have been otherwise.

There is a great deal of original data in this book for which we owe credit to many contributors. Thanks to Dr Sayoko Takano and Mr Ichiro Fujimoto at ATR (Kyoto, Japan) for the MRI images of Ian Wilson, to Dr John Houde at the University of California (San Francisco) for the MRI images of Donald Derrick, and to Dr Elaine Orpe at the University of British Columbia School of Dentistry for the CT images of Ian Wilson. We are grateful to Dr Sverre Stausland Johnsen for the image of Norwegian lip rounding in Chapter 10, to Dr Richard Watts for fMRI data used in Figure 2.9, and to Chenhao Chiu for EMG data used in Figure 3.6. Many thanks to Dr Amanda Miller for the click data upon which the click images in Chapter 11 are based. Special thanks to Jenggu Rooi Fransisko, speaker of Mangetti Dune !Xung, whose speech provided the information for those click images. We are grateful to Scott Moisik, Dr John Esling, and colleagues for the use of their high-speed laryngoscope data in Chapters 5 and 6, and to Dr Penelope Bacsfalvi for her helpful input on cleft palate speech in Chapter 7.

We are grateful to the phonetics students at the 2009 LSA Linguistic Institute at UC Berkeley, and to generations of Linguistics and Speech Science students at the University of British Columbia (Department of

Linguistics) for patiently working with earlier, rougher versions of this book. In particular, thanks to the UBC Linguistics 316 students for helpful feedback, and many thanks to Taucha Gretzinger and Priscilla Riegel for detailed comments on the very early drafts of the textbook.

Thanks to Dr Guy Carden for teaching all of us about speech science and for developing the original clay tongue exercise we have modified for this text, and to Vocal Process (UK) for the idea of creating a paper larynx exercise. Special thanks to Chenhao Chiu for pulling together the chapter assignments from various sources and cleaning them up, and for contributions and suggestions throughout the text.

We couldn't have done it without Danielle Descoteaux and Julia Kirk at Wiley-Blackwell, as well as the anonymous reviewers. This book is the result of a dynamic collaborative process; we the authors jointly reserve responsibility for all inconsistencies, oversights, errors, and omissions.

At many junctures in this book there simply were not satisfying answers to even quite basic questions. As such, we have done a good deal of original research to confirm or underscore many points in this book. Part of this research was funded by a Discovery Grant from the Natural Sciences and Engineering Council of Canada (NSERC) to Bryan Gick, by National Institutes of Health (NIH) Grant DC-02717 to Haskins Laboratories, and by Japan Society for the Promotion of Science (JSPS) "kakenhi" grant 19520355 to Ian Wilson.

Finally, to our families and loved ones who have sacrificed so many hours together and provided support in so many ways in the creation of this textbook . . . Thank you!

Introduction

The goal of this book is to provide a short, non-technical introduction to articulatory phonetics. We focus especially on (1) the basic anatomy and physiology of speech, (2) how different kinds of speech sounds are made, and (3) how to measure the vocal tract to learn about these speech sounds. This book was conceived of and written to function as a companion to Keith Johnson's *Acoustic and Auditory Phonetics* (also published by Wiley-Blackwell). It is intended as a supplement or follow-up to a general introduction to phonetics or speech science for students of linguistic phonetics, speech science, and the psychology of speech.

Part I of this book, entitled "Getting to Sounds," leads the reader through the speech production system up to the point where simple vocal sounds are produced. Chapter 1 introduces the speech chain and basic terms and concepts that will be useful in the rest of the book; this chapter also introduces anatomical terminology and an overview of tools used to measure anatomy. Chapters 2 and 3 walk the reader from thought to action, starting with the brain in Chapter 2, following through the peripheral nervous system and ending with muscle movement in Chapter 3. Chapter 4 continues from muscle action to airflow, describing respiratory anatomy and physiology. Chapter 5 moves from airflow to sound by describing laryngeal anatomy and physiology and introducing basic phonation.

Part II, entitled "Articulating Sounds," continues through the speech system, introducing more anatomy and tools along the way, but giving more focus to particular sounds of speech. Chapter 6 introduces more advanced phonation types and airstream mechanisms, and describes the hyoid bone and supporting muscles. Chapter 7 introduces the nasopharynx, skull, and palate, and the sphincter mechanisms that allow the description of velic sounds. Chapter 8 describes how vowel sounds are made, introducing the jaw and jaw muscles, and the extrinsic muscles of the tongue, with special emphasis on hydrostatics and the inverse problem of speech. Chapter 9 describes how lingual consonant sounds are made, introducing the intrinsic muscles of the tongue and the concepts of ballistics, overshoot, and constriction degree and location. Chapter 10 covers labial sounds, introducing lip and face anatomy and the visual modality in speech. Chapter 11 wraps up by considering what happens when we combine the articulations discussed throughout the book. It starts by talking about context-sensitive versus context-invariant models of coordinating sounds, describes complex sounds including liquids and clicks, and finishes with coarticulation. At the very end of the book, there is a list of all abbreviations used, as well as a table of muscles with their innervations and attachment points. While this book follows a logical flow, it is possible to cover some parts in a different order. In particular, Chapter 2, which deals with the brain, is designed so that it can be read either in the order presented, or at the end of the book.

While there is very little math in this textbook, many of the questions and assignments at the end of each chapter and in the online material (www.wiley.com/go/articulatoryphonetics) require making measurements, and often require a basic knowledge of descriptive statistics and the use of t-tests. Students who study articulatory phonetics are strongly encouraged to study statistics for psychological or motor behavior experiments, as our field often requires the use of more complex statistics such as those offered in more advanced courses.

One important note about this book: some traditions identify articulatory phonetics with a general description of how sounds are made, or with a focus on recognizing, producing or transcribing sounds using systems such as the International Phonetic Alphabet (IPA). We do not. Rather, this textbook sets out to give students the basic content and conceptual grounding they will need to understand how articulation works, and to navigate the kinds of research conducted by practitioners in the field of articulatory phonetics. IPA symbols are used throughout the text, and students are expected to use other sources to learn how to pronounce such sounds and transcribe acoustic data.

Semi-related stuff in boxes

Our textbook includes semi-related topics in gray boxes. These boxes give us a place to point out some of the many interesting side notes relating to articulatory phonetics that we would otherwise not have the space to cover. Don't be surprised if you find that the boxes contain some of the most interesting material in this book.

Part I
Getting to Sounds

Chapter 1

The Speech System and Basic Anatomy

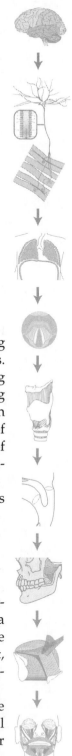

Sound is movement. You can see or feel an object even if it – and everything around it – is perfectly still, but you can only hear an object when it moves. When things move, they sometimes create disturbances in the surrounding air that can, in turn, move the eardrum, giving us the sensation of hearing (Keith Johnson's *Acoustic and Auditory Phonetics* discusses this topic in detail). In order to understand the sounds of speech (the central goal of phonetics as a whole), we must first understand how the different parts of the human body move to produce those sounds (the central goal of articulatory phonetics).

This chapter describes the roadmap we follow in this book, as well as some of the background basics you'll need to know.

1.1 The Speech Chain

Traditionally, scientists have described the process of producing and perceiving speech in terms of a mostly feed-forward system, represented by a linear speech chain (Denes and Pinson, 1993). A *feed-forward* system is one in which a plan (in this case a speech plan) is constructed and carried out, without paying attention to the results. If you were to draw a map of a feed-forward system, all the arrows would go in one direction (see Figure 1.1).

Thus, in a feed-forward *speech chain* model, a speaker's thoughts are converted into linguistic representations, which are organized into vocal tract movements – *articulations* – that produce acoustic output. A listener

Articulatory Phonetics, First Edition. Bryan Gick, Ian Wilson, and Donald Derrick.
© 2013 Bryan Gick, Ian Wilson, and Donald Derrick. Published 2013 by Blackwell Publishing Ltd.

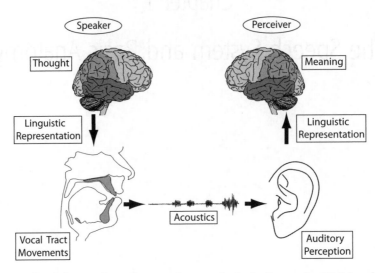

Figure 1.1   Feed-forward, auditory-only speech chain (image by W. Murphey and A. Yeung).

can then pick up this acoustic signal through hearing, or *audition*, after which it is perceived by the brain, converted into abstract linguistic representations and, finally, meaning.

Although the simplicity of a feed-forward model is appealing, we know that producing speech is not strictly linear and unidirectional. Rather, when we speak, we are also constantly monitoring and adjusting what we're doing as we move along the chain. We do this by using our senses to perceive what we are doing. This is called *feedback*. In a feedback system, control is based on observed results, rather than on a predetermined plan. The relationship between feedforward and feedback control in speech is complex. Also, speech perception feedback is *multimodal*. That is, we use not just our sense of hearing when we perceive and produce speech, but all of our sense modalities – even some you may not have heard of before. Thus, while the speech chain as a whole is generally linear, each link in the chain – and each step in the process of speech communication – is a loop (see Figure 1.2). We can think of each link of the chain as a *feedback loop*.

Multimodality and feedback

Speech production uses many different sensory mechanisms for feedback. The most commonly known feedback in speech is auditory feedback, though many senses are important in providing feedback in speech.

(Continued)

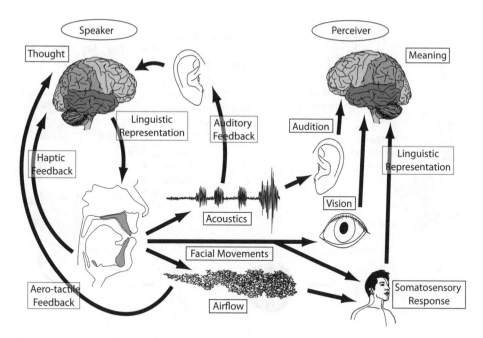

Figure 1.2 Multimodal speech chain with feedback loops (image by W. Murphey and A. Yeung).

Speech is often thought of largely in terms of sound. Sound is indeed an efficient medium for sharing information: it can be disconnected from its source, can travel a long distance through and around objects, and so on. As such, sound is a powerful modality for communication. Likewise, *auditory feedback* from sound provides a speaker with a constant flow of feedback about his or her speech.

Speech can also be perceived *visually*, by watching movements of the face and body. However, because one cannot normally see oneself speaking, vision is of little use for providing speech feedback from one's own articulators.

The *tactile*, or touch, senses can also be used to perceive speech. For example, perceivers are able to pick up *vibrotactile* and *aero-tactile* information from others' vibrations and airflow, respectively. Tactile information from one's own body can also be used as feedback. A related sense is the sense of *proprioception* (also known as *kinesthetic sense*), or the sense of body position and movement. The senses of touch and proprioception are often combined under the single term *haptic* (Greek, "grasp").

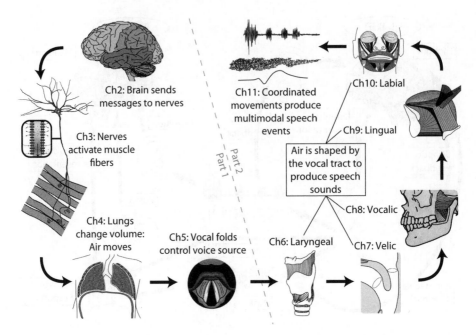

Figure 1.3 Speech production chain; the first half (left) takes you through Part I of the book, and the second half (right) covers Part II (image by D. Derrick and W. Murphey).

1.1.1   The speech production chain

Because this textbook is about articulatory phonetics, we'll focus mainly on the first part of the speech chain, just up to where speech sounds leave the mouth. This part of the chain has been called the *speech production chain* (see Figure 1.3). For simplicity's sake, this book will use a roadmap that follows along this feed-forward model of speech production, starting with the brain and moving in turn through the processes involved in making different speech sounds.

This is often how we think of speech: our brains come up with a speech plan, which is then sent through our bodies as nerve impulses. These nerve impulses reach muscles, causing them to contract. Muscle movements expand and contract our lungs, allowing us to move air. This air moves through our vocal tract, which we can shape with more muscle movements. By changing the shape of our vocal tract, we can block or release airflow, create vibrations or turbulence, change frequencies or resonances, and so on, all of which produce different speech sounds. The sound, air, vibrations and movements we produce through these actions can then be perceived by ourselves (through feedback) or by other people as speech.

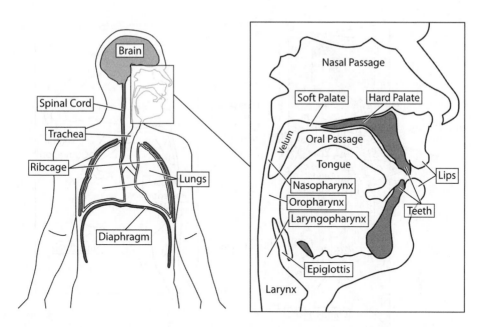

Figure 1.4 Anatomy overview: full body (left), vocal tract (right) (image by D. Derrick).

1.2 The Building Blocks of Articulatory Phonetics

The field of articulatory phonetics is all about the movements we make when we speak. So, in order to understand articulatory phonetics, you'll need to learn a good deal of anatomy. Figure 1.4 shows an overview of speech production anatomy. The speech production chain begins with the brain and other parts of the nervous system, and continues with the respiratory system, composed of the ribcage, lungs, trachea, and all the supporting muscles. Above the trachea is the larynx, and above that the pharynx, which is divided into the laryngeal, oral, and nasal parts. The upper vocal tract includes the nasal passages, and also the oral passage, which includes structures of the mouth such as the tongue and palate. The oral passage opens to the teeth and lips. The face is also intricately connected to the rest of the vocal tract, and is an important part of the visual and tactile communication of speech.

Scientists use many terms to describe anatomical structures, and anatomy diagrams often represent anatomical information along two-dimensional slices or planes (see Figure 1.5). A *midsagittal* plane divides a body down the middle into two halves: *dextrad* (Latin, "rightward") and *sinistrad* (Latin,

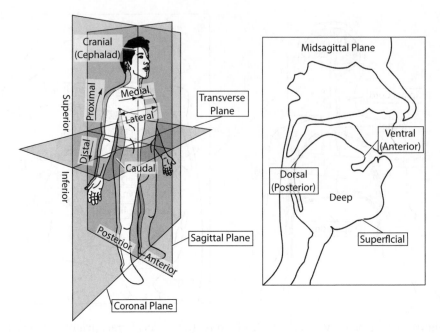

Figure 1.5   Anatomical planes and spatial relationships: full body (left), vocal tract (right) (image by D. Derrick).

"leftward"). The two axes of the *sagittal* plane are (a) vertical and (b) anterior-posterior. Midsagittal slices run down the midline of the body and are the most common cross-sections seen in articulatory phonetics. Structures near this midline are called *medial* or *mesial*, and structures along the edge are called *lateral*.

Coronal slices cut the body into *anterior* (front) and *posterior* (back) parts. The two axes of the *coronal* plane are (a) vertical and (b) side-to-side.

The *transverse* plane is horizontal, and cuts a body into *superior* (top) and *inferior* (bottom) parts.

The direction of the head is *cranial* or *cephalad*, and the direction of the tail is *caudal*. Also, *ventral* refers to the belly, and *dorsal* refers to the back. So, for creatures like humans that stand in an upright position, ventral is equivalent to anterior, and dorsal is equivalent to posterior. There are also terms that refer to locations relative to a center point rather than planes. Areas closer to the trunk are called *proximal*, while areas away from the trunk, like hands and feet, are *distal*.

Finally, structures in the body can also be described in terms of depth, with *superficial* structures being nearer the skin surface, and *deep* structures being closer to the center of the body.

1.2.1   Materials in the body

Anatomical structures are made up of several materials. Nerves make up the nervous system, and will be discussed in Chapters 2 and 3. As we are mostly interested in movement in this book, though, we'll mainly be learning about bones and muscles.

The "hard parts" of the body are made up of bones and cartilages. Bony, or *osseous* material is the hardest. The skull, ribs, and vertebrae are all composed of *bone*. These bones form the support structure of the vocal tract. *Cartilaginous* or *chondral* (Greek, "cartilage, grain") material is composed of semi-flexible material called *cartilage*. Cartilage is what makes up the stiff but flexible parts you can feel in your ears and nose. The larynx and ribcage contain several important cartilages for speech. Bones and cartilages are also the "hard parts" in the sense that you need to memorize their names, whereas most muscles are just named according to which hard parts they are attached to. For these reasons, we usually learn about the hard parts first, and then proceed to the muscles.

Muscles are made up of long strings of cells that have the specialized ability to contract (we'll look in more detail at how muscles work in Chapter 3). The word "muscle" comes from the Latin *musculus*, meaning "little mouse" (when you look at your biceps, it's not hard to imagine it's a little mouse moving under your skin!). In this textbook we'll study only striated, or skeletal, muscles. *Striated muscles* are often named by combining their *origin*, which is the larger, unmoving structure (usually a bone) to which they attach, and their *insertion*, which is usually the part that moves most when a muscle contracts. Many muscle names take the form "origin-insertion." For example, the muscle that originates at the *palate* and inserts in the *pharynx* is called the "palatopharyngeus" muscle (this is a real muscle you'll learn about later)! As you can see, if you know the origin and insertion of a muscle, then in many cases, you can guess its name.

Muscles seldom act alone. Most of the time, they interact in agonist-antagonist pairs. The *agonist* produces the main movement of an articulator, while the *antagonist* pulls in the opposite direction, lending control to the primary movement. Other muscles may also act as *synergists*. A synergist does not create movement, but lends stability to the system by preventing other unwanted motion.

Depending on whether a muscle is attached closer to or farther from a joint, it can have a higher or lower *mechanical advantage*. A muscle attached farther from a joint has a higher mechanical advantage, giving the muscle greater strength, but less speed and a smaller range of motion. A muscle attached closer to a joint has a lower mechanical advantage, reducing power but increasing speed and range of motion.

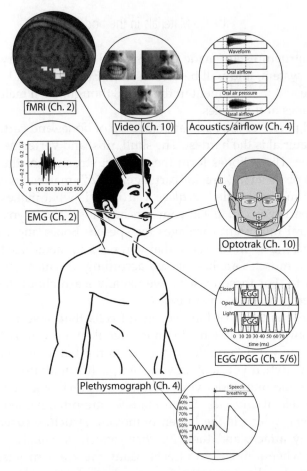

Figure 1.6a   Measurement Tools for Articulatory Phonetics (image by D. Derrick).

1.3   The Tools of Articulatory Phonetics

Scientists interested in articulatory phonetics use a wide array of tools to track and measure the movements of articulators. Some of these tools are shown in Figures 1.6a and 1.6b, including examples of data obtained using each tool. Each tool has important advantages and disadvantages, including time and space resolution, subject comfort, availability and setup time, data storage and analysis, and expense. The issues related to each tool are discussed in depth in their respective chapters.

Decades ago, when graphical computer games first came out, the objects on the screen made choppy movements and looked blocky. Their movements were choppy because it took a long time for early computers to redraw images on the screen, indicating poor temporal resolution. *Temporal resolution* is a term for how often an event happens, such as how often a

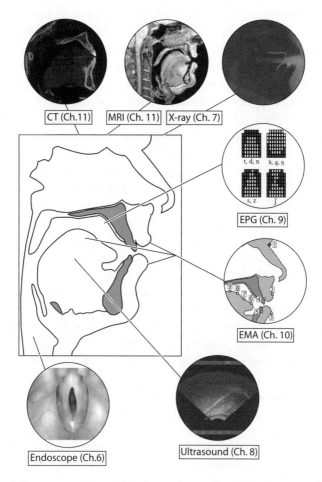

Figure 1.6b Measurement Tools for Articulatory Phonetics (image by D. Derrick).

recording, or sample, is taken. The term "temporal resolution" is often interchangeable with "sampling rate," and is often measured in samples per second, or *Hertz* (Hz). The "blocky" look was because only a few square pixels were used to represent an object, indicating low spatial resolution. From a measurement point of view, *spatial resolution* can be thought of as a term for how accurately you can identify or represent a specific location in space. Temporal and spatial resolution both draw on a computer's memory, as one involves recording more detail in time and the other requires recording more detail in space. Because of this, temporal and spatial resolution normally trade off, such that when one increases, the other will often decrease.

Many of the data-recording tools we'll look at in this book are ones that researchers use to measure anatomy relatively directly: imaging devices and point-tracking devices. *Imaging* devices take "pictures" of body structures, so that they tend to show more spatial detail, but often run more slowly than other kinds of devices. For example, using current ultrasound or x-ray technology, a two-dimensional view of the tongue can be captured no faster than about 100 times per second, but a more common rate is about 30 times per second, as in standard movie-quality video (relatively low temporal resolution). These tools allow the measurement of slower articulator motion but show a picture of an entire section of the vocal tract (high spatial resolution). Imaging tools we'll look at in this book include: functional magnetic resonance imaging (fMRI), positron emission tomography (PET), and electroencephalography (EEG) (Chapter 2); endoscopy (Chapter 6); x-ray film (Chapter 7); ultrasound (Chapter 8); electropalatography (EPG) (Chapter 9); video (Chapter 10); and computed tomography (CT) and magnetic resonance imaging (MRI) (Chapter 11). While most of these produce 2D images, some of them, such as CT and MRI, provide many slices of 2D information that can be combined to create 3D shapes. Electropalatography (EPG), which shows tongue-palate contact, has the highest temporal resolution of the imaging tools, but records only a few dozen points, giving it the lowest spatial resolution.

Unlike imaging devices, *point-tracking* systems track the motion of a small number of fixed points or markers very accurately, giving them high spatial resolution for only those points, and they can often capture this information at 1000 or more times per second, giving them high temporal resolution as well. Optotrak, Vicon MX, x-ray microbeam, and electromagnetic articulometers (EMA) (all discussed in Chapter 10) are all point-tracking systems.

We'll also look at other measurement devices in this book. These typically have higher temporal resolution, but may not directly convey any spatial information at all. For instance, a CD-quality sound file contains audio information captured 44,100 times per second. Electromyographs (EMG) (Chapter 3), airflow meters, plethysmographs (Chapter 4), and electroglottographs (EGG) (Chapter 5) are other measurement tools that can capture information at many thousands of times per second.

Now that we have some basic background, and an idea of where we're headed, the next chapter will start with the central nervous system, looking at the first steps of how the brain converts ideas into movement commands.

Exercises

Sufficient jargon

Define the following terms: feed-forward, speech chain, articulations, audition, feedback, multimodal, feedback loop, auditory feedback, vibrotactile feedback, aero-tactile feedback, proprioception (kinesthetic sense), haptic, speech production chain, midsagittal, dextrad, sinistrad, sagittal plane, medial (mesial), lateral, coronal plane, anterior, posterior, transverse plane, superior, inferior, cranial (cephalad), caudal, ventral, dorsal, proximal, distal, superficial, deep, bone (osseous), cartilage (chondral), striated muscle, origin, insertion, agonist, antagonist, synergist, mechanical advantage, temporal resolution, spatial resolution, imaging devices, point-tracking systems.

Short-answer questions

1 Which anatomical plane(s) can show parts of both eyes in the same plane?
2 When perceiving speech, one can use vision as well as audition. List ten English consonants that normally provide clearly visible cues (use IPA where possible; where the IPA character is not available on a standard keyboard, standard English digraphs and/or broad phonetic descriptions are acceptable; for example, some English vowels could be listed as follows: a, u, lax u, open o, schwa, caret).
3 The *sternohyoid* muscle connects the *sternum* (a bone in the chest) and the *hyoid* (a bone in the neck). Which of these bones is the origin? Which is the insertion? What do you think is the name of the muscle that originates at the sternum and inserts into the *thyroid* (a cartilage in the neck)? What muscle originates at the thyroid cartilage and inserts into the hyoid bone? If the *palatoglossus* muscle runs between the palate and the tongue, what muscle inserts into the tongue and originates at the hyoid bone?
4 According to the above definition of spatial resolution, rank the following tools in terms of their spatial resolution (from lowest to highest): electropalatograph, Optotrak, ultrasound.

References

Denes, P. B. and Pinson, E. N. (1993). *The Speech Chain: The Physics and Biology of Spoken Language* (2nd edition). New York: W. H. Freeman.
Johnson, K. (2011). *Acoustic and Auditory Phonetics* (3rd edition). Chichester, UK: Wiley-Blackwell.

Chapter 2

Where It All Starts: The Central Nervous System

Think before you speak! It takes commands from the brain to start the vocal tract moving to create speech. This chapter describes the brain and the way signals are sent out when you want to move your body. To understand how this happens, we will need to learn about the parts of the central nervous system: the brain and the spinal cord.

2.1 The Basic Units of the Nervous System

Before we can understand how humans produce the sounds they use to communicate, we'll first need to discuss how messages get communicated within the body. This means getting acquainted with the basic parts of the nervous system. The nervous system is segmented into two main parts: the central nervous system and the peripheral nervous system (see Figure 2.1). The *central nervous system* (CNS) includes the brain and spinal cord. The *peripheral nervous system* (PNS) encompasses a widely distributed network that runs throughout the organs and muscles of the body, allowing the body to communicate and coordinate with the brain.

Given the complexity of the nervous system, you may be surprised to learn that the entire nervous system is composed of only two types of cells: *neurons* (electrically active cells that collect and transmit information throughout the body) and *glia* (surrounding cells that perform various

Articulatory Phonetics, First Edition. Bryan Gick, Ian Wilson, and Donald Derrick.
© 2013 Bryan Gick, Ian Wilson, and Donald Derrick. Published 2013 by Blackwell Publishing Ltd.

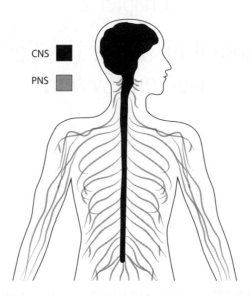

Figure 2.1 Central nervous system (CNS) versus peripheral nervous system: coronal view with sagittal head view (PNS) (image by A. Klenin).

supporting roles for neurons). For the purposes of this book, we will only need to discuss neurons.

Neurons are highly compartmentalized cells, meaning that different parts of the cells have distinct functions. Neurons typically have three parts: dendrites, a cell body, and an axon (see Figure 2.2). *Dendrites* (Greek, "tree-like"), the in-roads of a neuron, are short branches that pick up signals from other neurons and carry them to the nucleus. The *cell body*, also called the *soma* (Greek, "body"), contains the cell's nucleus; it acts as the control center, processing signals brought in by the dendrites and sending new signals out along the axon. The *axon* (Greek, "axis") is a neuron's out-road, a single branch of varying length and width that carries signals out to other cells (either muscle cells or other neurons). Some axons are made for distance, and are covered in a protective *myelin sheath*. This fatty, white myelin sheath insulates the axon and allows signals to transmit at maximum strength and speed, and so helps with long-distance travel (a single axon can stretch all the way from the spinal cord to the bottom of the feet!). Axons end in several terminals that nearly touch the dendrites of other neurons. The tiny space between one neuron's *axon terminal* and another neuron's dendrite is called a *synapse* (Greek, "junction"). Neurons communicate by sending chemicals from the axon terminals into the synapses, which in turn stimulate the dendrites of the next neuron. It is through these synaptic connections that neurons can communicate with each other, enabling them to function as a system.

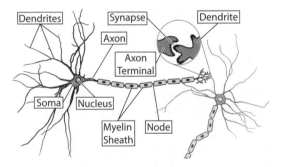

Figure 2.2   A myelinated neuron (image by D. Derrick).

It's all gray and white

You've probably heard of the "gray matter" and "white matter" in the brain. By itself, the tissue that makes up the nervous system appears gray. However, some parts of the nervous system appear whitish because they contain a large proportion of neurons with myelin coatings on the axons.

The white-colored parts – the long strings of protected nerves that function as the body's "information highways" or "wires" – can be called either nerves or tracts. *Nerves* and *tracts* are more or less the same thing, both being bundles of neurons with myelinated axons; however, tracts are located in the CNS while nerves are located in the PNS.

The gray-colored parts of the nervous system – the clusters of nerves that act as "information centers" or "computers" in the body – can be called either *nuclei* or *ganglia* (singular *ganglion*; Greek, "tumor"). As with nerves and tracts, nuclei and ganglia are pretty much the same things, except that nuclei are in the CNS while ganglia are (usually) in the PNS.

Now, back to gray matter vs. white matter. Normally, the terms "gray matter" and "white matter" only refer to parts of the brain. Thus, *white matter* refers only to tracts: brain areas with a high concentration of axons covered in myelin. *Gray matter*, on the other hand, refers to nuclei: brain areas with high neuron cell body density (in particular the outer layer, or cortex, of the brain).

So, in the rest of this book, just remember: when we're talking about tracts and nuclei, we're usually talking about the brain; and when we're talking about nerves and ganglia, we're usually talking about the body (Warning: a notable exception to this rule is the basal ganglia, which is part of the brain! – more on this in Section 2.2.1.3).

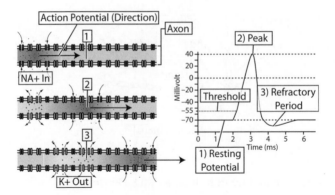

Figure 2.3 An action potential and its chemical reactions (image by D. Derrick).

2.1.1 The action potential: how the nervous system communicates

Axons are the nervous system's wires, transmitting information via an electrical impulse, or *action potential*. Action potentials are passed along by local chemical reactions that transfer electrically charged ions across the axon's cell membrane (Barnett and Larkman, 2007) (see Figure 2.3). This movement is analogous to doing "the wave" at a sports game: the wave itself moves all the way around the stadium, even though each individual stays in their place as they raise and lower their arms (similar to the opening and closing of the channels).

An axon at rest is filled with positively charged potassium and negatively charged particles, or *anions*, while on the outside it is surrounded by a salty solution containing positively charged sodium. When the axon is at rest, the net charge inside is negative, while the net charge outside is positive. This balance – with potassium on the inside and sodium on the outside – is maintained by the cell membrane. When part of an axon receives an electrical impulse that is at least as high as a *threshold*, tiny sodium gateways, or channels, open in that part of the axon, allowing sodium to rush from the outside to the inside. This influx of positively charged sodium changes the axon's electric charge, or potential, from negative to positive. Once the axon nears its peak positive potential, potassium channels open allowing positively charged potassium ions to flow from the inside of the axon to the outside. When the axon loses this positive charge, its potential becomes more negative once again. After this exchange, the system returns to near-baseline, with a net negative charge inside the axon, but now the sodium and potassium in this part of the axon have switched places, with sodium on the inside and potassium on the outside! During the next and final phase of the process, called the *refractory period*, tiny pumps exchange sodium and potassium, and the system returns to rest. During the refractory period, the sodium and potassium channels stay closed at that segment of the axon, so that each time this reaction takes place, it passes the action potential a little farther along the axon; this is how an electric charge moves along the axon, even though the chemical changes all occur locally.

Firing range

The length of time it takes for neurons to restore their electrochemical balance, or refractory period, limits the rate at which the neurons can fire. Each neuron can fire at 200 times per second – and as fast as 1000 times per second in specialized neurons.

Also, the speed of an impulse moving along an axon varies, depending on axon thickness and the thickness of the myelin sheath: potentials travel faster in thicker axons with more insulation. In motor neurons with 12 μm-thick axons, potentials travel at around 70 m/s, while potentials travel much faster, at 120 m/s, in motor neurons with 20 μm-thick axons (Kiernan, 1998).

Why do potentials travel so fast along myelinated neurons? It's because of saltatory conduction. *Saltatory conduction* (Tasaki, 1939; Huxley and Stämpfli, 1949) (from Latin *saltare*, "leap," related to the "-sault" part of the English word "somersault") happens when the impulse in an axon jumps along a myelinated neuron from one node to the next, skipping past the slower chemical transfers needed to propagate the impulse within the axon.

2.2 The Central Nervous System

The brain, which dominates the CNS, controls every aspect of articulation. It is where concepts and utterances are formed, and where motor plans are created and sent out to the body to become the movements we use to communicate. The brain also receives and processes communicative information from our environment.

Although this is a book about articulating speech sounds, perception is an important part of articulation: just as we pick up information from others, we pick up similar information from within ourselves, monitoring and adjusting our own production through perceptual feedback systems. For this reason, we'll review language areas of the brain that are considered important both for production and perception.

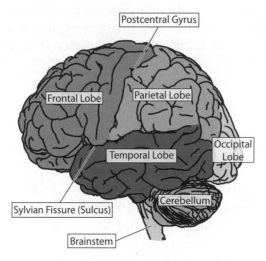

Figure 2.4a Gross anatomy of the brain: left side view of gyri, sulci, and lobes (image by A. Yeung).

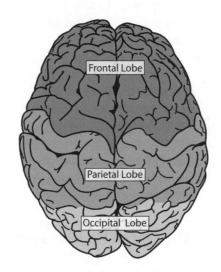

Figure 2.4b Gross anatomy of the brain: top view (image by E. Komova).

The main part of the brain is called the *cerebrum* (Latin, "brain"). One of the most striking features of the cerebrum is the wrinkled or convoluted appearance of its outer layer, or *cortex* (Latin, "bark"). Deeper parts of the brain include subcortical structures, the cerebellum, and the brainstem. We'll discuss all of these areas in Section 2.2.1, and you can see where they are in Figures 2.4a and 2.4b. The cerebral cortex controls many of the "higher" brain functions of humans, and its size has steadily increased over the course of human evolution.

Huge head or wrinkly cortex?

The area of an average modern human cortex is about 2500 cm². To accommodate such a large cortex, however, humans would need to have huge heads, over 50 cm in diameter! Besides being incredibly cumbersome, such gargantuan heads would introduce more immediate problems for reproduction: such giant-headed humans would produce babies that would never have fit through the human birth canal. Nature's solution: wrinkles! A brain with a wrinkled surface can have a greater surface area without the need to increase the size of the skull. It also allows unrelated areas to be physically closer to each other, aiding parallel processing.

The bumpy curves or ridges in the cortex are called *gyri* (singular *gyrus*; via Latin, from Greek "ring") while the valleys or spaces between the gyri are known as *sulci* (singular *sulcus*; Latin "wrinkle"). The term *fissure* is also used to describe long and deep sulci. The width and angles of the convolutions may vary from person to person, but the overall pattern remains the same.

The *longitudinal fissure* is the longest and deepest sulcus in the brain. It runs sagittally along the brain, splitting it into two symmetrical hemispheres (left and right, of course). Although the two hemispheres look somewhat alike, the brain is actually lateralized, meaning that each half is responsible for different functions. For example, the right half of the brain controls the muscles on the left side of the body, and vice versa. Another example of lateralization is that at least three quarters of humans have language specialization in the left hemisphere. For those people, though, the right hemisphere handles prosody. We'll talk more about speech areas in the brain in Section 2.2.1. Each hemisphere created by the longitudinal fissure is subdivided into four *lobes* (via Latin, from Greek "pod"): the frontal lobe, the parietal lobe, the temporal lobe, and the occipital lobe.

The *frontal lobe* is the most anterior of the four lobes, covering much of the front part of the brain. The frontal lobe extends from the anterior tip of the brain back to a deep rift called the *central sulcus*, which splits each hemisphere, more or less, into front and back parts. The lower boundary of the frontal lobe is the *Sylvian fissure (lateral sulcus)*, a deep sulcus that runs front-to-back along the lateral surface of the cortex.

The *parietal* (Latin, "wall") *lobe* covers much of the dorsal surface of the brain. It begins posterior to the central sulcus and extends back to the occipital lobe (there are no distinct sulci segregating the parietal lobe from the occipital lobe so don't worry about knowing exactly where the parietal lobe ends). Similar to the frontal lobe, the ventral border of the parietal lobe is the Sylvian fissure.

The *temporal* (Latin, pertaining to the "temples" on the sides of the head) *lobe* covers the lateral surface of the brain, below the frontal and parietal lobes (i.e., bounded above by the Sylvian fissure) and anterior to the occipital lobe (which again, does not have a distinct landmark).

The boundaries of the *occipital* (Latin, *ob-* "opposite" + *caput* "top, head") *lobe* are not as distinguishable as the boundaries of the other three lobes, but this small lobe is the most posterior of the four.

2.2.1   Speech areas in the brain

It is a common misconception that there is a one-to-one relationship between brain areas and their functions. That is, it's often assumed that there is exactly one place in the brain for processing vision, one for smelling, one for language, and so on. In fact, most brain functions are far more complicated and interconnected than that, and speech is no exception. Speech and language areas are widely distributed throughout the brain, with important centers in every part of the brain.

Because of the highly distributed way the brain works, it is impossible to trace a single, clean line starting with a thought and ending with language output. However, let's consider first some of the "higher-level" language-related functions of the brain that take place in the cortex. Later, we'll look at some "lower-level" functions that take place below the cortex.

2.2.1.1   The language zone   The areas of the cortex most frequently associated with language are located in the *perisylvian language zone* of the dominant language hemisphere (almost always the left hemisphere, which controls speech for 96% of right-handed people, and 70% of left-handed people; Stemmer and Whitaker, 2008). "Perisylvian" refers to areas around the Sylvian fissure, including: the auditory cortex, Wernicke's area, Broca's area, and the angular gyrus (see Figure 2.5).

In speech perception, information about sounds is processed first mainly by the *auditory cortex*. The auditory cortex is located bilaterally on the *superior temporal gyrus* (STG), within the Sylvian fissure. The auditory cortex primarily processes auditory information, but it has also been shown to respond to visual information from faces during lip reading, as well as to some somatosensory information (e.g., in macaques; Fu *et al.*, 2003).

After being processed in the auditory cortex, speech information is sent to *Wernicke's area*, a brain region considered largely responsible for conscious speech comprehension. Wernicke's area is located on the left STG,

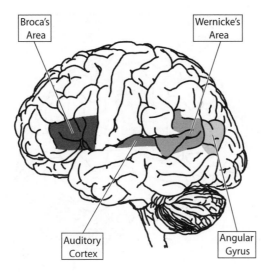

Figure 2.5 The perisylvian language zone of the brain: left side view (image by D. Derrick and A. Yeung).

just posterior to the auditory cortex (Wernicke, 1874). Incidentally, the STG is also important for social cognition. A tract (white matter) beneath the cortex known as the *arcuate fasciculus* (Latin, "curved bundle") connects Wernicke's area to Broca's area. This tract allows the two structures to coordinate and cooperate. Damage to Wernicke's area can result in *Wernicke's aphasia* (Greek, *a-* "not" + *phanai* "speak"), a speech disorder characterized by fluent nonsense speech and poor comprehension, but relatively well-preserved syntax production.

The *angular gyrus*, located bilaterally in the parietal lobe near the superior edge of the temporal lobe, is responsible for conveying high-level meaning through metaphor and irony. It is also largely responsible for the ability to read and write, and plays a perception role in multimodal integration of speech information.

While most language-related areas of the brain play some role in both perceiving and producing speech, some are more specifically geared toward production. Conscious speech plans are generated in *Broca's area*, which is in the inferior frontal gyrus of the left hemisphere (Broca, 1861). If this area is damaged, *Broca's aphasia* can result, which is characterized by labored speech or loss of syntax production skills, but preservation of speech comprehension. Broca's aphasics often produce short, disfluent utterances. Because Broca's aphasia doesn't interfere with perception so much, people with this disorder can often understand their own speech deficiencies, and can become very frustrated with their inability to communicate effectively.

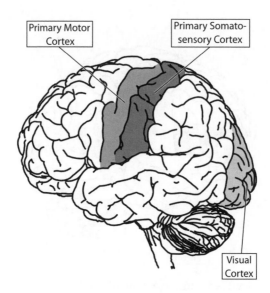

Figure 2.6 Motor cortex, somatosensory cortex, and visual cortex of the brain: left side view (image by D. Derrick and A. Yeung).

2.2.1.2 Other language-related areas of the cortex Other cortical areas, outside of the perisylvian language zone, are also involved in speech perception and/or production. Such areas include: the visual cortex, the primary somatosensory cortex, and the primary motor cortex (see Figure 2.6).

The *visual cortex* is located bilaterally in the occipital lobe in the posterior end of the brain. The visual cortex mainly processes visual information, some of which can facilitate speech comprehension. You may find that it's difficult to carry on a conversation at a loud party or concert when you're not looking directly at the person you are conversing with. Additionally, you may have noticed it's more difficult to talk on the phone with people than it is to talk face to face. This is because you lack the visual information you would otherwise use to facilitate communication.

The *primary somatosensory cortex*, or *postcentral gyrus*, is located bilaterally along the lateral surface of the parietal lobe, posterior to the central sulcus. The somatosensory system processes information having to do with touch, temperature, and proprioception (body position). This area is important both in processing external tactile information in speech perception (e.g., gross movements, vibrations, airflow), and as part of the feedback system in speech production.

Homunculus, homunculi

Your leg is bigger than your finger, so it should have more brainpower dedicated to it, right? Well, from the brain's point of view, not all parts of the body are treated equally. For example, disproportionately large areas of the somatosensory cortex and motor cortex are dedicated to controlling and receiving information from the mouth, hands, and feet. If you were to draw a person's body with its proportions in terms of cortical space, it would look very strange, with a huge mouth, hands, and feet. This kind of representation is called a *homunculus*. Think of it as a way of visualizing your body as your brain sees it.

For the somatosensory cortex, the amount of surface area dedicated to a body part is proportionate to the *sensory resolution* of that body part, meaning that body parts with more dedicated cortical area can feel with more detail than other parts. A representation of this distribution of cortical real estate is called a *sensory homunculus*. In humans, the hands, feet, and speech articulators represent the largest areas of the sensory homunculus.

Like the somatosensory cortex, the primary motor cortex dedicates surface area in proportion to the degree of *motor resolution*, or how fine or gross a muscle's actions are, for each part of the body. A visual representation of this is called a *motor homunculus*. In a motor homunculus, the face and speech articulators, along with the hands and feet, have the largest areas, indicating a greater degree of fine motor control (Penfield and Roberts, 1959). A sensory homunculus and a motor homunculus can be seen on the left and right sides, respectively, of Figure 2.7.

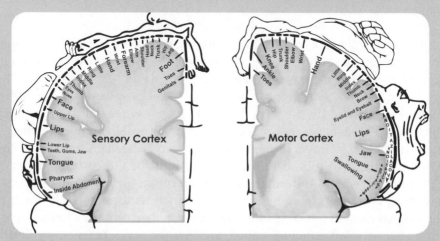

Figure 2.7 Sensory and motor homunculi: coronal view of brain (image adapted from Penfield and Rasmussen, 1950, Wikimedia Commons public domain).

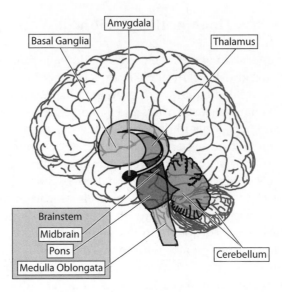

Figure 2.8 Deeper structures of the brain: left side view (image by D. Derrick and A. Yeung).

The *primary motor cortex*, or *precentral gyrus*, is anterior and parallel to the primary somatosensory cortex. It is located bilaterally along the lateral surface of the posterior portion of the frontal lobe, anterior to the central sulcus. The speech plan produced in Broca's area is projected to the primary motor cortex, after which it will be sent to lower parts of the brain, and ultimately distributed to the different parts of the body that will produce movements.

2.2.1.3 Subcortical speech areas Beneath the surface of the cortex (i.e., in *sub-cortical* areas) are several deeper structures in the brain that are involved in speech, including the basal ganglia and amygdalae (see Figure 2.8). The *basal ganglia* are a symmetrical system of nuclei deep beneath the cortex (don't be confused by the term "ganglia" here – we're still talking about the CNS!). These nuclei are connected by symmetrical loops of tracts allow-ing information to travel throughout the system. The main function of the basal ganglia is to modulate the motor output of the cortex. The basal ganglia receive motor information from the cortex (primary motor cortex) and make necessary changes to movements in order to successfully execute the desired motor plan. This fine-tuned plan is then sent back to the motor cortex via a relay structure called the *thalamus* (via Latin, from Greek "chamber").

The *amygdalae* (singular *amygdala*; via Latin, from Greek, "almond") are a pair of small, almond-shaped nuclei nestled deep within the anterior portion of the temporal lobe. These structures are found in many lower-order animals, and are a piece of the "old" part of the brain. The amygdalae send information to other nuclei in the basal ganglia, and are considered the "emotion center" of the brain. Some functions of the amygdalae pertain to processing emotional aspects of language and forming long-term memories (Stemmer and Whitaker, 2008). They are also involved in multimodal processing and determining the importance of incoming information, and have links to autism spectrum disorders.

2.2.1.4 The cerebellum and brainstem The *cerebellum* (Latin, "little brain") is a structure attached to the brainstem, inferior and posterior to the cerebrum. It looks like a miniature brain with deeper sulci and more compact folds. The cerebellum gets input from sensory systems and from other parts of the brain and spinal cord, then sends messages up to the motor cortex that help with the fine-tuning of skilled motor activities. Since the cerebellum and basal ganglia are responsible for neuromuscular control and the storage of skills-based knowledge, these structures have long been thought to coordinate low-level planning and timing of speech (Lassen *et al.*, 1978).

The *brainstem* is a small cluster of structures that makes up the lowest part of the brain. At the top of the brainstem is the *midbrain* or *mesencephalon* (Greek, "middle brain"), below the midbrain is the *pons* (Latin, "bridge") and at the base of the brainstem is the *medulla oblongata* (Latin, "long core"), which becomes the top of the spinal cord. The medulla oblongata is the final point of contact before a motor plan is sent out to the rest of the body – and the first point of contact for incoming sensory messages. While the brainstem regulates many vital basic functions of the body via the spinal cord, it is also important in that it is the source of the "cranial nerves" (more on these in Chapter 3) that directly innervate the face and neck.

2.3 Measuring the Brain: fMRI, PET, EEG, MEG, TMS

Originally, scientists learned which parts of the brain do what by performing autopsies on people who had had various brain-related disorders or injuries. Researchers would relate the freshly uncovered brain lesions to the impaired functions. This is how both Broca and Wernicke discovered the brain areas bearing their names (Broca, 1861; Wernicke, 1874).

In the modern era, we have many tools to help us understand brain function. Tools like functional magnetic resonance imaging (fMRI), positron emission tomography (PET), electroencephalography (EEG), and magnetoencephalography (MEG) use different mechanisms to measure the function, rather than the anatomy, of the brain. It's important to note that these tools don't show the structure of the brain – they just measure activity.

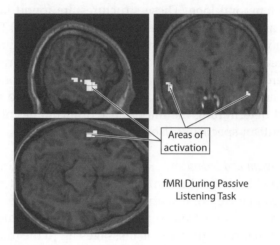

Figure 2.9 Structural MRI image with fMRI overlay of areas of activation (in white): sagittal (top left), coronal (top right), transverse (bottom) (image by D. Derrick, with data from R. Watts).

In order to *localize* brain activity (i.e., to show where in the brain the activity is happening), these tools must be coupled with imaging tools that can show the physical structure – the "map" – of the brain. There are several tools that can provide structural images of the brain, but we won't get to these until Chapter 11. For now, let's look at the tools we have for monitoring brain activity.

Functional magnetic resonance imaging (fMRI) is one of the most commonly used tools for mapping brain activity (see Figure 2.9). It works because it can detect different magnetic properties in blood. When a part of the brain is active, blood flow to that area increases to bring more oxygen. In red blood cells, oxygen is carried in protein molecules called *hemoglobin*. As the oxygen is used, the hemoglobin changes magnetically, from repelling a magnetic field to being able to receive magnetism. This process takes a few seconds. In 1990, Japanese neuroscientist Seiji Ogawa discovered that fMRI could detect the magnetic difference between hemoglobin with and without oxygen, making it possible to use an MRI machine to map brain function. Ogawa's "blood-oxygen-level dependent" (*BOLD*) technique has revolutionized brain activity research (Huettel *et al.*, 2009). fMRI provides good spatial (~1–2 mm) and reasonably good temporal (~500 Hz) resolution, and has the great advantage of being easily coupled with structural MRI, which can simultaneously provide the structural "map" of the brain. On the down side, participants often find the experience of MRI unpleasant, as the space inside the scanner is very small and the machine is extremely loud. One way to significantly reduce the impact of MRI noise, though, is by using MRI-safe, noise-canceling headphones.

Positron emission tomography (PET) scans work by reading traces of radioactive particles introduced into a participant's blood stream (Ter-Pogossian *et al.*, 1975; Phelps *et al.*, 1975). Usually, a radioactive analog of glucose is used, allowing PET scans to detect metabolic rates in various parts of the brain. PET scans are quieter and not susceptible to data loss from motion in speech articulation. As a result, while fMRI is popular for brain imaging studies, PET scans are sometimes still preferred for language studies. PET couples well with a structural imaging technique known as computed tomography (CT), which also images radioactivity (see Chapter 11). However, the need to introduce radioactive isotopes into the blood of the research participant is a serious downside to this technique.

If you've ever seen a picture of someone with electrodes attached all over their scalp, they were probably participating in an *electroencephalography* (EEG) session (Niedermeyer and da Silva, 2004). EEG directly measures *event-related potentials* (ERPs), or the electrical signals generated within neurons relating to a specific event (such as being presented with a visual or auditory stimulus, or making a speech error). EEG can be useful in identifying details of speech production since the presentation of speech with various semantic, syntactic, phonological, and phonetic errors can produce distinct ERPs related to specific parts of the brain. Also, because EEG passively measures signals produced by the brain, it is completely non-invasive, safe, and quiet.

Magnetoencephalography (MEG) is another technique that can be used safely and non-invasively to measure electrical signals produced by the brain (Cohen, 1968). This technique uses arrays of *superconducting quantum interference devices* (SQUIDs) to pick up on the electromagnetic fields the brain puts out during activation. MEG has high temporal resolution, and while it has relatively poor spatial resolution, MEG results are not degraded by the presence of skull, skin, and membranes surrounding the brain. Because the fields produced by brain activity are so weak, the SQUIDs have to be incredibly sensitive, making it very difficult to screen out other ambient electromagnetic noise. As a result, MEG sessions are always conducted in a carefully controlled magnetically shielded environment.

One way of mapping regions of brain function that's completely different from those above is *transcranial magnetic stimulation* (TMS). TMS uses magnetic induction to introduce electricity into a specific region of the brain, which can artificially trigger weak nerve activity (Barker *et al.*, 1985). With this electric shock, TMS can temporarily activate a portion of the brain, or can create temporary artificial lesions that prevent the affected area of the brain from functioning. In this way, the regions of speech control and comprehension can be studied by observing which functions are activated or disabled.

Stuttering and singing

Stuttering is a speech disturbance involving stumbling on or repeating parts of words. Speakers who stutter know what they want to say, but have difficulty producing fluent speech. Surprisingly, many stutterers do not stutter while singing, possibly because speaking and singing are processed in somewhat different parts of the brain. Part of this may have to do with differences in planning: When you speak a language, you generally have to plan out utterances at the same time as you produce them (more on this in Chapter 11). It has been observed that stuttering can be reduced by rehearsing or carefully timing what is going to be said. Except in extemporaneous singing, a singer's "utterances" are already planned, carefully timed, and can easily be rehearsed.

Exercises

Sufficient jargon

Define the following terms: central nervous system (CNS), peripheral nervous system (PNS), neurons, glia, dendrites, cell body (soma), axon, myelin sheath, axon terminal, synapse, nerves, tracts, nuclei, ganglia, white matter, gray matter, action potential, anions, threshold, refractory period, saltatory conduction, cerebrum, (cerebral) cortex, gyri, sulci, longitudinal fissure, frontal lobe, central sulcus, Sylvian fissure (lateral sulcus), parietal lobe, temporal lobe, occipital lobe, perisylvian language zone, auditory cortex, superior temporal gyrus (STG), Wernicke's area, arcuate fasciculus, Wernicke's aphasia, angular gyrus, Broca's area, Broca's aphasia, visual cortex, primary somatosensory cortex (postcentral gyrus), homunculus, sensory resolution, sensory homunculus, motor resolution, motor homunculus, primary motor cortex (precentral gyrus), subcortical, basal ganglia, thalamus, amygdalae, cerebellum, brainstem, midbrain (mesencephalon), pons, medulla oblongata, localize, functional magnetic resonance imaging (fMRI), hemoglobin, BOLD technique, positron emission tomography (PET), electroencephalography (EEG), event-related potentials (ERPs), magnetoencephalography (MEG), superconducting quantum interference devices (SQUIDs), transcranial magnetic stimulation (TMS), stuttering.

Short-answer questions

1   What is the last part of the brain from which motor plans exit to travel to various parts of the body (be specific)?

2   Unlike Wernicke's aphasia, patients with Broca's aphasia sometimes complain that their mouths do not work properly. Explain why in terms of brain anatomy.

3   For each of the following tools used to study the brain, find and cite one speech research paper not mentioned in this book: (1) fMRI, (2) TMS, and (3) EEG. Follow the reference formatting used in the references section at the end of each chapter.

Practical assignment

Part of learning to do articulatory phonetics research is learning how to work with anatomical and physiological data. Our understanding of vocal tract anatomy and physiology informs the kinds of research questions we ask in order to understand speech better. By now, you know enough to start analyzing the kinds of data researchers collect for their experiments.

For each chapter, this text has online assignments (at www.wiley.com/go/articulatoryphonetics) that either provide research data for analysis, or practical tools for understanding vocal tract anatomy. For Chapter 2, you will look at the setup for a simple electroencephalograph (EEG) device, along with EEG data. The assignment is designed to help you relate physiological data to real-world events. The assignment and the related assignment images can be found in the online materials for this textbook under *Chapter 2*.

References

Barker, A. T., Jalinous, R., and Freeston, I. L. (1985). Non-invasive magnetic stimulation of human motor cortex. *The Lancet*, *1*(8437), 1106–1107.

Barnett, M. W. and Larkman, P. M. (2007). The action potential. *Practical Neurology*, *7*(3), 192–197.

Broca, P. (1861). Remarques sur le siège de la faculté du langage articulé, suivies d'une observation d'aphémie (perte de la parole). *Bulletins de la Société Anatomique de Paris*, *36*, 330–357.

Cohen, D. (1968). Magnetoencephalography: Evidence of magnetic fields produced by alpha rhythm currents. *Science*, *161*, 784–786.

Fu, K.-M. G., Johnston, T. A., Shah, A. S., Arnold, L., Smiley, J., Hackett, T. A., Garraghty, P. E., and Schroeder, C. E. (2003). Auditory cortical neurons respond to somatosensory stimulation. *Journal of Neuroscience*, *23*, 7510–7515.

Huettel, S. A., Song, A. W., and McCarthy, G. (2009). *Functional Magnetic Resonance Imaging* (2nd edition). Massachusetts: Sinauer.

Huxley, A. F. and Stämpfli, R. (1949). Evidence for saltatory conduction in peripheral myelinated nerve fibres. *Journal of Physiology*, *108*, 315–339.

Kiernan, J. A. (1998). *Barr's the Human Nervous System: An Anatomical Viewpoint* (7th edition). Philadelphia, PA: Lippincott-Raven.

Lassen, N. A., Ingvar, D. H., and Skinhoj, E. (1978). Brain function and blood flow. *Scientific American, 239*(4), 62–71.

Niedermeyer E. and da Silva F. L. (2004). *Electroencephalography: Basic Principles, Clinical Applications, and Related Fields*. Baltimore, MD: Lippincott Williams & Wilkins.

Penfield, W. and Rasmussen, T. (1950). *The Cerebral Cortex of Man*. New York: Macmillan.

Penfield, W. and Roberts, L. (1959). *Speech and Brain-Mechanisms*. Princeton, NJ: Princeton University Press.

Phelps, M. E., Hoffman, E. J., Mullani, N. A., and Ter-Pogossian, M. M. (1975). Application of annihilation coincidence detection to transaxial reconstruction tomography. *Journal of Nuclear Medicine, 16*(3), 210–224.

Stemmer, B. and Whitaker, H. A. (eds) (2008). *Handbook of the Neuroscience of Language*. San Diego, CA: Academic Press.

Tasaki, I. (1939). The electro-saltatory transmission of the nerve impulse and the effect of narcosis upon the nerve fiber. *American Journal of Physiology, 127*, 211–227.

Ter-Pogossian, M. M., Phelps, M. E., Hoffman, E. J., and Mullani, N. A. (1975). A positron-emission transaxial tomograph for nuclear imaging (PET). *Radiology 114*(1), 89–98.

Wernicke, C. (1874). *Der Aphasische Symptomenkomplex*. Breslau: Max Cohn & Weigert.

Chapter 3

From Thought to Movement: The Peripheral Nervous System

In the previous chapter, we looked at how the brain creates and sends out signals to start the chain of events leading to speech. We also learned about methods scientists use to measure the brain's activities. In this chapter, we'll learn how signals get from the brain out to the different parts of the body, and once they arrive, how they make muscles move.

3.1   The Peripheral Nervous System

As you'll recall, the peripheral nervous system is made up of all of the neural fibers in the body that are not part of the brain or spinal cord. When a peripheral nerve is damaged, quite different parts of the body can be affected. This is because the complex network of nerves in the body links together different parts of the anatomy.

Some nerves carry motor commands out of the CNS, while others carry sensory information into the CNS. The *motor*, or *efferent* (Latin *ex-* "out" + *ferrent* "carrying"), nerves carry messages out of the CNS to different muscles in the body. The *sensory*, or *afferent* (Latin *ad-* "toward" + *ferrent* "carrying"), nerves carry sensations such as touch, pain, pressure, heat, and cold to the CNS.

There are two main types of peripheral nerves in the body: *cranial nerves*, which emerge directly from the brainstem, and *spinal nerves*, which exit from the spinal cord at regular intervals. All of the nerves are summarized in a table at the end of this book.

Articulatory Phonetics, First Edition. Bryan Gick, Ian Wilson, and Donald Derrick.
© 2013 Bryan Gick, Ian Wilson, and Donald Derrick. Published 2013 by Blackwell Publishing Ltd.

3.1.1   Cranial nerves

The first peripheral nerves to leave the central nervous system are the *cranial nerves*. These emerge directly from the brainstem. There are 12 pairs of cranial nerves in total (a member of each pair emerges from either side of the brainstem): some are exclusively sensory, some are exclusively motor, and some are mixed. In addition to their standard anatomical names, each cranial nerve is also known by a Roman numeral I through XII, assigned roughly in the order (from top to bottom) in which they leave the brainstem.

In this book, we'll look at six of the cranial nerves that are particularly important for speech articulation: V, VII, IX, X, XI, and XII. As you may guess from their higher numbers, all of these nerves originate from lower parts of the brainstem (the pons or the medulla oblongata), and form many branches. We'll discuss each of these six nerves (but only a few of their branches) in detail below – each one is shown in a separate part of Figure 3.1.

The *trigeminal* (Latin, "three-branched") nerve (CN V) is primarily used for sensation. The trigeminal nerve emerges from the pons (in the middle of the brainstem) and separates into three branches at the *trigeminal ganglion*. One branch of this nerve, known as the *mandibular* nerve, is important for articulation, as it provides motor innervation to the jaw muscles. The other two branches (known as the ophthalmic nerve and the maxillary nerve) are purely sensory nerves.

The *facial* nerve (CN VII) emerges between the pons and the medulla oblongata to provide motor innervation to the face, including control of the lips. This nerve is important for communicative facial expression, and for consonants and vowels that involve opening, closing, and rounding the lips.

Another important cranial nerve for speech is the *glossopharyngeal* nerve (CN IX), which exits the medulla oblongata just anterior to the vagus nerve. This nerve feeds into a complex network of nerves called the *pharyngeal plexus*, responsible for innervating several of the pharyngeal muscles.

The *vagus* (Latin, "wandering") nerve (CN X) innervates the larynx, pharynx and velum. The vagus nerve gets its name from its circuitous pathway through the body: one important branch of the vagus nerve, known as the *recurrent laryngeal* nerve (because it travels down and then up again), descends from the medulla oblongata down into the chest cavity, looping around major blood vessels (the left branch loops around the aortic arch while the right branch loops around the right subclavian artery), only to "wander" back up to the larynx. The pharyngeal branch of the vagus nerve takes a somewhat less roundabout route to the pharynx and velum. The *superior laryngeal* nerve branches off directly to the larynx (without looping downward), and is important in pitch control.

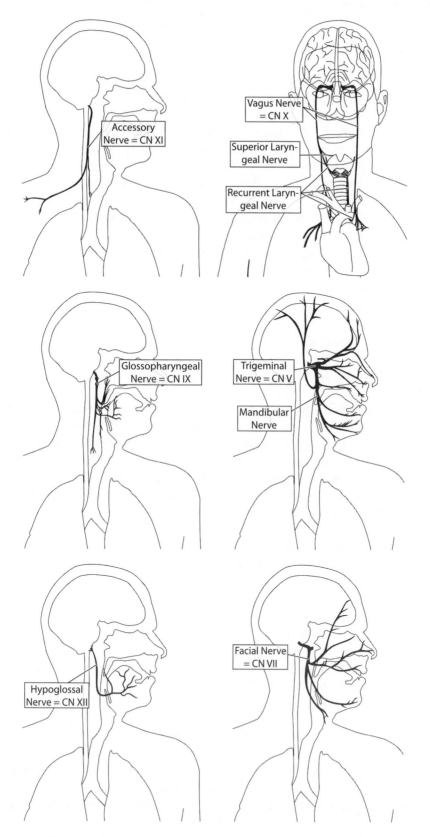

Figure 3.1 Cranial nerves (left to right and top to bottom: Accessory, Vagus, Glossopharyngeal, Trigeminal, Hypoglossal, and Facial) (image by W. Murphey).

Although respiration is mainly controlled by spinal nerves (which we'll discuss in Section 3.1.2), it also uses the *accessory* nerve (CN XI) to power the sternocleidomastoid muscle, a neck muscle that sometimes aids in deep or heavy breathing. CN XI also contributes to innervation in the pharynx.

Finally, the tongue is almost entirely innervated by the *hypoglossal* (Greek, "under the tongue") nerve (CN XII). The hypoglossal nerve emerges from the medulla oblongata (as well as spinal nerves C1–C3) to connect into the tongue.

It can be hard to remember all of these cranial nerves and their Roman numerals. Try coming up with a mnemonic to help you remember their order. Here they are again, in Roman numeral order:

Trigeminal (V; jaw)
Facial (VII; lips and face)
Glossopharyngeal (IX; pharynx)
Vagus (X; larynx, pharynx, velum)
Accessory (XI; respiration)
Hypoglossal (XII; tongue)

While the Roman numeral system for cranial nerves may make sense in terms of brain anatomy, their order tells us little about their function in speech. A different way to think about the cranial nerves is in the order in which they take part in the speech production chain described in this book (i.e., starting with respiration, and ending with the facial muscles). By reordering the cranial nerves in order of their speech function we might get something like this:

Accessory (XI; respiration)
Vagus (X; larynx, pharynx, velum)
Glossopharyngeal (IX; pharynx)
Trigeminal (V; jaw)
Hypoglossal (XII; tongue)
Facial (VII; lips and face)

A useful mnemonic for remembering these nerves in order of their speech function is: "A Very Good Talking Happy Face!"

3.1.2   Spinal nerves

Speech movement begins with respiration, which is controlled mainly via the *spinal* nerves (see Figure 3.2). Each spinal nerve has both motor and sensory components. At the level of each vertebra in the spine, nerves

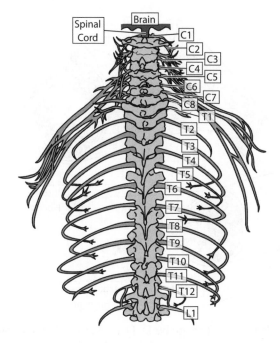

Figure 3.2   Spinal nerves: posterior view (image by W. Murphey and A. Yeung).

emerge from the front and back of the spinal cord. The dorsal (posterior) roots give rise to the afferent portion of each spinal nerve, while the ventral (anterior) roots give rise to the efferent portion of each spinal nerve. A tip for remembering what portion of the spinal cord is responsible for what kind of information is to remember the acronym AMPS: Anterior = Motor; Posterior = Sensory (i.e., Anterior roots carry Motor information; Posterior roots carry Sensory information). Or, for a more dramatic visual aid, picture someone being shot in the back with an arrow (ouch!), with the arrow going in the back of the spine, and out the front.

Spinal nerves are named according to their associated vertebrae. There are eight *cervical* (Latin, "neck") nerves (C1–C8). C1 emerges from below the base of the skull, while C2 through C8 emerge below the seven vertebrae in the neck. Of these, C3–C5 are the most significant for speech because they merge together to form the *phrenic* (Greek, "diaphragm") nerve, which innervates the diaphragm, an important muscle for breathing. Below these are 12 *thoracic* (Greek, "chest") nerves, corresponding to the 12 vertebrae of the chest cavity. All of these are used in breathing, and hence in speech: T1–T11 innervate muscles attached to ribs, with T7–T11 also innervating abdominal muscles. T12 and the lumbar nerve L1 innervate abdominal muscles, too – more on this in Chapter 4.

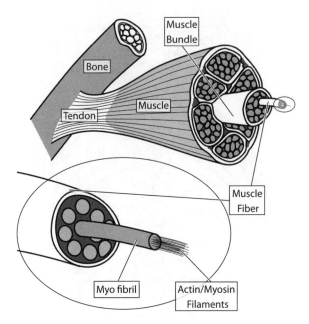

Figure 3.3 Muscle bundles (image by D. Derrick, from United States government public domain).

3.2 How Muscles Move

After its long journey from the brain down through the peripheral nervous system, an action potential (see Chapter 2) finally reaches a muscle. Now all that remains is for the muscle to turn this electrochemical energy into movement.

All the muscles used for speech – indeed, for any voluntary movement – are striated or skeletal muscles. *Skeletal muscles* are really just bundles within bundles within bundles of parallel fibers. Looking closely at a muscle, you can see the fibers that run all along its length (see Figure 3.3). These are actually sheathed bundles of smaller *muscle fibers*. Inside each of these tiny muscle fibers are smaller bundles of microscopically thin *myofibrils* (via Latin, from Greek, *myo-* "mouse/muscle" + *fibril* "little filament"). Within each myofibril are the moving parts that make contraction happen.

First, let's look at how the energy is distributed to these fibers, and then we'll think about the mechanics going on within each fiber.

Action potentials are distributed to groups of muscle fibers called motor units. A *motor unit* consists of a single motor neuron and all the muscle fibers the neuron innervates (see Figure 3.4). The spacing of motor units is such that each unit controls sparsely spaced muscle fibers, intermingled with fibers belonging to other motor units. The number of muscle fibers in a motor unit can vary greatly, from several hundred in leg muscles to fewer

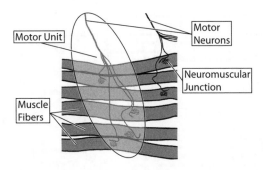

Figure 3.4 Motor unit and muscle fibers (image by D. Derrick).

than ten fibers in specialized fine-motor systems like the eye muscles, intrinsic finger muscles or laryngeal muscles. Since all the muscle fibers contract when a given motor unit is activated, motor units that connect to a smaller number of fibers provide more precise motor control to that part of the body.

Within a muscle, motor units with the smallest number of fibers are activated first, and then larger motor units are recruited, as more muscle force is needed. This is known as *Henneman's Size Principle* (Henneman *et al.*, 1965). Because muscle fibers can only be contracted for a short period of time, motor units switch on and off rapidly, allowing a muscle to maintain a consistent level of contraction for an extended period of time.

As we mentioned earlier in this section, it is the internal structure of myofibrils that allows muscles to shorten. The tremendous power generated when a muscle contracts is the result of millions of microscopic interactions happening at the same time. By way of analogy, imagine millions of tiny, sticky hands drawing on a rope of filament in a kind of hand-over-hand movement, causing the filaments inside a myofibril to slide relative to each other. This process is often described in terms of the *sliding filament model* (Huxley and Neidergerke, 1954; Huxley and Hanson, 1954) (see Figure 3.5).

According to the sliding filament model, muscles work because myofibrils contain two very different kinds of filaments, each made of a different kind of protein molecule. The long, thin filaments are made up of the protein *actin* (you can think of the actin filament as the strong rope, the passive player in our analogy) and the short, flexible, thick filaments are made up of the protein *myosin* (you can think of the myosin filament as the active player – the one with the sticky hands that pull on the rope). Because myosin molecules do all the pulling, let's briefly discuss how myosin works.

Myosin filaments are made up of long myosin protein molecules all intertwined. Each myosin molecule looks like an elongated tadpole, with a globular *head* (the "sticky hands" in our analogy), a flexible neck, and a long, snake-like tail. Millions of these molecules twine their tails together into a long thread, with their heads sticking out along the thread's entire length.

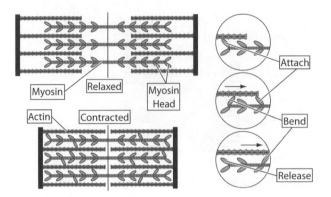

Figure 3.5 Sliding filament model (image by D. Derrick).

When an action potential reaches a muscle fiber, several electrochemical changes take place in sequence: first, binding sites on the actin molecules open up, attracting nearby myosin heads which immediately attach to the actin (the *attach* phase). Second, the myosin necks bend, causing the actin filament to slide alongside the myosin filament, thus microscopically shortening the whole fiber (the *bend* phase). Finally, the myosin releases the actin (the *release* phase). With this sequence happening millions of times within a single fiber – Attach-Bend-Release, Attach-Bend-Release – the whole muscle shortens substantially.

ATP and rigor mortis

Rigor mortis (Latin, "stiffness of death") is a stiffness that occurs in a body during the hours after death. It is what happens when a body's muscles undergo the "Attach" and "Bend" phases, but not the "Release" phase. While the "Release" phase of muscle contraction may seem passive or automatic, it is in fact an active process kick-started by a specific chemical: *Adenosine triphosphate* (commonly known as *ATP*). ATP is a molecule that helps the body transfer energy, and it is often called the body's "molecular unit of currency." After the "Bend" phase of muscle contraction, while myosin heads are attached to actin, they take up ATP. It is this ATP that allows them to detach from the binding sites.

After death, the body loses oxygen, which is needed to make ATP. With no more ATP, the myosin cannot detach, resulting in rigor mortis. Muscles stay contracted like this until, after about 3 days, muscle tissue begins to break down.

3.3   Measuring Muscles: EMG

Electromyography (EMG) is a technique for measuring muscle activation indirectly by picking up the electric charge produced by an action potential just as it reaches a muscle. This electrical charge can extend as far as a few centimeters away from the source (though its strength decreases logarithmically as it gets farther away), and can be measured by testing the voltage difference between two nearby wires. It's possible to place the two wires so close together that the motor action potential to an individual muscle fiber can be measured. For speech, electrodes are often larger and farther apart because speech researchers are interested in the action potentials of a whole muscle or muscle region.

There are two current techniques for electromyography, surface EMG and intramuscular EMG. *Surface EMG* picks up voltage changes on the surface of the skin and only works properly on superficial muscles. One problem with surface EMG is that muscles move underneath the skin, and therefore move relative to the electrodes. As a result, surface EMG may pick up signals from different muscles or portions of muscle, sometimes with confusing results. Surface EMG is used because it is safe, painless, and easy to use, requiring no medical supervision.

In contrast, *intramuscular EMG* uses *hooked-wire electrodes*, which are inserted directly into the relevant muscle and require local anesthetics, proper medical hygiene, and medical supervision. Results from properly placed hooked-wire electrodes can be extremely precise and very reliable. Obviously, hooked-wire electrodes can also cause some discomfort and therefore require more involved ethics approval for research use.

Since there is no widely accepted and standardized method of relating microvolts (the typical units of measurement for EMG) to muscle activation strength, the relationship between an EMG reading and the action of a muscle is best thought of in relative terms. One reason for this is that it is nearly impossible to know how close the electrode is to the motor nerve(s) providing the electric signal. This makes it very difficult or even impossible to compare the strengths of the muscle activations of two muscles, or even compare two separate wire insertions into the same muscle. Even a single electrode can change in signal strength over the span of just a few minutes: a wire insertion will read weaker signals for similar events as scar tissue forms around the wire and interferes with electrical conduction.

The output of EMG readings, which can be seen in the left image of Figure 3.6a, can appear very noisy, often containing tiny, high-frequency variations related to subtle activation patterns or movements of nearby muscles. Also, EMG signals contain both positive and negative voltages indicating muscle activation. As a result of these factors, EMG signals are

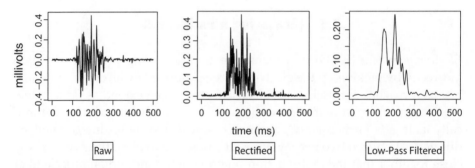

Figure 3.6a EMG signal of the left sternocleidomastoid muscle during startle response. On the left is the raw signal. In the center is that same raw signal rectified. On the right is the rectified image after low-pass filtering (image by D. Derrick, from data provided by C. Chiu).

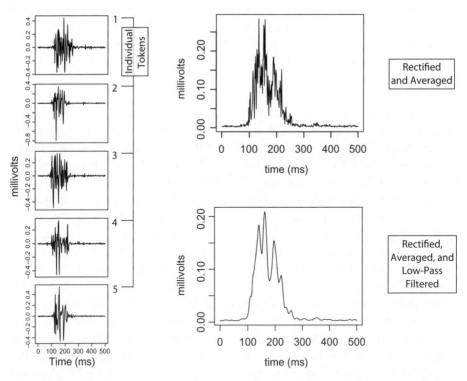

Figure 3.6b EMG signal of the left sternocleidomastoid muscle during startle response. On the left are 5 raw signals. The top-right image shows those 5 signals after they have been rectified and then averaged. The bottom-right image is after low-pass filtering (image by D. Derrick, from data provided by C. Chiu).

often *rectified*, or converted to absolute values (seen in the center image of Figure 3.6a), *averaged* over many recordings (the top-right image of Figure 3.6b), and *smoothed* using a *low pass filter* to remove the high-frequency variations that make EMG signals look jagged and irregular (the bottom-right image of Figure 3.6b). This postprocessing allows scientists to see clearly when important events take place in a muscle.

The shocking history of electric eels and EMG

As far back as 2750 BC, electricity was noticed in a living creature: the ancient Egyptians described a Nile catfish that could shock and stun at a distance (Finger and Piccolino, 2011). Over 4000 years later, in 1666, Francesco Redi (a court physician to the Medici rulers of Tuscany, most famous for demonstrating that maggots are not spontaneously generated from rotting meat) discovered the source of electricity in the South American electric eel: a specialized muscle.

More than a century later in 1792, the Italian physician Luigi Galvani demonstrated that this same electricity could also contract muscles (Galvani, 1792). By 1849, Emil du Bois-Reymond, a German physician, discovered action potentials and that the electrical activity that generates a muscle contraction could be recorded. Finally, in 1890, Etienne-Jules Marey gave electromyography its name, and made the first EMG recordings.

3.3.1   The speed of thought to movement

Now we know how neurons transmit information through electrochemical reactions, and how muscles contract through even more complex reactions. Because our bodies use electrochemical processes to think and act, our response times to outside *stimuli*, or information, are not instantaneous and can be measured in terms of *latencies*, or the amount of time it takes for each part of the process to happen.

Auditory stimuli are transmitted through rapid physical mechanisms, which reach the cerebrum in 8–10 ms (about one hundredth of a second). Visual information is transmitted to the brain through slower chemical processes, and so reaches the cerebrum in 20–40 ms. Tactile stimuli are transmitted through a chemical process that takes an amount of time in between those required for audition and vision.

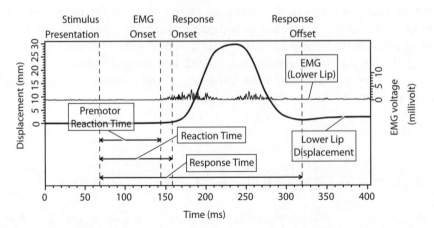

Figure 3.7   Reaction and response times based on EMG of the lower lip and lower lip displacement (image by C. Chiu and D. Derrick).

The cerebral cortex takes a minimum of 65–70 ms to process one piece of information, longer if there is more information. It takes an additional 60 ms or so (depending on distance from the brain) for information to be processed by the brainstem and spinal centers and travel through the peripheral nervous system to reach the muscles. Muscles then take their own time to move in response to motor neuron action potentials. For example, muscles in the wrist take about 50 ms to move; smaller muscle sets can respond faster.

Response times (see Figure 3.7) represent the time it takes to receive outside stimuli, mentally process it, initiate action potentials to motor units, contract muscles, and complete the motion. *Premotor reaction times* represent the time from thought to the initiation of action potentials in motor units. Premotor reaction times are measured using EMG.

When all of these processing times are put together, premotor reaction times of 180 ms are typical with visual stimuli, premotor reaction times of 155 ms are typical with tactile stimuli, depending on how far away from the brain the affected area of the body is, and premotor reaction times of 140 ms are typical for auditory stimuli (Brebner and Welford, 1980).

Premotor reaction times as fast as 65 ms, or even faster, can be observed by bypassing the cerebral cortex completely. This has been suggested to occur when movements are pre-planned and stored subcortically, or with reflexes like the startle response (Valls-Solé *et al.*, 1999).

So, the time from the beginning of a thought to the first muscle motions in a speech act can be measured in milliseconds, and that time depends on many factors, including the type of stimulus prompting the thought in the first place.

Exercises

Sufficient jargon

Define the following terms: motor (efferent) nerves, sensory (afferent) nerves, cranial nerves, spinal nerves, CN V (trigeminal nerve), trigeminal ganglion, mandibular nerve, CN VII (facial nerve), CN IX (glossopharyngeal nerve), pharyngeal plexus, CN X (vagus nerve), recurrent laryngeal nerve, superior laryngeal nerve, CN XI (accessory nerve), CN XII (hypoglossal nerve), cervical nerves C1–C8, phrenic nerve, thoracic nerves T1–T12, lumbar nerve L1, skeletal muscles, muscle fibers, myofibrils, motor unit, Henneman's Size Principle, sliding filament model, actin, myosin, myosin head, attach phase, bend phase, release phase, rigor mortis, Adenosine triphosphate (ATP), electromyography (EMG), surface EMG, intramuscular EMG, hooked-wire electrodes, rectified/averaged/ smoothed signals, low pass filter, stimuli, latencies, response times, premotor reaction times.

Short-answer questions

1 Name three cranial nerves that are necessary for saying the English word "I"; name three cranial nerves that are necessary for saying the English word "you."
2 When using EMG to compare the actions of two different muscles, which of the following can we determine conclusively: timing of the action or strength of the action? Explain.
3 Your friend is standing near you looking in your direction, and you want to get her attention as quickly as possible; will it be faster for you to (A) wave your hand or (B) make a clicking sound with your tongue? Give two reasons for your answer in terms of human physiology.
4 Find and cite two speech research papers not mentioned in this book in which EMG is used. Follow the reference formatting used in the references section at the end of each chapter.

Practical assignment

For each chapter of this book, there are online assignments that either provide research data for analysis, or practical tools for understanding vocal tract anatomy. For Chapter 3, you will perform hands-on data analysis of EMG signals taken from research participants in control and experimental conditions.

The *control condition* is used to provide a baseline from which the experimental condition is measured. For most control conditions, the researcher takes a measurement while a participant is doing something they understand, so it can be compared to a measurement of a behavior they are trying to study that is not yet understood. For instance, if you want to understand the effect of an unknown medicine, this is compared to the effect of a placebo.

Your analysis will include some of the functions you see in Figure 3.6, such as rectifying and graphing the signal, and you will answer questions about the results of this experiment. The assignment and the related assignment images can be found in the online materials for this textbook under *Chapter 3* (www.wiley.com/go/articulatoryphonetics).

References

Brebner, J. M. T. and Welford, A. T. (1980). Introduction: An historical background sketch. In A. T. Welford (ed.), *Reaction Times*, London, UK: Academic Press, 1–23.

Finger, S. and Piccolino, M. (2011). *The Shocking History of Electric Fishes: From Ancient Epochs to the Birth of Modern Neurophysiology*. Oxford, UK: Oxford University Press.

Galvani, L. (1792). *De Viribus Electricitatis in Motu Musculari Commentarius*. Bologna, Italy: Ex typographia Instituti Scientiarum.

Henneman, E., Somjen, G., and Carpenter, D. O. (1965). Functional significance of cell size in spinal motoneurons. *Journal of Neurophysiology*, *28*, 560–580.

Huxley, A. F. and Niedergerke, R. (1954). Structural changes in muscle during contraction: Interference microscopy of living muscle fibres. *Nature*, *173*(4412), 971–973.

Huxley, H. and Hanson, J. (1954). Changes in the cross-striations of muscle during contraction and stretch and their structural interpretation. *Nature*, *173*(4412), 973–976.

Valls-Solé, J., Rothwell, J. C., Goulart, F., Cossu, G., and Muñoz, E. (1999). Patterned ballistic movements triggered by a startle in healthy humans. *Journal of Physiology*, *516*, 931–938.

Chapter 4

From Movement to Flow: Respiration

In the previous chapter, we learned how the nervous system sends electrical commands to muscles, and how muscles convert those commands into movements. Now, to get speech to happen, we need to get some air moving. Many muscles need to act in precise coordination to move the air we need for speech. This movement of air through the body is called *respiration*. In this chapter, we will examine how speech respiration works.

4.1 Breathing Basics

The respiratory system acts like a bellows, a device you may have used to blow air onto a fire (see Figure 4.1). A bellows consists of an airtight flexible bladder attached to two hinged paddles. A small tube exits the hinge end to allow air to flow in and out of the bellows. When the handles of the bellows are pulled apart, the volume of the bladder increases and air rushes in to fill the space; when the handles are pushed together, the volume of the bladder is reduced and air is pushed out.

4.1.1   Two principles for respiration

Two important principles help explain how the bellows works. The first of these principles is referred to as *Boyle's Law*. Boyle's Law says that, in a

Articulatory Phonetics, First Edition. Bryan Gick, Ian Wilson, and Donald Derrick.
© 2013 Bryan Gick, Ian Wilson, and Donald Derrick. Published 2013 by Blackwell Publishing Ltd.

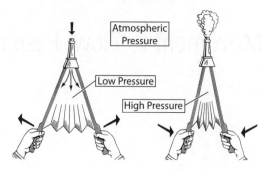

Figure 4.1   A bellows (based on public domain image by Pearson Scott Foresman).

closed system, air pressure and volume are inversely proportional. This relationship can be stated using a simple equation like this:

$$P_1V_1 = P_2V_2$$

That is, if you measure the air in a closed space, you can always multiply the pressure (*P*) by the volume (*V*), and get the same answer (assuming the temperature doesn't change). This means that if the volume of the cavity increases, the pressure will have to drop, and vice versa. So, when the volume of the bellows increases, the air pressure inside decreases, creating a relative vacuum; and when the volume of the bellows decreases, the air pressure inside increases.

The second principle is *equalization of pressure*, which says that air always flows from a region of higher pressure to a region of lower pressure. When the air pressure inside the bellows becomes lower than *atmospheric pressure*, or the pressure of the ambient air outside the system, the outside air rushes into the bellows until the pressure in the two regions is the same. Conversely, when the volume of the bellows is reduced by pushing the handles, the air pressure inside becomes greater than the outside pressure, causing air to rush out until the pressure is the same.

4.1.2   Lung volumes

Respiration works very much the same way as the bellows. Muscles of the chest cavity, or *thorax* (Greek, "chest"), increase and decrease the volume of the lungs, causing air to move in and out to equalize pressure. This action, creating a vacuum to suck air into the lungs, is known as *negative-pressure breathing*. Figure 4.2 shows different types of breathing and how the amount of air in the lungs changes over time.

Quiet, or *tidal*, breathing is the regular kind of breathing people do when they're relaxed. Tidal breathing follows a rhythmical, roughly sinusoidal

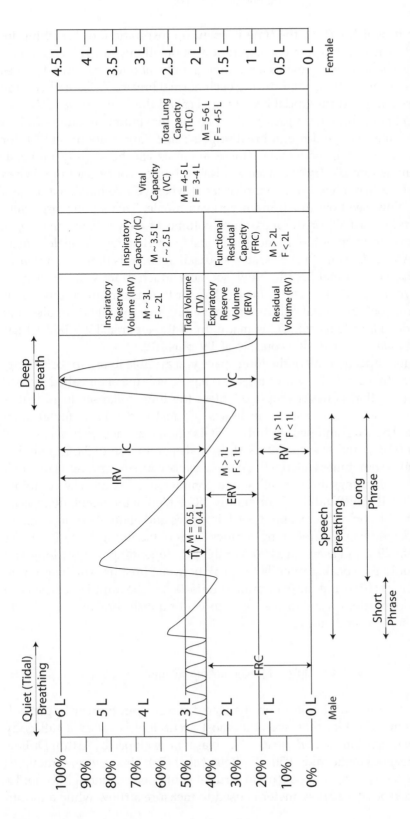

Figure 4.2 Respiration volumes and graphs for tidal breathing, speech breathing, and maximum breathing (See Marieb and Hoehn, 2010) (image by D. Derrick).

pattern in which 40% of the time is spent on inspiration, or breathing in, and 60% of the time is spent on expiration, or breathing out. Tidal breathing is quite shallow, with males exchanging only about 0.5 L and females exchanging about 0.4 L of air during each normal breath. This small volume of air exchanged during tidal breathing is called the *tidal volume* (TV).

In contrast, the *vital capacity* (VC), or the maximum amount of air a person can exchange through breathing, is much larger, about 4 to 5 L for males, and 3 to 4 L for females (these amounts can be slightly higher if breathing is forced). Try this exercise: Relax. Notice your breathing. When you've breathed a few cycles, stop yourself when you've inhaled a normal breath. Now, see how much more you can inhale. That's your *inspiratory reserve volume* (IRV), or the maximum volume of air you can inhale *after* tidal inspiration (about 3 L in males and just over 2 L in females). Now relax again. After a few breath cycles, stop yourself again, this time when you've just exhaled a normal breath. Now, see how much more you can exhale. That's your *expiratory reserve volume* (ERV), or the maximum volume of air you can expel after tidal expiration (averaging just over 1 L in males and just under 1 L in females). VC is made up of three parts: TV + IRV + ERV. The *inspiratory capacity* (IC) consists of TV plus IRV.

So, vital capacity is all of the lung space you are able to use for breathing. However, that's not all – your lungs also have a volume of air called *residual volume* (RV) that is never emptied unless the lung collapses (e.g., if it is punctured). RV is just over 1 L in males and just under 1 L in females, on average. The RV combined with the ERV is known as the *functional residual capacity* (FRC), and averages 2 to 3 L in males and close to 2 L in females. FRC is also sometimes called *relaxation volume* because it represents the total volume of the lungs after exhaling and completely relaxing. The combination of TV, IRV, ERV, and RV (or simply VC + RV!) is the *total lung capacity* (TLC), and is, on average, about 5–6 L in males and about 4–5 L in females.

Speech breathing is different from other kinds of breathing. Speech can use as little as 25% and as much as 70% of the VC, depending on how long and how loudly the speaker intends to speak between breaths. The inspiration time is short (10%) and the expiration time is 90% of the duration of a speech respiration cycle, owing to the need to continuously breathe out slowly during speech production.

4.1.3   Measuring lung volume

The exact amount of air volume exchanged during respiration can be difficult to measure. The tool that does this most accurately is called a full body *plethysmograph* (Greek, *plethysmos* = "increase"), developed by Arthur DuBois and colleagues in the mid-1950s (DuBois *et al.*, 1956). This device, sometimes called a "body box," consists of an airtight container big enough to hold a whole person. An airflow meter is used to measure airflow while a mouth

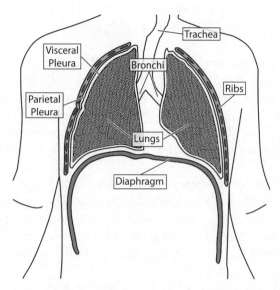

Figure 4.3 Overview of the respiratory system: coronal cross-section (image by D. Derrick).

pressure transducer measures lung pressure. Plethysmographs allow very accurate measurements of a person's vital capacity and also allow the measurement of the exact rate of respiration and oral pressure during speech. As a result, the devices are usually used in medical diagnosis of respiratory problems, but they can also be paired with EMG measurements in speech research to track when muscles are recruited during the respiratory cycle.

4.2 The Anatomy of Breathing

The bellows analogy for the respiratory system is useful when thinking about the basic mechanics of breathing. There are a few important structural details we'll want to know about respiration for speech (see Figure 4.3 for an overview).

4.2.1 The lungs

Inside the thorax are two *lungs*, which fulfill the function of the leather bladder of the bellows. But unlike the empty inside of a bellows, the lungs themselves contain more than just air. The lungs are composed of a very light airy tissue with pockets of air giving it a very spongy texture. This spongy material is made up of some 300 million *alveoli* (Latin, "small cavities") that fill with air, and that are surrounded by an intricate network of blood vessels for the exchange of oxygen and carbon dioxide.

Why lungs collapse

We've all heard the term "collapsed lung." The lungs themselves are very elastic, and standing alone, they would collapse like a deflated balloon. For breathing to work at all – that is, for the lungs to expand as the ribcage expands – the lungs must somehow be connected to the inner walls of the thorax. In fact, the lungs are not physically attached to the walls of the thorax at all. So . . . how does this work? Suction.

A double layer of waterproof membrane called the *pleura* (via Latin, from Greek, "side, rib") surrounds each lung. The inner layer, which is attached to the lungs, is the *visceral* (Latin, "organs") *pleura*, while the outer layer, attached to inside wall of the thorax, is called the *parietal* (Latin, "wall") *pleura*. A thin film of fluid separates these two membranes.

Just as two microscope glass plates can be made to adhere to each other with a thin film of water, a thin film of fluid keeps the two pleural membranes stuck together by the force of suction.

Now we can understand why lungs collapse: if the pleural sac were punctured (as in Figure 4.4), the fluid would leak out, releasing the suction, and the lungs would collapse to their deflated state.

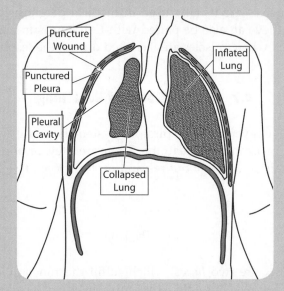

Figure 4.4   Collapsed lung: coronal cross-section (image by D. Derrick).

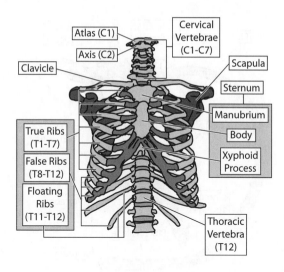

Figure 4.5a Bones and cartilages of respiration: anterior view (image by A. Yeung).

Like the bellows, the lungs have a tube that connects to the outside. This tube, commonly known as the windpipe, is called the *trachea* (Greek, "rough" – because of its uneven surface). The trachea doesn't connect directly to the alveolar sacs; there are multiple branches of tubes connecting the two levels. Groups of tiny alveoli connect together to feed into small tubes called *bronchioles* (Greek, "small windpipes"), which themselves connect together to form two large *bronchi* (Greek, "windpipes") that join together, one from the left lung and one from the right, to form the trachea. The trachea connects up to the larynx, discussed in Chapter 5, and forms the base of the vocal tract, opening up into the mouth and nose. In this way, the lungs have direct access to the outside, but can be left open or shut off at will by structures in the upper airway.

4.2.2 The hard parts: bones and cartilages of respiration

Now, back to our bellows analogy. Recall that, in order for the bladder to expand, it has to be attached to two stiff paddles. The bones and cartilages surrounding the lungs provide the structural support for respiration (see Figure 4.5a).

The spine, or spinal column, is the tower of small bones that makes up the central support system for the body: the ribs attach to it, the skull rests upon it, and the hollow space running down the middle of it is the protective passageway that houses the spinal cord.

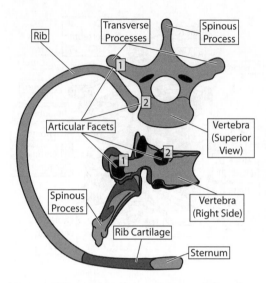

Figure 4.5b Superior view of vertebra and rib (with right side view of vertebra in the center) (image by D. Derrick).

The small bones that make up the spine are called *vertebrae* (related to Latin, "to turn") – see Figure 4.5b. The spinal column is made up of several different types of bones. From the top down, these are: the *cervical* (Latin, "neck") vertebrae in the neck, the *thoracic* vertebrae in the upper back, the *lumbar* vertebrae in the lower back, the *sacrum*, a triangular bone in the lower back made up of fused vertebrae, and finally the *coccyx*, or tailbone, at the bottom. The most important of these bones for speech are the cervical and thoracic vertebrae.

The skull rests on top of the *atlas*, or C1 vertebra – the topmost of the cervical vertebrae. The atlas in turn rests on the *axis* (Greek, "pivot"), or C2 vertebra. The axis and atlas are shaped and positioned to allow a wide range of movement, enabling the head to nod and rotate. There are seven cervical vertebrae in all (C1–C7). Aside from the skull, no other bones attach to the cervical vertebrae. In contrast, the 12 thoracic vertebrae (T1–T12) are built to attach to the 12 ribs. Each thoracic vertebra has two wing-like *transverse processes*, or sideward protrusions, that stick out laterally and a *spinous process* that sticks out posteriorly, like a dorsal fin on a shark. There are two indentations on each side of each thoracic vertebra. These indentations, called *articular facets*, are the points of contact for the ribs, with each pair of facets acting as hinges around which the ribs can rotate.

The ribs, sometimes called *costae* (Latin, "ribs"), are long, flattish bones that connect to each thoracic vertebra and wrap around toward the front of the thorax. The uppermost seven ribs, also called the *true ribs*, originate from T1–T7 and connect to a thick, flat bone around the front of the thorax called the sternum; the connection between these ribs and the sternum is cartilaginous and adds to the flexibility of the ribcage. Beneath the seven true ribs are five *false ribs*, originating from T8–T12. The false ribs do not connect directly to the sternum. The top three of these, originating from T8, T9, and T10, connect to cartilages that merge into the cartilage of the seventh rib. The bottom two ribs (11–12) do not connect to the sternum at all, and thus are referred to as the *floating ribs*.

In addition to the spine and ribs, several other bones of the thorax play roles in breathing. The *sternum* (Latin, from Greek, "breastbone") is actually three connected bones: the *manubrium* (Latin, "handle," related to *manus* "hand") on top; the long, thin *body* below that; and the small *xyphoid* (Greek, "sword-shaped") *process* at the bottom. The two *clavicles* (Latin, "small key"), or collarbones, attach to the sides of the manubrium and extend laterally to the shoulders. Around the back are two broad, flat bones – the *scapulae* (via Latin, related to the Greek word for "spade"), or shoulder blades, each of which connects to the clavicle and the upper arm.

Pump handles and bucket handles

The human ribcage can expand in two different directions: front-to-back (by lifting the whole ribcage) and side-to-side (by flaring out the ribs). Scientists who work with respiration often describe the movements that allow the ribcage to expand in these two directions as "pump handle" motion and "bucket handle" motion (see Figure 4.6).

Of course, the ribcage is made of bones, which don't themselves expand and contract, so how do we increase and decrease the volume inside the ribcage? The key is in the curved nature of the ribs. What's more, they don't stand outward like the rings of a barrel; rather, they – and the whole ribcage – rest downward, like your arms do when you clasp your hands and rest them on your stomach (try this!).

"Pump handle" movement describes the front-to-back expansion of the lungs. You can feel this if you lean back and look up – notice that your sternum lifts (pulled by muscles in your neck) and air flows into your lungs. This lifting of the sternum can be likened to lifting an old-fashioned water pump handle (it might help to remember that "manubrium" means handle!), with the hinge at your spine. Another way to picture this motion is with your arms: starting with your hands clasped in front of you and resting on your stomach, lift your

(Continued)

hands up, hinging at the shoulders and being sure to keep your arms stiff. Notice that the space between your arms and body gets bigger as the arms move up and forward. When the ribcage and sternum move upward in this way, hinging at the vertebrae, the lungs expand forward and so gain volume.

In contrast, the term "bucket handle" describes the motion that allows the lungs to expand side-to-side. Start again with your hands clasped across your stomach and your elbows resting against your sides. This time, lift your elbows only, keeping your hands touching your stomach. As your elbows lift away from your body, the sideways expansion of the lungs can be likened to lifting a bucket handle that is lying on the top of a bucket, hinged at two points: the sternum in the front, and the vertebrae in the back. Another way to picture this motion is to clasp your hands in front of you in line with your chest and let your elbows relax against your sides. If you lift your elbows up and outward while keeping your hands stationary, the gap between your arms expands sideways. If the entire ribcage does this, the lungs expand laterally and so gain volume.

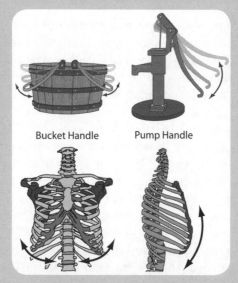

Figure 4.6 Pump handle and bucket handle motions of the ribcage: anterior view (left), right side view (right) (image by D. Derrick, E. Komova, W. Murphey, and A. Yeung).

4.2.3   Passive forces of breathing

There are three key passive forces that are balanced in respiration: torque, elasticity, and gravity. The bones of the respiratory system, especially the ribs, are semi-flexible and have a preferred rest position. When they are moved out of that rest position, they are somewhat twisted; this twisting force is called *torque*. Since the lungs adhere to the inside of the ribcage, the internal *elasticity* of the soft tissues (lung tissue and respiratory muscles) and rib torque oppose each other, resulting in a rest position that keeps the lungs partially inflated. *Gravity*, the last of the three passive forces, affects the rest volume of the lungs to a different degree, depending on whether someone is standing, sitting, or lying down. This is because the body's posture affects the amount of force the abdominal contents can exert on the diaphragm (see Section 4.2.4.1) and, hence, on thoracic volume.

Although the body at rest will always find a state of equilibrium, balancing its passive forces, the actions of respiratory muscles are constantly pulling the body out of this state of equilibrium. When this happens, the body needs only to relax to bring itself back into balance.

It's easy to demonstrate this: if you take in a deep breath, then relax, you'll see that you automatically *exhale* the excess air in your lungs; on the other hand, if you push out as much of the air in your lungs as possible, then relax, you'll see that relaxing causes you to *inhale* until your body's passive forces are in equilibrium again.

4.2.4   Inspiratory muscles

Several different muscles and muscle groups are important in expanding the lungs for *inspiration*, or breathing in. Some of these contribute to "pump handle" motion, some to "bucket handle" motion, while one muscle, the diaphragm, does neither, expanding the lungs from below instead.

4.2.4.1   The diaphragm   While the lungs are surrounded on their sides by the ribs, below the lungs is a large, dome-shaped sheet of muscle called the *diaphragm* (via Latin, from Greek, "partition"), shown in Figure 4.7. The diaphragm forms the barrier between the thorax above and the abdomen beneath. Because the diaphragm originates at the upper lumbar vertebrae and domes upward, when it contracts, the dome pulls downward, lowering the floor of the thorax and expanding the volume of the lungs. Thus, the diaphragm is an inspiratory muscle. As mentioned in the previous chapter, the diaphragm is innervated by the phrenic nerve, which begins with a merger of cervical nerves from C3, C4, and C5 and runs downward through the thorax.

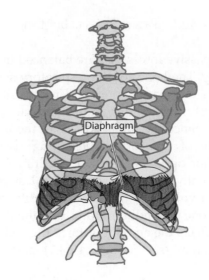

Diaphragm

Figure 4.7 Diaphragm: anterior view (image by W. Murphey and A. Yeung).

Use your diaphragm!

If you have ever studied singing or public speaking, someone has probably told you to "use your diaphragm." But, wait – your articulatory phonetics textbook says that the diaphragm can only contract for inhalation. Was your teacher wrong? Is your textbook wrong? Perhaps a slightly different choice of words would help to clarify.

The kind of breathing that pushes up and pulls down on the bottom of the lungs is variously called "diaphragmatic breathing," "abdominal breathing," or "belly breathing." The diaphragm contributes to this kind of breathing by pulling down on the bottom of the lungs, expanding them for inhalation. When your diaphragm pushes down, however, it squishes your abdominal contents, or guts, downward, making your belly bulge out.

You can think of your abdomen as a big water balloon. Because of its fixed volume, if you squeeze a water balloon in one direction it has to bulge out somewhere else. This is the key to how exhalation works in diaphragmatic breathing: you can use your abdominal muscles to squeeze inward on the guts, forcing them to expand upward into the ribcage, which compresses the lungs.

There are two reasons why your teacher might want you to use diaphragmatic breathing rather than expanding and contracting the ribcage for "chest breathing." First, the abdominal muscles are

(Continued)

incredibly strong, enabling strong and consistent contraction of the lungs. Second, many of the muscles we use to expand and contract the ribcage connect up to the muscles of the neck, directly or indirectly linking them to the larynx and speech articulators. Tensing these muscles for respiration can tense up these higher structures, making them less flexible for singing and speaking.

Hint: If you want to practice your "belly breathing," just lie down – most people breathe diaphragmatically when lying on their backs!

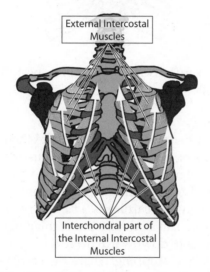

Figure 4.8 Vectors of the EI and III muscles: anterior view (image by W. Murphey and A. Yeung).

4.2.4.2 The intercostals The *intercostal* (Latin, "between ribs") muscles make up a two-layered system of muscles running between the ribs, wrapping around the thorax in different directions. Some subgroups of the intercostal muscles are inspiratory muscles and some are expiratory. All intercostals contribute to "bucket handle" motion. The vectors of the inspiratory inter-costal muscles are shown in Figure 4.8.

The *external intercostal* (EI) muscles run between the ribs along the outside (superficial) surface of the bones, with the muscle fibers forming a network linking downward and *obliquely*, or diagonally, away from the vertebrae. The EI muscles do not extend all the way to the sternum, but stop when they reach the cartilages at the front of the ribcage. Viewed as a system, the external intercostals link the ribcage up to higher points along the spine, so that when these strong muscles contract, they flange the ribcage up and

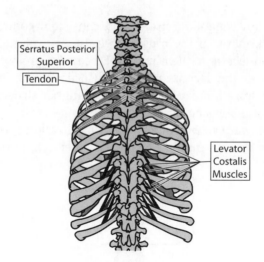

Figure 4.9 Some accessory muscles of inspiration: posterior view (image by W. Murphey and A. Yeung).

sideways in a "bucket handle" movement. Since there are 12 ribs on each side, there are 11 pairs of external intercostal muscles, each innervated by their respective thoracic nerves (T1–T11).

The other intercostal muscles that are important for inspiration are the *interchondral* (Latin, "between cartilages") *parts of the internal intercostal* (III) muscles. These muscles run between the cartilaginous parts of ribs 1–8, connecting obliquely and downward from the sternum along the inner surface of the ribcage and stopping where the cartilage and bone of each rib meet. As a system, the III muscles link the ribcage to higher points on the sternum, so that when these muscles contract, they pull the lower cartilages up and away from the center of the body in a "bucket handle" motion. Thoracic nerves (T1–T7) innervate their respective III muscles.

4.2.4.3 Accessory muscles: forced inspiration   Some inspiratory muscles are activated only during extreme or forced inspiration, as when gasping for air or taking an extremely deep breath. Some of these accessory muscles are shown in Figure 4.9.

The *serratus posterior superior* muscles comprise four thin muscles along the spine that originate at C7 to T2 and insert into the second through fifth ribs respectively. They are innervated by T2–T5 and may be used to augment "bucket handle" motion during forced inspiration. The *levator costalis* muscles also originate in the vertebrae and insert into the ribs. Each levator costalis muscle inserts into the rib that is immediately below the vertebra of origin. A third example of a forced inspiratory muscle is the *sternocleido-mastoid* (SCM) muscle, or the "head-turn" muscle. This is the muscle in your neck that you can see extending downward and forward from behind your ear when you turn your head to the side (try this with a mirror or a friend!). This large muscle originates in two places – the manubrium of the sternum and the middle of the clavicle – and runs upward to the mastoid processes, which are paired bumps in the skull that can be felt behind and below the ears. While the SCM muscles are usually used to tilt or move the head forward, if the head is held stiff, contracting the SCM can also raise the sternum for "pump handle" movement in forced inspiration. The SCM is innervated by the spinal part of the accessory nerve (CN XI). The infrahyoid or "strap" muscles – thin, strap-like muscles that attach to the larynx and tongue root above – can also be used to raise the sternum for forced inspiration; these muscles will be discussed in detail in Chapter 6.

4.2.5 Expiratory muscles

If inspiratory muscles act like someone pulling the handles of the bellows apart, then *expiratory* muscles act like someone pushing the handles closer together. Reducing the air volume in the system increases the air pressure in the lungs, causing air to rush out.

4.2.5.1 The intercostals The *internal intercostal* (II) muscles run between the bony parts of the ribs. These are technically the *interosseus* parts of the II muscles, but you normally only need to specify this to distinguish them from the III muscles. They represent the main sections of the internal inter-costal muscles, and function differently from their interchondral counter-parts. The II muscles are deeper than the EI muscles, originating along the inner (deep) edge of each lower rib and inserting into the inner edge of the next upper rib obliquely, but perpendicular to the direction of the externals (see Figure 4.10). Taken as a system, the II muscles create a strong sheet linking the ribcage to lower points in the direction of the spine. Thus, when these muscles contract, they pull the ribs downward in a bucket handle motion, reducing the volume of the sides of the ribcage and lungs for expiration. Like the EI muscles, each II muscle is innervated by its cor-responding thoracic nerve, T1–T11.

4.2.5.2 Abdominal muscles Abdominal muscles also play a major role in expi-ration during speech breathing. Going from the most superficial to the deepest, they are: rectus abdominis, external oblique, internal oblique, and transversus abdominis (see Figure 4.11).

The *rectus abdominis* (RA) muscle is the outermost anterior abdominal muscle, extending from the top of the pelvic bone in the groin area, to the lower costal cartilages that connect ribs 5–7 to the sternum. When this muscle contracts, it pulls the ribs down and inward in a pump handle

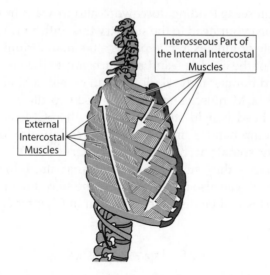

Figure 4.10 II muscle vectors with EI muscle overlay: right side view (image by W. Murphey and A. Yeung).

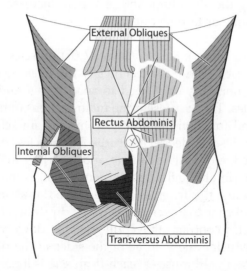

Figure 4.11 Abdominal muscles: anterior view (image by W. Murphey).

motion, thereby aiding in forced expiration. The rectus abdominis is innervated by the lower thoracic nerves T6 (or T7, depending on the person) to T12.

The *external oblique* (EO) muscles are covered by the rectus abdominis muscles in the front, but make up the outermost abdominal layer on the sides of the body. These muscles are broad and thin, connecting from just under the sides of the rectus abdominis in the front and running around to the back in an upward angle. The EO muscles contract to squeeze the guts into the abdominal cavity, pushing the diaphragm upward against the bottom of the lungs and resulting in exhalation. The external obliques are innervated by thoracic nerves T5 to T12.

The *internal oblique* (IO) muscles make up the middle layer of muscles in the sides of the abdomen. They run perpendicular to the external obliques from the back in a triangular shape to the top of the pelvic bone and halfway up the chest along the midline or *inguinal* (Latin, "groin") ligament. Functionally, the internal obliques act the same as the external obliques, squeezing the guts into the abdomen, pushing them upward against the diaphragm and the bottom of the lungs. The internal obliques are innervated by the lower thoracic nerves T7 to T12 as well as L1, the nerve of the first lumbar vertebra.

The *transversus abdominis* (TVA) is the deepest of the abdominal muscles. It wraps horizontally around the front of the body, originating in a line along the crest of the pelvis and the lower edge of the ribcage, and inserting into the *linea alba* (Latin, "white line"), a line of white connective tissue that runs up and down along the frontal midline of the stomach. Like the obliques, the TVA contracts to squeeze the guts, pushing them upward against the diaphragm, resulting in exhalation. The TVA is innervated by T6 or T7 to T12, and L1.

As with forced inspiration, many muscles can be recruited to force out the last bit of air from the lungs. These include the *latissimus dorsi*, commonly known as the "lats," and the *serratus posterior inferior* muscles (see Figures 4.12a and 4.12b). The serratus posterior inferior muscles are irregular quadrilateral muscles that originate in the T11 to L3 vertebrae and insert

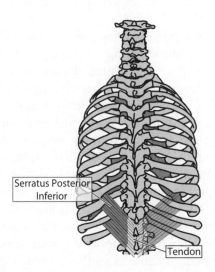

Figure 4.12a Accessory muscles of expiration: deep accessory muscles, posterior view (image by W. Murphey and A. Yeung).

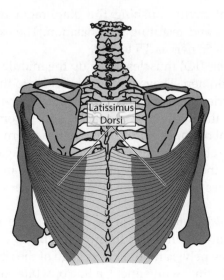

Figure 4.12b Accessory muscles of expiration: shallow accessory muscles, posterior view (image by W. Murphey and A. Yeung).

into the 9th through 12th ribs. They contract to pull the ribs down and backward in a bucket handle motion for expiration, and are innervated by T9 to T12.

4.2.6   The respiratory cycle revisited

Because of the passive forces described above, most of the time we don't need to do very much active exhaling – we can just breathe in, then use the muscles of *inspiration* to slow and control the return to equilibrium. During speech breathing, however, sometimes much larger volumes of air need to be exchanged in each respiration cycle (depending on the length of the utterance), and as a result more muscles must be recruited.

During speech respiration (shown in Figure 4.13), the external intercostals, interchondral internal intercostals, diaphragm, and levator costalis muscles are all recruited to take in lots of air in a short time for inspiration. During expiration, all these muscles stay active to slow the contraction of the lungs and allow air to escape in a controlled manner. As the system relaxes and the passive forces decrease, the diaphragm is contracted less and less and then the intercostal muscles are contracted less and less. At a particular instant, the equilibrium is reached, where air pressure outside is balanced with the desired subglottal air pressure (see Section 4.3 for more

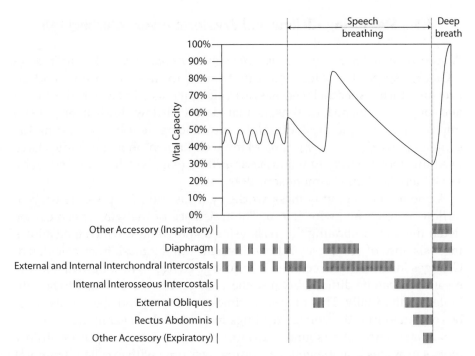

Figure 4.13 The respiratory cycle and muscle activation (image by D. Derrick, based in part on ideas in Ladefoged, 1967).

on this term) in the lungs, and for just that moment, neither inspiratory nor expiratory muscles are active. Immediately after this, the interosseous parts of the internal intercostal muscles are recruited to continue expiration. Now the torque in the bones and force of gravity on the guts exceed the forces of gravity on the ribcage and elasticity, and muscle force is needed to make up the difference.

As more air is expired, the abdominal muscles are recruited, beginning with the superficial muscles. Only when almost all the air that can be forced out is removed are the muscles of forced expiration such as the lats and serratus posterior inferior recruited to get the last of the expiratory reserve volume out.

Once the speech cycle ends, the passive torque is allowed to work, and gravity is allowed to pull the guts downward, until the lungs reach relaxation volume, and then the regular muscles of inspiration are recruited again. If the speaker is out of breath, s/he may now recruit the SCM and serratus posterior superior muscles for forced inspiration. In this way, expiration in speech breathing is slow and controlled, while inspiration is faster and less controlled.

4.3 Measuring Airflow and Pressure: Pneumotachograph

A speech *airflow meter* or *pneumotachograph* (*pneumo-* = Greek, "air"; *tacho-* = Greek, "speed") is a tool that can be used to measure airflow and air pressure during speech. It consists of an airtight mask that covers the mouth and/or nose attached to sensors that detect airflow. Rothenberg (1973) improved the simple mask design by introducing vent holes, creating the commonly used *Rothenberg mask*. Many well-known phonetic studies have used this tool to study oral and nasal airflow (e.g., Ní Chasaide and Gobl, 1993; Merrifield and Edmondson, 1999).

A pneumotachography mask works by measuring the pressure drop of airflow across a fine wire screen. The resistance of the wire screen can be determined by calibrating the mask using a known flow, which then allows the resistance of an unknown flow directed into the mask to be calculated. Changes in airflow are recorded as a voltage change. Working with airflow meter data can be difficult because the voltage transducers need to be calibrated individually. This process is time-consuming and the results must be computed into the voltage readings in order to be meaningful.

Similar to acoustic (sound pressure) recordings, the output of airflow meters provides a single voltage reading over time with excellent temporal resolution (see Figure 4.14). Airflow meters are also quite affordable, costing only a few thousand dollars for the best equipment. However, while airflow meters are not medically invasive, using a mask to cover the face may be unpleasant for some participants. Also, airflow meters interfere with audio recording, distorting amplitudes above about 1000 Hz (Badin *et al.*, 1990).

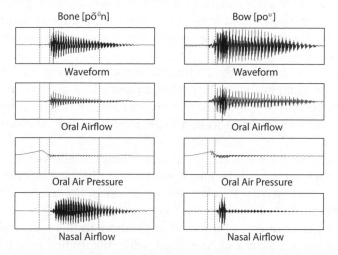

Figure 4.14 Acoustic waveform, oral airflow, oral air pressure, and nasal airflow (top to bottom) as measured by an airflow meter (image by D. Derrick).

As mentioned, airflow is measured by calculating the air pressure drop across a wire screen. Air pressure is measured using a *pressure transducer* that reacts to the strain of compressed air and records this strain as voltage changes. Pressure transducers are calibrated using known air pressure measurements from a *u-tube manometer*. The pressure transducer is attached to one end of a u-shaped tube, and the pressure is changed by a known amount and recorded on the manometer. This information is used to provide a conversion between the voltage measured by the transducer and known air pressures. As with airflow, air pressure recordings can be paired with acoustic or other recordings and analyzed statistically.

The two kinds of air pressure measurement that are useful for speech research both make reference to the *glottis*, the space between the vocal folds (see Chapter 5 for more on this): supraglottal pressure and subglottal pressure. *Supraglottal* (or *intra-oral*) *pressure* (P_{IO}), the pressure above the glottis, is easy to measure at the lips by inserting a tube into the mouth during speech. It's more difficult when measuring the pressure behind a farther-back constriction, in which case the tube may be fed in through the nose. *Subglottal pressure* (P_{SG}) can be measured by puncturing the cricothyroid space with a needle (Isshiki, 1964), or by threading a catheter down the throat and below the larynx (Cranen and Boves, 1985). Both techniques are invasive, and not all people can tolerate them. Another technique involves placing a balloon-like device down the esophagus and measuring the pressure through the device (Lieberman, 1968). To avoid invasive procedures, subglottal air pressure can be inferred from measurements of supraglottal air pressure during labial stops, because the subglottal and supraglottal air pressure has a chance to equalize. If the subglottal pressure during phonation is also measured, the glottal resistance during phonation can be calculated as the quotient between pressure and flow (Isshiki, 1964; Schutte, 1980).

The results of airflow and air pressure recordings can be segmented along with synchronized acoustic recordings and then analyzed statistically. Airflow or pressure meters can be stand-alone devices, or can be used with plethysmographs as described in Section 4.1.3, or with other tools.

4.4 Sounds

4.4.1 /h/

Now that we have a relatively thorough understanding of how the body makes air move, we can consider how we use this ability to make the sounds of human language. This moving air will allow us to make any speech sound. However, one sound in particular is associated with just the sound of turbulent air moving through the vocal tract. This sound changes its character depending on the shape of the upper airway. The sound, of course, is /h/.

As long as there is no narrow closure of the upper vocal tract to block the flow of air, a simple exhalation will enable you to produce this sound. Of course, in many languages and populations, /h/ is not quite this simple. Some languages use a constriction in the glottis, or even in the upper vocal tract, to create more turbulence to make the /h/ sound louder. Also, in some languages or for some speakers, an /h/ between vowels may not be voiceless at all – it may simply be a more breathy period in the middle of the voicing. In English, this pattern is typical of adult male speakers (Koenig, 2000).

4.4.2   Pitch and loudness

Regardless of the muscles we use, carefully controlling air pressure is very important for speech. This is partly because features of speech like pitch and loudness are affected by air pressure. For loudness, this is particularly true: because the lungs are very large compared to the vocal tract, a doubling of air pressure in the lungs leads to a fourfold increase in sound pressure, which people experience as loudness. Functions such as loudness or pitch are part of how we voice, or *phonate*, and will be discussed in the next chapter.

Exercises

Sufficient jargon

Define the following terms: respiration, Boyle's Law, equalization of pressure, atmospheric pressure, thorax, negative-pressure breathing, tidal breathing, tidal volume (TV), vital capacity (VC), inspiratory reserve volume (IRV), expiratory reserve volume (ERV), inspiratory capacity (IC), residual volume (RV), functional residual capacity (FRC), relaxation volume, total lung capacity (TLC), speech breathing, plethysmograph, lungs, alveoli, collapsed lung, visceral pleura, parietal pleura, trachea, bronchioles, bronchi, cervical vertebrae, thoracic vertebrae, lumbar vertebrae, sacrum, coccyx, atlas, axis, transverse processes, spinous process, articular facets, costae (ribs), true ribs, false ribs, floating ribs, sternum, manubrium of the sternum, body of the sternum, xyphoid process, clavicle, scapulae, passive forces of respiration (torque, elasticity, and gravity), exhale, inhale, inspiration, diaphragm, external intercostal (EI) muscles, obliquely, interchondral parts of the internal intercostal muscles (III), serratus posterior superior, levator costalis muscles, sternocleidomastoid (SCM), expiration, internal intercostal muscles (II), internal intercostal (II) muscles, rectus abdominis (RA) muscle, external oblique (EO) muscles, internal oblique (IO) muscles, inguinal ligament, transversus abdominis (TVA), linea alba, latissimus dorsi, serratus posterior inferior, airflow meter (pneumotachograph), Rothenberg mask, air pressure transducer, u-tube manometer, glottis, supraglottal pressure (P_{IO}), subglottal pressure (P_{SG}).

Short-answer questions

1   If someone has damage to spinal nerves C4–C5, describe how the production of speech would be most affected. How about someone with damage to spinal nerves T1–T6?
2   Describe how the diaphragm can act to increase the loudness of speech.
3   If the pressure times volume in a closed space is equal to 100 (don't worry about the units), what would the pressure times volume be if the pressure were then doubled (warning: this is a trick question!)?
4   For each of the following measurement techniques, find and cite one speech research paper not mentioned in this book in which the following techniques are used: plethysmograph oral airflow meter. Follow the reference formatting used in the references section at the end of each chapter.

Practical assignment

For each chapter, this text has online assignments (at www.wiley.com/go/articulatoryphonetics) that either provide research data for analysis, or practical tools for understanding vocal tract anatomy. For Chapter 4, you will perform hands-on data analysis of Airflow data of a person speaking their native language (L1) and a language they learned later in life (L2).

For this assignment you will have two tasks: The first is to write methods, results and discussion as though you were the author of a short experimental paper. The second is to figure out how to address realistic data that is difficult to interpret. The assignment and the related assignment images can be found in the online materials for this textbook under *Chapter 4*.

References

Badin, P., Hertegard, S., and Karlsson, I. (1990). "Notes on the Rothenberg mask," *KTH Speech, Music and Hearing Quarterly Progress and Status Report (STL-QPSR)*, *31*, 1–7.

Cranen, B. and Boves, L. (1985). Pressure measurements during speech production using semiconductor miniature pressure transducers: Impact on models for speech production. *Journal of the Acoustical Society of America*, *77*, 1543–1551.

DuBois, A. B., Botelho, S. Y., and Comroe, J. H., Jr (1956). A new method for measuring airway resistance in man using a body plethysmograph: Values in normal subjects and in patients with respiratory disease. *The Journal of Clinical Investigation*, 35, 327–335.

Guyton, A. C. and Hall, J. E. (2005). *Textbook of Medical Physiology* (11th edition). Philadelphia: Saunders.

Isshiki, N. (1964). Regulatory mechanism of voice intensity variation. *Journal of Speech and Hearing Research*, 7, 17–29.

Koenig, L. L. (2000). Laryngeal factors in voiceless consonant production in men, women, and 5-year-olds. *Journal of Speech, Language, and Hearing Research*, 43, 1211–1228.

Ladefoged, P. (1967). *Three Areas in Experimental Phonetics*. Oxford, UK: Oxford University Press.

Lieberman, P. (1968). Direct comparison of subglottal and esophageal pressure during speech. *Journal of the Acoustical Society of America*, 43, 1157–1164.

Marieb, E. N. and Hoehn, K. (2010). *Human Anatomy and Physiology* (8th edition). San Francisco: Pearson Benjamin Cummings.

Merrifield, W. R. and Edmondson, J. A. (1999). Palantla Chinantec: phonetic experiments on nasalization, stress, and tone. *International Journal of American Linguistics*, 65, 303–323.

Ní Chasaide, A. and Gobl, C. (1993). Contextual variation of the vowel voice source as a function of adjacent consonants. *Language and Speech*, 36, 303–330.

Rothenberg, M. (1973). A new inverse-filtering technique for deriving the glottal air flow waveform during voicing. *Journal of the Acoustical Society of America*, 53, 1632–1645.

Schutte, H. K. (1980). The efficiency of voice production. PhD thesis. University of Groningen.

Chapter 5

From Flow to Sound

In Chapter 4, we saw how the body gets air flowing from the lungs into the trachea. Now, let's look at how that moving air can be used to create the sound of the voice. Specifically, we'll look at phonation, the most common speech mechanism for converting air motion into vibration.

Phonation, or voicing, creates a buzzing sound in the throat, and that sound is then amplified and changed by our articulators to produce many of the sounds of speech. Phonation only occurs when conditions are right for it. Particularly important for phonation is the correct positioning of the muscles and cartilages of the larynx, or voicebox. The amount and speed of airflow also contributes to the type and quality of phonation, and to whether phonation will occur at all.

In this chapter, we'll describe the *intrinsic* anatomy of the larynx, and look at how we use the larynx for basic phonation and pitch control.

5.1 Intrinsic Laryngeal Anatomy

The *larynx* is a complex and adjustable tube of cartilage, muscles, and ligaments, suspended between the trachea below and the pharyngeal opening and hyoid bone above. The larynx houses and protects the two small fleshy folds known as the *vocal folds*, or "vocal cords," which vibrate to produce the phonation that enables us to speak, and which give the larynx its common name, the "voicebox." As mentioned in Chapter 4, the small space between the vocal folds is called the glottis.

Articulatory Phonetics, First Edition. Bryan Gick, Ian Wilson, and Donald Derrick.
© 2013 Bryan Gick, Ian Wilson, and Donald Derrick. Published 2013 by Blackwell Publishing Ltd.

In this section, we'll discuss the tiny cartilages and muscles that make up the larynx itself. We'll get to the hyoid bone and other *extrinsic* structures that surround and support the larynx in Chapter 6.

5.1.1   The hard parts

There are no bones in the larynx: the hard structures of the larynx are all cartilaginous. The main cartilages of the larynx are the cricoid, the thyroid, the two arytenoids, and the epiglottis (see Figures 5.1a and 5.1b).

The trachea, briefly mentioned in Chapter 4, is a tube of horseshoe-shaped cartilages with openings at the back. Interconnecting ligaments and mucous membranes between the cartilages make the trachea airtight. The thin back wall of the trachea is attached to the esophagus behind, and the tubes run parallel until the trachea diverts to the lungs and the esophagus diverts to the stomach.

Attached to the top of the trachea is the base of the larynx – the *cricoid* (Greek, "ring-like") cartilage, which is shaped like a signet ring, with the larger, flat part of the ring facing back toward the spine.

On top of the cricoid cartilage sits the *thyroid* (Greek, "shield-like") cartilage, the largest of the laryngeal cartilages. It is composed of right and left plates that fuse at the front to form the shield-like structure from which the thyroid cartilage gets its name. The two plates fuse together to form a triangular-shaped notch, or *angle*, that can be felt from the outside. This angle, called the *thyroid prominence*, has a more common nickname: the "Adam's apple." The angle of the thyroid is wider in women than in men (Zemlin, 1998), resulting in a more distinct thyroid prominence in men. At the back of the thyroid cartilage are two superior horns and two inferior horns. The *inferior horns* rest on the surface of the cricoid cartilage so that the two cartilages can rock back and forth relative to one another, while the *superior horns* connect the larynx upward to the hyoid, a small bone in the root of the tongue (see Chapter 6).

Just below the thyroid angle, the anterior ends of the *vocal ligaments* (the innermost part of the vocal folds) connect to the inside of the thyroid angle. The posterior ends of the vocal ligaments connect to the two *arytenoid* (Greek, "ladle-like") cartilages that rest on the thick part of the cricoid cartilage at the back of the larynx. The two tiny arytenoid cartilages are roughly pyramid-shaped, but hollowed out on one side like a ladle. The fronts of the arytenoids end in small protrusions called the *vocal processes*, which are the rear attachment points for the vocal folds. The *muscular processes* stick out behind and laterally, providing attachments for some of the intrinsic muscles of the larynx. The arytenoid cartilages have two primary movements: they can pivot on the cricoid cartilage or slide along its edge. Two miniscule bits of cartilage, the *cuneiform* (Latin, "wedge-shaped") and

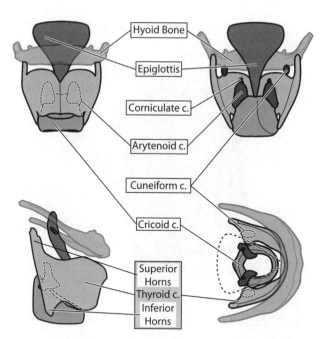

Figure 5.1a Major cartilages of the larynx: anterior view (top left), posterior view (top right), right side view (bottom left), top view (bottom right) (image by D. Derrick).

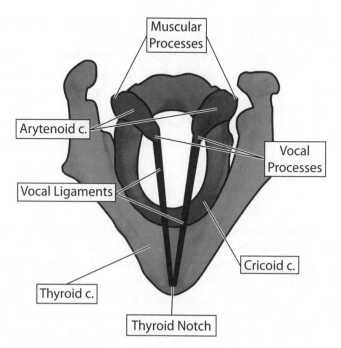

Figure 5.1b Larynx: top view (image by A. Yeung).

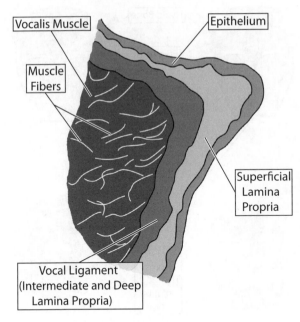

Figure 5.2 Internal structure of a vocal fold: coronal cross-section (image by W. Murphey).

corniculate (Latin, "horned") cartilages, sit atop each arytenoid, adding structure to the aryepiglottic folds (see Figure 5.1a).

The *epiglottis* is a flap of cartilage attached behind the angle of the thyroid near the root of the tongue, and projecting upward behind the tongue. During swallowing, the larynx is raised, and the epiglottis folds over to keep food from going down the trachea.

Now that you know the names of the hard structures of the larynx, it will be easy to learn the names of the muscles that connect them.

5.1.2   Intrinsic laryngeal muscles

Several small but important muscles connect the main cartilages of the larynx to one another. These are called the *intrinsic* muscles of the larynx.

The vocal folds, despite their small size, are actually very complex (see Figure 5.2). Medially to laterally (right to left in the figure), they are made up of: two covering membranes called the epithelium and the superficial lamina propria, both of which contribute to the vibrations of the folds, the vocal ligament, and finally a thin vocal fold muscle called the *vocalis* muscle, which is actually the lateral part of the *thyroary-tenoid* (TA) muscle.

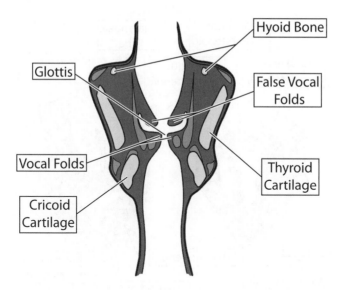

Hyoid Bone

Glottis

False Vocal
Folds

Vocal Folds

Thyroid
Cartilage

Cricoid
Cartilage

Figure 5.3   Coronal cross-section of the vocal folds and false vocal folds (image by W. Murphey).

The *false vocal folds* lie above the "true" vocal folds (see Figure 5.3) and the open space between the two sets of folds is called the *ventricle* (Latin, "small belly"). As such, the false vocal folds are often called the *ventricular folds*. The false vocal folds contain no muscles, and hence are not under direct muscular control, but in some speakers they can vibrate along with the true vocal folds, intentionally or unintentionally, which may result in a rough-sounding voice. Generally, however, the function of the ventricular folds in speech is not well understood.

The *posterior cricoarytenoid* (PCA) muscles originate at the back of the cricoid cartilage and insert into the muscular processes, the protrusions along the back lateral surface of the arytenoid cartilages (see Figures 5.4 and 5.5). When the PCA muscles contract, they tilt and pivot the arytenoids back, separating, or *abducting*, the vocal processes outward (see Figure 5.6).

The *lateral cricoarytenoid* (LCA) muscles originate along the outside edges of the cricoid cartilage and insert into the muscular processes. When these muscles contract, they pivot the arytenoid cartilages so that the vocal processes turn inward, *adducting*, or moving the vocal folds together (see Figure 5.6). In this way, tensing the LCA muscles creates *medial compression*, or pressure forcing the middle of the vocal folds together. Contracting the LCA muscles to just the right degree is important when attempting to phonate – the vocal folds must be close enough together (but not pressed too tightly against one another) for phonation to occur.

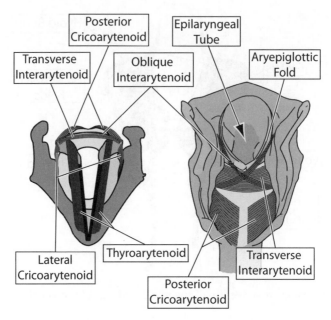

Figure 5.4 Intrinsic muscles of the larynx: top view (left), posterior view (right) (image by W. Murphey and A. Yeung).

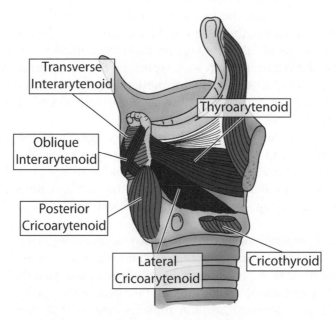

Figure 5.5 Intrinsic muscles of the larynx: right side view (image by E. Komova, based on Gray, 1918).

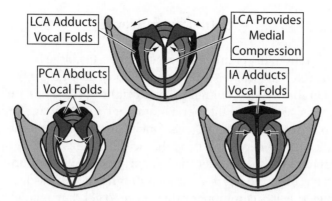

Figure 5.6 Schematic showing functions of the laryngeal muscles: top view of the larynx (image by D. Derrick).

The arytenoid cartilages are connected to each other by the interarytenoid (IA) muscles: the *transverse interarytenoid* (IAt) muscle, a single muscle that connects the backs of the arytenoid cartilages horizontally, and the *oblique interarytenoid* (IAo) muscles, which connect diagonally behind the IAt muscle. The IA muscles can, in conjunction with the LCA muscles, tense to close the vocal folds completely (see Figure 5.6).

The IAo muscles each continue upward to connect to the top of the epiglottis. These extensions of the IAo muscles are sometimes called the *aryepiglottic* muscles, and they form part of the *aryepiglottic folds*, the largest of the folds in the larynx. The aryepiglottic folds (at the sides), the epiglottis (in front), and the arytenoid cartilages (at the back) make up the *epilaryngeal tube*. Because the tube starts at the false vocal folds (at the sides), these also contribute to part of the tube. Each aryepiglottic fold wraps around to the back of the larynx to envelop the cuneiform and corniculate cartilages, which look like white areas protruding along the upper posterior edges of the folds. These cartilages increase the rigidity of the aryepiglottic folds and add characteristic irregularities to aryepiglottic vibration.

All of the above intrinsic laryngeal muscles are innervated by the recurrent (inferior) laryngeal nerve, which extends from the vagus nerve (CN X).

The *cricothyroid* (CT) muscle originates at the front of the cricoid cartilage and inserts into two places on the thyroid cartilage, the inferior horn and the lower surface. The CT muscle is the only intrinsic laryngeal muscle innervated by the external branch of the superior laryngeal nerve, which itself extends from the vagus nerve. This muscle is of primary importance in pitch control.

Ortner's syndrome

During gestation, the cranial nerves all extend from the brain in a line, but as the fetus grows, the shape of the body changes from the form of a typical four-legged animal to the upright posture of a human. As well, organs form near the nerves and get in the way, forcing the nerves to grow around the organs. One such case is the left branch of the vagus nerve where growth of the heart requires the left recurrent laryngeal nerve to loop under the left aorta. Since it is not unusual for people have multiple heart attacks and high blood pressure for years before they die, it is common for this nerve to get damaged along with the heart. This causes paralysis of the left side of the larynx, making it difficult to close the vocal folds during phonation. People with this kind of paralysis, called *Ortner's syndrome*, have breathy or hoarse speech, and the syndrome can be life threatening, as an inability to close the vocal folds can lead to aspiration of food and subsequent lung damage (Brasnu, 2000).

5.2 Sounds: The Voice

Now that we've covered the anatomy of the larynx, we have the tools we need to understand phonation, the buzzing sound (the source of many speech sounds) at the vocal folds, more commonly known as the "voice." As mentioned above, once air leaves the lungs and passes through the trachea, it encounters the larynx. Within the larynx are the two ligament-muscle sets that make up the vocal folds, which can move together to form a fleshy wall with an air slit – the glottis – in the center (see Figure 5.7). During speech, the glottis opens and closes in a regular, or *periodic* manner (just as the lower lip and tongue will do when one produces a "raspberry" or "Bronx cheer" – more on this in Chapter 10). The sound of this vibration is what we call *voicing*.

5.2.1 Modal phonation

Modal voice is the most common type of phonation, used in every spoken language in the world. It is the kind of phonation that is produced when air pressure and vocal fold configuration are optimized for maximum vibration (Ladefoged and Maddieson, 1996). During modal voicing, the vocal folds open wide and close tightly, spending about the same amount of time

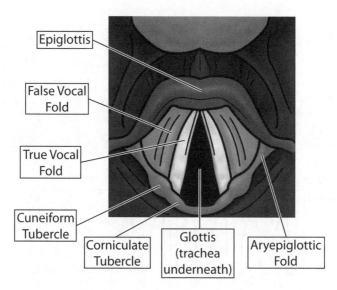

Figure 5.7 Top view of the glottis (image by E. Komova, based on Rohen *et al.*, 1998).

open and closed (though the duration of closure is longer at lower frequencies). As a result of this maximal vibration, modal voicing is comparatively louder than other forms of phonation (van den Berg, 1963). Because modal voice involves total closure of the vocal folds, it is limited by the maximum frequency at which a given speaker can maintain total periodic closure (Greene and Mathieson, 2001).

During modal voicing, the vocal folds are kept relatively thick, so that they don't simply open and close. Rather, they open and close in a complex cycle. In the opening phase of the cycle, the vocal folds open from the bottom upward, and from the back forward; the closing phase also proceeds from the bottom upward, but often moves from the middle outward to the front and back. This complex cycle of vibration results in a rich sound that can be easily shaped by movements at higher points in the vocal tract.

Figure 5.8 shows photographs of the vocal folds (images 1 through 10), with an *electroglottography* (EGG) signal plotted below (see the end of this chapter for more details about EGG). Electroglottography measures contact area between the vocal folds, so that higher values show more contact (i.e., closure), while lower values show less contact (i.e., opening). As you can see from the gentle downward slope starting at point 1 in Figure 5.8, the opening phase in modal voice happens gradually, then drops off quickly as the vocal folds pull apart (you can see this gradual pulling apart in Figure 5.11 as well). After this, the vocal folds stay open for nearly half of their cycle (the low period starting around point 6 in Figure 5.8), and then very rapidly smack together (note the very sharp rise in contact area at point 10).

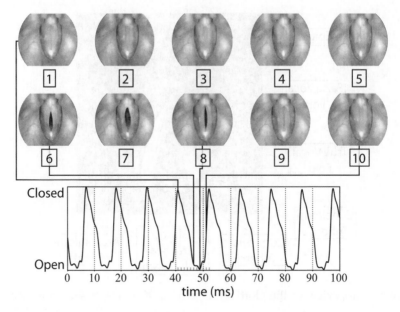

Figure 5.8 High-speed laryngograph images of modal voice cycle with typical EGG: top view. Note that the EGG image does not come from the same person, and has been added for illustrative purposes (image by D. Derrick, full video available on YouTube by tjduetsch).

The rest of this chapter explains how theories of phonation can help us to understand this complex pattern.

5.2.2   Theories of modal phonation

For more than three hundred years, people have come up with various theories to explain how phonation works. We'll have a brief look at some of the earlier ideas and then focus on the theories that are most widely believed today.

During the eighteenth century, Ferrein (1741), a French physician, argued that the vocal folds worked like the vibrating strings of a violin to produce sound. To demonstrate why this is not a good explanation of phonation, imagine plucking the string of a violin while covering the two resonance holes (*f-holes*) on the top of the violin. The violin will sound much quieter than normal. While the vocal tract has resonant properties that are important for speech, they do not amplify sound enough for this theory to be plausible.

If the vocal folds are not like vibrating strings, perhaps they are controlled like the wings of a hummingbird – with each flap of the wings controlled by its own muscle contractions. In the mid-twentieth century, the *neurochronaxic* theory (Husson, 1950) argued that each vocal fold vibration resulted from the deliberate motion of muscles in the vocal folds contracting and relaxing. However, during speech, the vocal folds can vibrate from about 80 to over 500 times per second (Hz). These vibrations occur much faster than the human brain can activate and relax muscles (even a hummingbird's wings can only beat up to about 200 times per second). Also, it is possible to produce phonation by blowing air through a larynx from a cadaver, i.e., without any muscle contractions at all. These two observations led Henry Rubin to publish a refutation of the neurochronaxic theory (Rubin, 1960).

5.2.2.1 Myoelastic aerodynamic theory of phonation

Rubin argued that van den Berg's (1958) *myoelastic aerodynamic theory* was a more accurate account of phonation. As is clear from its name, this theory combines two different components. The term "myoelastic" refers to the internal elastic forces that cause muscles to want to spring back to their resting position, while the term "aerodynamic" reflects how airflow creates the periodic vibrations of phonation.

Aerodynamically, the most important thing to know about the glottis is that it is narrower than the channels above and below it, and so forms a constriction. Intuition might suggest that airflow at a constriction would slow down, like cars in a traffic jam, or that pressure would increase as the air tries to force its way through the narrow point. However, two important, and perhaps surprising, things happen when air flows through a constriction: first, air moves *faster*, and second, air pressure on the surrounding walls *decreases*.

To understand the aerodynamics part of the theory, we'll need to learn a bit about *fluid dynamics*, the branch of physics that deals with how fluids (like air) flow. At the core of fluid dynamics are several laws, or basic assumptions, known as the *conservation laws*. Two of these that are important for phonation are *conservation of mass* and *conservation of energy*. These laws simply state that, in a closed system (like the vocal tract), mass and energy, respectively, must remain constant.

First, let's consider what *conservation of mass* means for air in the vocal tract. In simple terms, it means that the amount of air going in one end of the tract should be the same as the amount coming out the other in the same amount of time. This seems straightforward enough. However, what happens when there's a narrow point in the tube? If we imagine air as individual particles, conservation of mass suggests that the number of air particles going into the tube has to match the number coming out in the same amount of time. Even if there's a constriction, the air particles have to continue moving through. Since there's less area in a constriction for particles to pass through, the particles have to move *faster* to get past the constriction. As such, the speed of laminar airflow through a constriction is inversely proportional to cross-sectional area; that is, the smaller the diameter of the constriction, the faster air moves through it. You can see this clearly when you put your thumb over the end of a garden hose, making a narrow constriction: the water coming out of the hose speeds up.

Which way the wind blows

A fluid (like air or water) can move in different ways: it can flow smoothly along or it can churn and break. Scientists distinguish these two types of movement with the terms laminar and turbulent. Figure 5.9 shows airflow of these two types.

Laminar (Latin, "layered") flow occurs when a fluid (like air) flows smoothly in parallel layers, with no disruption between the layers. During laminar airflow in a tube, the air next to the walls of the tube flows slowly, while the speed of flow is fastest in the center of the tube, just as water flows in a slow-moving stream or river. In laminar flow, this pattern, as well as pressure and velocity, are stable over time. Acoustically, laminar airflow is silent or causes periodic vibrations.

In contrast, *turbulent* airflow is characterized by chaotic change, and it moves faster, not slower, next to solid boundaries. Turbulent airflow has a lot of randomness in individual particle motion, as well as eddies, or curls of fluid motion, as you can see when cigarette smoke is exhaled. Turbulent airflow therefore has rapid variations in pressure and velocity in space and time, like river rapids. Acoustically, turbulent airflow produces partially random, or *aperiodic*, noise.

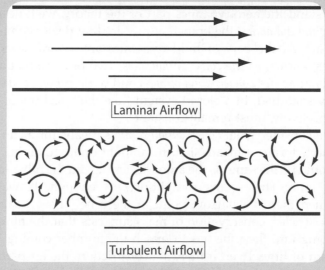

Figure 5.9 Laminar (above) and turbulent (below) airflow (image by D. Derrick).

Second, to explain why there's less pressure exerted on the sides of the tube at the constriction, we need to use the other law, *conservation of energy*. Imagine that each air particle is normally free to move around, such that it spends some of its energy bouncing off the side walls as it makes its way down the length of the tube. Each bounce contributes to the overall air pressure pushing outward on the inside of the tube. When a particle is moving through the narrow constriction, however, some of its side-to-side movement energy is spent moving quickly forward through the narrow segment of the tube, giving it less energy to bounce off the walls, resulting in less pressure on the tube walls. This relationship between velocity and pressure in fluid flow was famously expressed by the Swiss scientist Daniel Bernoulli (1700–1782). His formulation, known as *Bernoulli's principle*, states that for laminar flow of a fluid, when the speed of flow increases, pressure perpendicular to the flow decreases, and vice versa. This effect applies anywhere there is fluid flowing – not just in a vocal tract or a tube. Another scientist, the Italian physicist Giovanni Battista Venturi (1746–1822), explored how this principle worked in a tube. His observation, known as the *Venturi effect* (sometimes called "Bernoulli in a tube"), specifically shows that pressure drops when fluid moves through a constriction in a tube (see the left side of Figure 5.10).

Demonstrating Bernoulli's principle (try this!)

Rip a long, narrow piece of paper, and curve the top edge around your index finger. Put the sheet up to your lower lip so that the top edge is right next to the top of your lower lip (as in the top diagram on the right side of Figure 5.10). Now blow forward, parallel to the top surface of the paper, and watch as the drop in air pressure above the sheet causes it to rise.

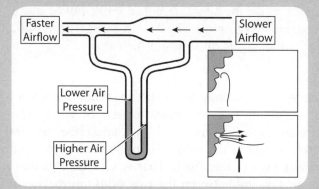

Figure 5.10 The Venturi tube (left); demonstrating the Bernoulli effect by blowing over a sheet of paper (right) (image by D. Derrick).

Now that we have some principles to work with, we can walk through how the vocal folds vibrate. When speech is initiated, the lungs are compressed, increasing subglottal air pressure (P_{SG}). If this happens while the vocal folds are held loosely together, P_{SG} continues to build, pushing upward on the vocal folds. Once the pressure from below is sufficiently greater than the supraglottal or intra-oral air pressure (P_{IO}) and strong enough to overcome the myoelasticity of the vocal folds, the folds are blown open (from the bottom up and the back forward). Even when the glottis is wide open, its area is still only about half the diameter of the trachea, so that the vocal folds themselves form a constriction in the vocal tract. Recall that the vocal folds during modal voicing are kept relatively slack and thick, making the glottis a constriction with some length. Because of conservation of mass, we know that air moving through this glottal constriction moves relatively faster, and based on conservation of energy (as expressed by Bernoulli's principle and the Venturi effect), the lateral air pressure on the vocal folds is relatively lower, than in the areas above and below the glottis. The relative vacuum created by this air pressure difference, combined with the elasticity of the vocal folds themselves, causes the vocal folds to be pulled together.

Hold your nose!

The difference between the air pressure below the glottis (P_{SG}) and that above the glottis (P_{IO}) is the *delta*, or change, in air pressure (ΔP). Phonation requires a minimum ΔP of about 2 centimeters of water (cm H_2O; a centimeter of water is defined as the pressure exerted by a column of water 1 cm in height at 4°C in Earth's standard gravity). About 7 cm H_2O is standard for conversational voicing, and with any ΔP less than 2 cm H_2O, phonation stops. To experience this effect, try to continually voice the labial nasal [m] while holding your nose. As the air pressure in your mouth builds up and ΔP decreases, the sound from the vibrations gets quieter and then stops.

5.2.2.2 The missing piece: modeling the vocal folds While the myoelastic aerodynamic theory explains two important aspects of what drives phonation (myoelasticity and aerodynamics), it does not describe the vocal folds themselves in detail. In fact, if the theory is applied to simple, uniform folds of flesh, it critically fails (Titze, 1988). That is, as a constriction narrows, the speed of the air flowing between the two sides approaches infinity – and the pressure approaches zero (i.e., a total vacuum). If vocal folds worked this way, they would be sucked shut as soon as they opened. The vocal folds can only vibrate the way they do because each fold is not simply one

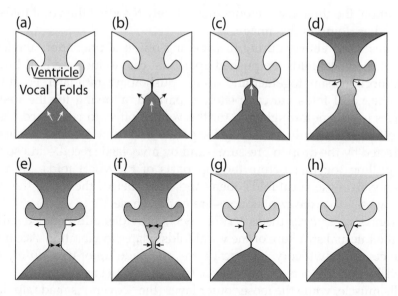

Figure 5.11 A schematic of vocal fold vibration: coronal view (image from Reetz and Jongman, 2008).

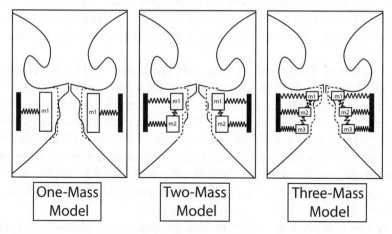

Figure 5.12 One-, two-, and three-mass models generate different predictions (dotted lines) for the motion of the vocal folds: coronal view (image by D. Derrick).

uniform mass of muscle but is instead many layered, creating multiple masses that can vibrate semi-independently. This concept was originally described as the *two-mass theory* of vocal fold vibration (Ishizaka and Flanagan, 1972), and you can see it in Figure 5.11. Researchers quickly adopted much more complex vocal fold models which included as many as 16 or more semi-independent masses (Titze, 1973, 1974) – you can see the differences between a one-, two-, and three-mass model in Figure 5.12. The predicted shape of the vocal folds is indicated by the dotted lines. In this illustration, the three-mass model most closely fits what the vocal folds are depicted as doing in this image.

As described above, during the opening phase of phonation, the lower parts of the vocal folds are pushed apart first due to increased ΔP, but the upper portions stay together and do not push apart until later. For a brief time, the vocal folds are completely separated, allowing for the first air particles to stream through, and for the Venturi effect to take place. Just as the bottom parts of the vocal folds separate first, they are also the first to be affected by the drop in pressure – and by myoelastic recoil – and so they start pulling together before the top parts of the vocal folds. Since the bottom part of the vocal folds opens and closes before the top of the vocal folds, we say that the two motions are out of phase.

Hirano's *cover body* theory (1974, 1985) provides additional detail on how the internal structure of the vocal folds relates to vibration. According to the cover body theory, the vocal folds are made up of two loosely connected layers: the denser inner layer (the "body") consists mainly of the vocalis muscle, while the looser outer layer (the "cover") is made up of the mucous membrane on the surface of the vocal folds. We now know there are several important layers in the vocal folds.

The multiple-mass and cover body theories show how a better understanding of the vocal folds themselves can help account both for periodic vibration and for some of the complex acoustic characteristics of phonation.

5.2.2.3 Adjustments to the model   The aerodynamic part of the myoelastic aerodynamic theory depends on laminar airflow. This works well for air and water, which are "thin" fluids. However, the outer film of mucous covering the vocal folds is "thick," or *viscous*. The effects of this viscosity on phonation are described as the *muco-viscose* effect (Broad, 1979). This theory describes how the air and viscous boundaries interact in complex ways, creating random vibrations or flutters on the vocal folds' surfaces, further adding to the complexity of vibratory patterns the vocal folds produce (see Figure 5.13).

A further adjustment to the model, Ishizaka and Matsudaira's (1972) *flow separation* theory, questions whether laminar flow alone is sufficient to describe phonation. In their model, *eddies*, or swirling flows of turbulent air, form at the edges of the vocal folds, helping to force the vocal folds apart.

5.2.3   Pitch control

The overall rate, or frequency, at which a body vibrates is its *fundamental frequency* (f_0). When the vocal folds vibrate more slowly, or at a lower f_0, we perceive this as lower pitch. We use adjustments of the intrinsic laryngeal

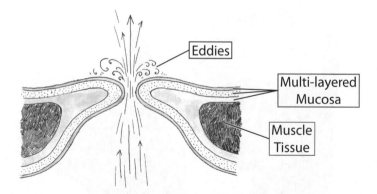

Figure 5.13 Flow separation theory: coronal view of the vocal folds (image from Reetz and Jongman, 2008).

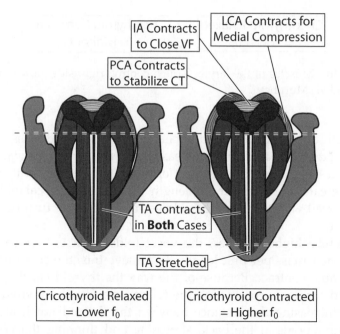

Figure 5.14a Muscles of the larynx – pitch control: top view (image by D. Derrick and W. Murphey).

muscles to change pitch during modal voicing, as shown in Figures 5.14a and 5.14b.

More massive things vibrate more slowly. To achieve the slower vibration needed to produce a lower pitch, parts of the thyroarytenoid (TA) muscles contract, shortening the vocal folds and making them thicker and heavier. It is not, however, the length alone that changes pitch. As the mass of the vocal folds remains more or less constant during modal voicing, changing

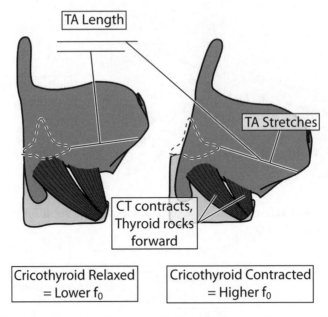

Figure 5.14b Muscles of the larynx – pitch control: right side view (image by D. Derrick and W. Murphey).

their length does not substantially change their absolute mass. However, shortening the vocal folds does increase their *mass per unit length*. Mass per unit length has a much larger effect on the rate of vibration than tension does: the greater the mass per unit length, the slower the vocal folds vibrate. Slower overall vibration equates to lower f_0, which is in turn perceived as lower pitch.

To produce higher pitches, the vocal folds must be stretched out to decrease their mass per unit length. To achieve this, the cricothyroid (CT) muscles must contract. Because of the way the thyroid cartilage rests on the cricoid cartilage, contracting the CT muscle tilts the thyroid cartilage forward, increasing the distance between the thyroid notch at the front and the arytenoids at the back, stretching and thinning the vocal folds. While the CT muscles contract, the TA muscles can also help to increase the frequency of vibration. Recall that the TA muscles, acting alone, will shorten the vocal folds to lower pitch. If, however, the TA muscles contract simultaneously with the CT muscles, creating an opposition, the vocal folds stiffen, which can contribute to raising f_0. The PCA muscles, normally used for abducting the vocal folds, also play a synergistic role in stabilizing the vocal folds as they stretch. When the CT muscle contracts, the PCA must contract somewhat as well to prevent the arytenoid cartilages from sliding forward, as any such sliding would hinder vocal fold lengthening, making it more difficult to increase f_0.

If the vocal folds stretch too much, the glottis can open up too wide to allow the complete closure needed for modal voice. In order to maintain modal voice at both high and low frequencies, the lateral cricoarytenoid (LCA) muscles must contract enough to provide medial compression. In addition, the interarytenoid (IA) muscles must contract to maintain a similar closure at the back of the vocal folds (Vennard, 1967).

The muscle contractions we've described above are not the only ways to change pitch. In fact, most people who lose control of one or two of the key muscles that control pitch can at least partially compensate using some other mechanism (Hirano et al., 1970). One alternative way of changing pitch is to change the height of the larynx. It has long been observed that raising and lowering the larynx is often associated with raising and lowering (respectively) voice pitch. Exactly how – and whether – this mechanism works is not well understood. One study (Nissenbaum et al., 2002) used high-speed MRI to show that in some languages, larynx raising and lowering is a regular mechanism for pitch control, independent of tilting the thyroid cartilage forward or backward relative to the cricoid cartilage.

Finally, in addition to changing the configuration of the larynx, it is also possible to change f_0 by changing subglottal pressure, such that an increase in P_{SG} – and the resulting increase in air flowing through the glottis – will often raise f_0. If all else is kept equal, louder speech (which often results from higher P_{SG}) will also have a somewhat higher pitch.

While aspects of speech such as tone, intonation, and prominence are often associated with pitch, these pitch changes almost always go hand in hand with varying other aspects of voice, including loudness and voice quality. Laryngeal control of voice and airstream is very complex, with many interacting aerodynamic and physiological effects determining the rate and type of vibrations (Plant and Younger, 2000). These effects can produce various types of voice quality beyond modal voice, some of which we will talk about in Chapter 6.

5.2.4   Voicelessness

In all this discussion of voice, let's not forget that voiceless sounds, too, play a big part in speech. In fact, there are many types of constriction of the vocal folds that can be used for making sounds. As we have mentioned, during modal voice, the vocal folds must be closed enough to vibrate and create a buzzing sound. However, there are times when we don't want the vocal folds to be vibrating. For example, during inspiration for speech, the PCA muscles are contracted, and the vocal folds are opened very widely. This allows the most airflow possible through the glottis and is extremely important since the diameter of the open glottis is still only half that of the vocal tract above and below.

The vocal folds are also open for sounds like [h] and aspiration. During the production of other voiceless consonants, the glottis is also spread open, though less extremely than during inspiration. Voiceless vowels are used contrastively in some of the world's languages (e.g., some Amerindian languages of the Plains and Rockies, Bantu languages of the Congo basin, and Indo-Iranian languages of the border region). During these sounds, the vocal folds are also open, though to a lesser degree than during most voiceless consonants.

Another type of speech for which the vocal folds are apart is *whisper*. Whispering is speech without periodic sound. Instead of producing voicing, the vocal folds cycle between an open voiceless state and a more closed whisper state. Throughout the cycle, the vocal folds produce frication (Sihler, 1999). As such, during whispered speech, the IA muscles are contracted only very slightly, if at all, and the PCA muscles are contracted slightly in order to abduct the vocal folds just enough to prevent voiced sound. Whispering is inefficient and has a high ratio of ΔP to amplitude. As a result, whispering is most effective for quiet communication and is used to communicate with nearby people while excluding others. It is possible to whisper loudly, and this "stage whisper" is often used for effect in public performance, but one runs out of air very quickly when doing this.

Closing the glottis tightly can also prevent phonation, and is accomplished by contracting the IA and LCA muscles tightly. During speech, the glottis can be rapidly closed for the production of a glottal stop. The epiglottis can participate in a similar but more forceful stop, as in Dahalo, a Cushitic language spoken in Kenya. The role of the aryepiglottic folds will be covered more in the next chapter.

5.3 Measuring the Vocal Folds: EGG

A non-invasive and easy-to-use technique for measuring vocal fold closure, electroglottography (EGG), allows the researcher to attach an unobtrusive collar around the subject's throat with electrodes on either side of the thyroid notch. Since electricity passes through flesh much more easily than through air, measuring the electrical resistance between these two electrodes is an easy way to know whether the vocal folds are open or closed at any point in time (Fourcin and Abberton, 1971; Lecluse *et al.*, 1975). Because greater contact area transfers more electricity, EGG also gives good information about the degree of closure, but says nothing about the degree of opening. EGG provides very high temporal resolution, but it doesn't reveal the location of the opening or contact in the vocal folds the way that video endoscopy, a tool that will be described in Chapter 6, can. Another drawback of EGG is that if the larynx as a whole is moving substantially up or down during speech, the vocal folds can easily move above or below the range of the electrodes, and EGG won't work.

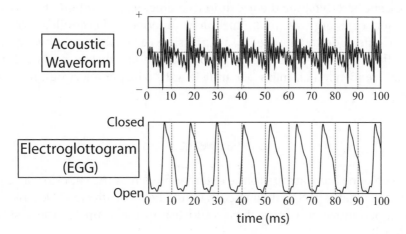

Figure 5.15 Comparison of glottal waveform from acoustics and EGG (image by D. Derrick).

Figure 5.15 shows acoustic data as well as EGG data. Here you can see that the same periods of opening and closure are apparent in the two signals. As in Figure 5.8, the EGG signal shows all of the characteristic patterns of opening and closure for modal phonation: 1) a gradual initial opening phase followed by a faster phase; 2) a sustained period where the glottis remains open, for roughly half of the cycle; and 3) a fast closure as the vocal folds smack together with the combined forces of elasticity and the Bernoulli effect.

Now that we understand the basics of modal phonation and the larynx, we are ready for Chapter 6, which describes other ways we can use the larynx to make the sounds of speech.

Exercises

Sufficient jargon

Define the following terms: phonation, larynx, vocal folds (vocal cords), cricoid cartilage, thyroid cartilage, thyroid prominence (angle), superior horn, inferior horn, vocal ligaments, arytenoid cartilage, vocal process, muscular process, cuneiform cartilage, corniculate cartilage, epiglottis, intrinsic laryngeal muscles, vocalis muscle, thyroarytenoid (TA) muscles, false vocal folds (ventricular folds), ventricle, posterior cricoarytenoid (PCA) muscles, abduct, lateral cricoarytenoid (LCA) muscles, adduct, medial compression, interarytenoid (IA) muscles, transverse interarytenoid (IAt) muscle, oblique interarytenoid (IAo) muscles, aryepiglottic muscles, aryepiglottic folds, epilaryngeal tube, cricothyroid (CT) muscle, Ortner's syndrome, periodic, voicing, modal voice, neurochronaxic theory, myoelastic aerodynamic theory, fluid dynamics, conservation of mass, conservation of energy, laminar, turbulent, aperiodic, Bernoulli's principle, Venturi effect, delta (change) in air pressure (ΔP), two-mass theory, cover body theory, muco-viscose effect, flow separation theory, eddies, fundamental frequency (f_0), mass per unit length, whisper, electroglottography (EGG).

Short-answer questions

1 If someone has damage to the external branch of the superior laryngeal nerve, what aspect of their speech would be most affected? Describe two compensatory strategies they could use to make up for the resulting deficit.
2 Describe the laryngeal muscle actions required for each of the following sounds: 1) opening the glottis wide for an /h/ sound, and 2) producing modal voice during the vowel /i/.
3 Rock singers sometimes develop nodules (small masses of tissue) on their vocal folds. Thinking of mass per unit length, how would you expect these extra growths to affect the sound of these singers' voices?
4 For the following measurement technique, find and cite two speech research papers not mentioned in this book in which that technique is used: electroglottography (EGG). Follow the reference formatting used in the references section at the end of each chapter.

Paper larynx exercise (see Figure 5.16)

For each chapter, this text has online assignments (at www.wiley.com/go/articulatoryphonetics) that either provide research data for analysis, or practical tools for understanding vocal tract anatomy. For Chapter 5, you will cut out and fold together a paper larynx, and then answer questions about the anatomical structures represented on the paper larynx. This assignment might seem easy, but the challenge of understanding anatomical structures in three dimensions should not be underestimated.

 Cutting and folding instructions:

0 Cut along all the solid lines (don't forget to make a small cut along the line marked with an arrow).
1 Fold along the three dotted lines that allow you to glue the tab marked "1" under the number "1"; this should form a triangular pyramid (the left arytenoid cartilage) with all the shaded markings and letters still visible.
(Note: the glue should go on the gray numbers).

Figure 5.16 Paper larynx (image by B. Gick). This figure is also available for download at www.wiley.com/go/articulatoryphonetics.

2 Do the same with the number "2" to form the right arytenoid cartilage.
3 Bend the paper into a ring so that you can glue the tab marked "3" under the number "3," keeping shaded areas on the outside. This forms the cricoid cartilage.
4 Fold up along the two dotted lines marked "4."
5 Bend the paper so that you can glue the tab marked "5" under the number "5"; crease lightly along the three dotted lines. Your thyroid cartilage and epiglottis are now in place.
6 Bend the tab marked "6" in a ring and tape under the number "6" to form the hyoid bone.

Paper larynx questions

1 What letters correspond to the origin and insertion locations of the muscle whose constriction primarily decreases pitch? Identify (a) origin (b) insertion.
2 What letters correspond to the origin and insertion locations of the muscle whose constriction primarily increases pitch? Identify (a) origin (b) insertion.
3 What letters correspond to the origin and insertion locations of the muscle whose activation abducts the vocal folds? Identify (a) origin (b) insertion.
4 What letters correspond to the origin and insertion locations of the muscle whose activation provides medial compression? Identify (a) origin (b) insertion.
5 Which letter corresponds to the attachments of a muscle that is bisected by the midsagittal plane?

References

Brasnu, D. F. (2000). Recurrent laryngeal nerve paralysis: Current concepts and treatment: Part I – phylogenesis and physiology. *Ear, Nose & Throat Journal*.
Broad, D. (1979). The new theories of vocal fold vibration. In N. Lass (ed.), *Speech and Language: Advances in Basic Research and Practice*. New York: Academic Press, 203–256.
Ferrein, M. A. (1741). *De la formation de la voix de l'homme*. Recueil de l'Académie Royale des Sciences de Paris, 402–432 [cited in Reetz and Jongman, 2008].
Fourcin, A. J. and Abberton, E. (1971). First applications of a new laryngograph. *Medical Biology Illustrated*, 21, 172–182.
Gray, H. (1918). *Anatomy of the Human Body*. Philadelphia: Lea & Febiger.
Greene, M. and Mathieson, L. (2001). *The Voice and its Disorders* (6th edition). London, UK: Whurr Publishers.

Hirano, M. (1974). Morphological structure of the vocal cord as a vibrator and its variations. *Folia Phoniatrica, 26*, 89–94.

Hirano, M. and Kakita, Y. (1985). Cover-body theory of vocal fold vibration. In R. G. Daniloff (ed.), *Speech Science: Recent Advances*. San Diego, CA: College-Hill Press, 1–46.

Hirano, M., Vennard, W., and Ohala, J. (1970). Regulation of register, pitch and intensity of voice, an electromyographic investigation of intrinsic laryngeal muscles. *Folia Phoniatrica, 22*, 1–20.

Husson, R. (1950). Étude des phénomènes physiologiques et acoustiques fonda-mentaux de la voix chantée. *Éditions de La revue scientifique*, Paris, 1–91.

Ishizaka, K. and Flanagan, J. (1972). Synthesis of voiced sounds from a two-mass model of the vocal cords. *The Bell System Technical Journal, 51*, 1233–1268.

Ishizaka, K. and Matsudaira, M. (1972). Fluid mechanical considerations for vocal-fold vibration. In *Speech Communication Research Lab, Monograph 8*, Santa Barbara, CA.

Ladefoged, P. and Maddieson, I. (1996). *The Sounds of the World's Languages*. Oxford, UK: Blackwell.

Lecluse, F. L. E., Brocaar, M. P., and Verschurre, J. (1975). The electoglottography and its relation to glottal activity. *Folia Phoniatrica et Logopaedica, 27*, 215–24.

Nissenbaum, J., Kirsch, J. E., Halle, M., Kobler, J. B., Curtin, H. D., and Hillman, R. E. (2002). High-speed MRI: A new means for assessing hypotheses concerning phonetic control of voicing and F0. In *Proceedings of the North East Linguistics Society*.

Plant, R. L. and Younger, R. M. (2000). The interrelationship of subglottic air pressure, fundamental frequency, and vocal intensity during speech. *Journal of Voice, 14*, 170–177.

Reetz, H. and Jongman, A. (2008). *Phonetics: Transcription, Production, Acoustics, and Perception*. Chichester, UK: Wiley-Blackwell.

Rohen, J. W., Yokochi, C., and Lütjen-Drecoll, E. (1998). *Color Atlas of Anatomy: A Photographic Study of the Human Body* (4th edition). New York: Williams & Wilkins.

Rubin, H. J. (1960). The neurochronaxic theory of voice production – a refutation. *Otolaryngology – Head & Neck Surgery, 71*, 913–920.

Sihler, A. L. (1999). *Language History: An Introduction*, Amsterdam: John Benjamins.

Titze, I. (1973). The human vocal cords: a mathematical model, part I. *Phonetica, 28*, 129–170.

Titze, I. (1974). The human vocal cords: a mathematical model, part II. *Phonetica, 29*, 1–21.

Titze, I. (1988). The physics of small-amplitude oscillation of the vocal folds. *Journal of the Acoustical Society of America, 83*, 1536–1552.

van den Berg, J. W. (1958). Myoelastic-aerodynamic theory of voice production. *Journal of Speech and Hearing Research, 1*, 227–244.

van den Berg, J. W. (1963). Vocal ligaments versus registers. *NATS Bulletin, 19*, 18.

Vennard, W. (1967). *Singing: The Mechanism and the Technic*, New York: Carl Fischer.

Zemlin, W. R. (1998). *Speech and Hearing Science: Anatomy and Physiology* (4th edition). Boston, MA: Allyn & Bacon.

Part II
Articulating Sounds

Chapter 6

Articulating Laryngeal Sounds

The last several chapters led us through the process of producing speech up to the point where we know how the body makes vocal sounds. From this point forward, the range of different kinds of sounds that can be produced will explode. The rest of the book continues along this path through the remainder of the speech production system, giving more and more attention to the different sounds the system can generate.

Chapter 5 described the larynx and covered the basics of modal phonation – the process by which the vocal folds vibrate to produce the sound of the voice. However, the vocal folds can do much more than produce modal phonation, and there is much more to the larynx than just the vocal folds. The larynx plays many important roles in speech, both phonatory and articulatory, such as producing different kinds of voice quality or making some of the more guttural speech sounds. For example, the different voice qualities you can hear in Louis Armstrong's growl or Marilyn Monroe's breathy voice are the result of different ways of using the larynx.

In this chapter, we discuss some of the different sounds we can produce using the larynx, first covering a number of "non-modal" types of phonation, and then moving on to laryngeal airstream mechanisms, or how we can make air move by raising and lowering the larynx (rather than using the lungs). Since some of these sounds require moving the entire larynx, we'll begin with the *extrinsic* anatomy of the larynx, or those structures that surround, support, and move the larynx from the outside.

Articulatory Phonetics, First Edition. Bryan Gick, Ian Wilson, and Donald Derrick.
© 2013 Bryan Gick, Ian Wilson, and Donald Derrick. Published 2013 by Blackwell Publishing Ltd.

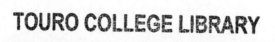

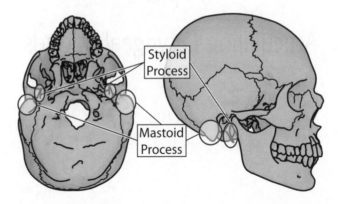

Figure 6.1 Skull: right side view (on right), bottom view (on left) showing styloid and mastoid processes (image by A. Yeung).

6.1 Extrinsic Laryngeal Anatomy

The larynx hangs suspended between hard structures both above and below. Below are the bones of the torso, which we have already described in Chapter 4; above are the bones of the head; and the suspension system in between is largely made up of the extrinsic laryngeal muscles.

6.1.1   The hard parts

We won't cover all of the bones of the head in this chapter. In fact, we'll discuss most of the skull in more detail in Chapter 7. In order to understand the system of muscles that supports and moves the larynx, though, we'll need to know about a couple of important connection points on the skull, as well as one tiny but very important bone – the hyoid bone, sometimes called the "tongue bone."

At the base of the skull, there are two sharp protrusions called the *styloid processes* (*styloid* = Greek, "stylus-shaped"). These inch-long, fang-like projections protrude from the bottom of the skull (see Figure 6.1), providing the origin point of several thin muscles that will be described in this and later chapters.

Lateral to the styloid processes, the skull also has two larger and smoother *mastoid processes* (*mastoid* = Greek, "breast-shaped"). You can feel these protruding at the base of your skull just behind your earlobes. These processes provide insertion points for the large sternocleidomastoid muscle described in Chapter 4, as well as some of the jaw muscles we'll get to in Chapter 8.

The last bone of the head we will cover in this chapter is a tiny but very important one for speech: the *hyoid* bone (*hyoid* = Greek "U-shaped"). The

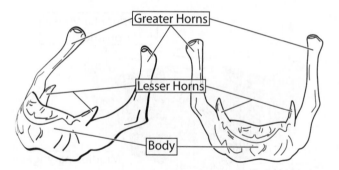

Figure 6.2 Hyoid bone: isomorphic view (left), anterior view (right) (image by W. Murphey).

hyoid, a small, horseshoe-shaped bone sometimes called the "lingual bone" or "tongue bone," is the only bone in the human body that does not make direct contact with some other bone. Rather, it hangs suspended near the level of the third cervical vertebra by a network of surrounding ligaments and muscles.

The hyoid bone has three distinct parts: the thicker *body*, the left and right *greater horns* (sometimes called *cornu*, from the Latin for "horn"), and the left and right *lesser horns* (see Figure 6.2). You can feel the body of your own hyoid bone by gently pressing into the crease where your neck and chin meet. Being the only solid part of the tongue, the hyoid bone gives the tongue essential structural support, and provides a vital anchor for the larynx below.

6.1.2 Extrinsic laryngeal muscles

Several muscle groups make up the *extrinsic laryngeal muscles*, the network of muscles that supports and moves the larynx from the outside. These are: the pharyngeal constrictors, the infrahyoids, the suprahyoids, and the pharyngeal elevators. Some of these muscle groups mainly provide support, while others are important for raising or lowering the larynx.

6.1.2.1 Pharyngeal constrictors The *pharynx* is the open space in the back of the throat, beginning at the top of the larynx and extending up into the nasal cavity. The *pharyngeal constrictor* muscles wrap around, forming the back and side walls of the tube-shaped pharynx, and giving support to the larynx and other structures (see Figure 6.3). There are three pharyngeal constrictors: inferior, middle, and superior. The first two of these – the inferior and middle constrictors – are an important part of the laryngeal support system, and so will be discussed here (we'll get to the superior constrictor in Chapter 7).

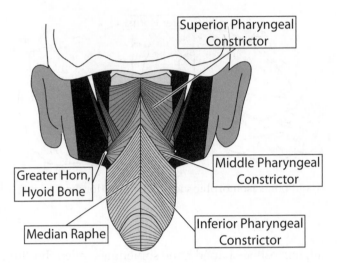

Figure 6.3 Pharyngeal constrictor muscles: posterior view (image by D. Derrick and W. Murphey).

The *inferior pharyngeal constrictor* muscles originate at the sides of the cricoid and thyroid cartilages, and wrap around to insert into the *median raphe* (Greek, "seam") of the pharynx, a vertical seam that runs midsagittally up and down the rear wall of the pharynx, where the left and right sides of the constrictors meet. Contracting the inferior constrictor pulls the whole larynx backward and raises it somewhat, while simultaneously narrowing the walls of the *laryngopharynx*, the lower segment of the pharynx. The inferior pharyngeal constrictor is innervated by the vagus nerve (CN X) via the pharyngeal plexus.

The *middle pharyngeal constrictor* muscles originate along the length of the greater horns and lesser horns of the hyoid bone, as well as from the stylohyoid ligament, and insert into the median raphe of the pharynx. Activating the middle constrictor retracts the hyoid bone and raises it somewhat, and narrows the walls of the oropharynx. Because it pulls back on the hyoid bone, the middle constrictor is also important for retracting the tongue root, and so will come up again in Chapter 8 where we discuss the tongue and jaw muscles. It is innervated by the vagus nerve (CN X) via the pharyngeal plexus.

6.1.2.2 Infrahyoid ("strap") muscles In Chapter 4 we mentioned the "strap" muscles – four ribbon-like muscles in the neck that can be recruited for forced inspiration. These muscles are also called the *infrahyoid* (Latin, "beneath the hyoid") muscles, because they all connect directly or indirectly to the hyoid bone from points beneath. Because of their position, they can be used to lower the larynx for certain speech sounds (though note that the

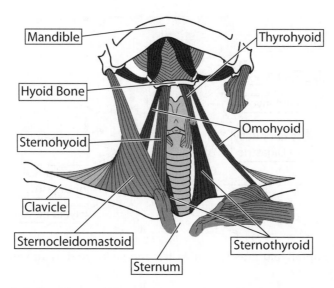

Figure 6.4 Infrahyoid muscles: anterior view (image by W. Murphey).

thyrohyoid, which links the thyroid and the hyoid, can either raise the larynx or lower the hyoid).

The four strap muscles, which can be seen in Figure 6.4, are: the *sternothyroid*, which originates at the manubrium of the sternum and inserts into the thyroid cartilage, the *sternohyoid*, which originates at the manubrium of the sternum and inserts into the hyoid bone, the *thyrohyoid*, which originates at the oblique line of the thyroid cartilage and inserts into the inferior border of the hyoid bone, and the *omohyoid* (*omo-* = Greek, "shoulder"), a muscle with two separate segments, or *bellies*, united by a short intermediate tendon (not unlike links of sausage); the inferior belly of the omohyoid connects to the scapula, the superior belly connects to the hyoid bone, and the short tendon is connected via fibrous tissue to the clavicle. All of the strap muscles get their innervation from cervical nerves C1 through C3.

6.1.2.3 *Suprahyoid muscles* The *suprahyoid* (Latin, "above the hyoid") muscles attach the hyoid to points above. All else being equal, substantially raising the hyoid bone will raise the larynx. While the infrahyoid (strap) muscles are all quite similar in form, the suprahyoid group is made up of four muscles of quite varied shape (see Figure 6.5).

The *digastric* (Greek, "two-bellied") muscle, like the omohyoid, has two bellies connected by a short tendon, with each belly innervated from a different source. The *anterior belly of the digastric* (ABD) muscle originates from a depression on the inner side of the lower border of the jaw, while the *posterior belly of the digastric* (PBD) originates at the mastoid processes. Both bellies insert into the short intermediate tendon, which is attached via a

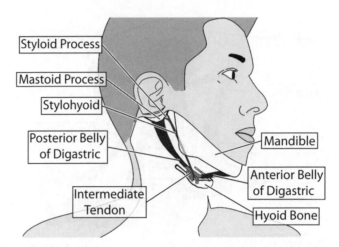

Figure 6.5 Suprahyoid muscles – digastric and stylohyoid: right view (image by W. Murphey).

tendinous loop to the body and greater horns of the hyoid bone. When both bellies contract, they form a sling that raises the larynx. Because the ABD attaches to the jaw, it is also an important muscle for jaw lowering (see Chapter 8). The trigeminal nerve (CN V) innervates the ABD, and the facial nerve (CN VII) innervates the PBD.

The *stylohyoid* muscle is a slender muscle that runs parallel to, and above and in front of, the PBD. As you may have guessed from its name, the stylohyoid originates in the styloid process and inserts into the hyoid bone. Contracting this muscle raises and retracts the hyoid bone. The stylohyoid is innervated by the facial nerve (CN VII).

The *mylohyoid* muscle is thin, flat and triangular. It is located just above the ABD, forming a sling-like floor beneath the tongue. It is a paired muscle (left and right sides) that originates from the length of the *mylohyoid line* along the inside of the jaw, and inserts into the hyoid bone (see Figure 6.6). Anterior fibers of the left and right mylohyoid often meet in a seam running midsagittally from the chin to the neck, forming a median raphe similar to the one seen in the pharyngeal constrictors. Contracting the mylohyoid raises the hyoid and stiffens the floor of the mouth. Like the ABD, the mylohyoid gets its innervation from the trigeminal nerve (CN V).

Just above (i.e., deeper than) the mylohyoid runs a narrow, paired muscle, the *geniohyoid* (geneion- = Greek, "chin"). The English word "chin" is related to the Greek *gen*, so that "chinny-o-hyoid" is a mnemonic that's both easy to remember and etymologically correct! This muscle originates from the inner surface of the chin (we'll talk about the jaw in more detail in Chapter 8), and inserts into the hyoid bone. Contracting the geniohyoid pulls the hyoid up and forward, making the floor of the mouth shorter and opening up the pharynx. C1, via the hypoglossal nerve, innervates the geniohyoid.

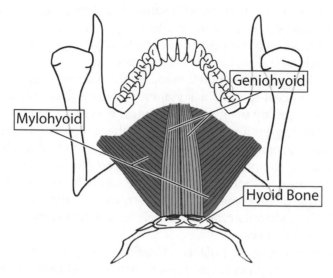

Figure 6.6 Suprahyoid muscles – mylohyoid and geniohyoid: posterior view (image by W. Murphey).

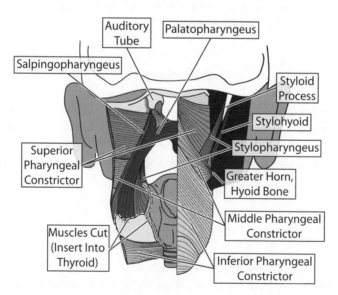

Figure 6.7 Pharyngeal elevator muscles. The pharyngeal constrictor muscles have been cut away on the left side to show deeper structures. Posterior view (image by D. Derrick and W. Murphey).

6.1.2.4 Pharyngeal elevators The larynx can also be raised by the pharyngeal elevators, a group of muscles that can pull up on the larynx and the walls of the laryngopharynx (see Figure 6.7).

The *stylopharyngeus* muscle is a thin muscle that originates at the styloid process and passes into the base of the pharynx between the superior and middle pharyngeal constrictors, with some fibers inserting into the pharyngeal constrictors and some directly into the posterior edge of the thyroid cartilage. The stylopharyngeus muscle elevates the larynx and laryngopharynx. Also, because the styloid processes are set wide apart, activating the stylopharyngeus can pull the sides of the pharynx laterally, widening the lower pharyngeal space. The stylopharyngeus is the only muscle in the pharynx innervated by the glossopharyngeal nerve (CN IX).

The *palatopharyngeus* muscle originates in the soft palate and merges into the stylopharyngeus muscle to insert into the thyroid cartilage. In addition to raising the larynx and laryngopharynx, because of its connection to the palate above, the palatopharyngeus muscle can help to lower and retract the velum, and so will come up again when we talk about velic sounds in Chapter 7. The palatopharyngeus muscle is innervated by the vagus (X) and accessory (XI) nerves.

The *salpingopharyngeus* (*salpinx* = Greek, "trumpet," referring to the opening of the Eustachian tubes) muscle originates at the ends of the Eustachian tubes and runs downward to insert into the palatopharyngeus muscle, and so helps to raise the laryngopharynx and larynx. The salpingopharyngeus muscle gets its motor innervation primarily from the vagus (X) nerve via the pharyngeal plexus.

6.2 Sounds

Chapter 5 introduced the most common type of phonation – modal voice. There are, however, many other kinds of sounds, both phonatory and otherwise, that we can produce using the larynx. We'll focus here on two of these in particular: non-modal phonation types, and glottalic airstream mechanisms.

6.2.1 Non-modal phonation types

In Chapter 5, we described modal voice as a type of phonation in which the vocal folds are held in the best possible configuration for maximum vibration. We also described voicelessness, when the vocal folds are spread apart. If the vocal folds are not held in the best possible position for phonation, but are nevertheless not spread widely apart, then they and other parts of the larynx can still vibrate when air passes through. This creates the possibility for many different types of phonation (hence the term "phonation types"). All of the different phonation types use the intrinsic and extrinsic muscles of the larynx to make adjustments to different parts of the larynx, creating a dramatic range of different voice qualities.

Only a handful of the *non-modal phonation types* that can result from laryngeal vibrations are commonly used in languages of the world. Aside from modal voice, the phonation types most widely used to make linguistic distinctions are breathy voice and creaky voice. While traditional descriptions of breathy and creaky voice have depicted them as being categorically distinct from modal voice, some work suggests that each of these may form a continuum with modal voice (Gerratt and Kreiman, 2001).

Other non-modal phonation types are more clearly distinct from modal voice, and are mostly used in different singing or speaking styles. These include growl and other subharmonic phonation types, and falsetto.

Alaryngeal phonation

Sometimes people use other parts of the vocal and alimentary tract than the larynx to produce *alaryngeal phonation*. People who have had laryngectomies (surgical removal of the larynx) may not breathe through their mouth or nose, but through a *tracheostoma* or tracheotomy tube, making them unable to phonate laryngeally. In lieu of an artificial larynx, controlling airflow through the esophagus (i.e., by swallowing and regurgitating air, or controlled belching), combined with proper constriction of the esophagus, produces *esophageal speech*.

Esophageal speech is difficult to produce, allowing only about 5 words per "breath." Such speech requires more effort and is quieter than laryngeal speech. Esophageal speech is produced by vibration of the large pharyngo-esophageal junction, and the frequency is very low at 50–100 Hz. Lower frequencies are quieter and easier to produce than high frequencies.

Very rarely, some speakers learn to use *buccal* (Latin, "cheek") speech, made famous by Clarence Charles "Ducky" Nash for the voice of Donald Duck (Weinberg and Westerhouse, 1971). Air is held between the upper jaw and a cheek, and forced through a gap behind the teeth and into the mouth. Because the source of air is so small, only two seconds of speech can be produced in each cheekful, and because the air source is in front of the nasopharynx, it is difficult to produce nasals with buccal phonation. Buccal phonation tends to have higher fundamental frequency than laryngeal phonation.

Creating an air supply using the tongue and pharyngeal wall produces pharyngeal phonation. This method is extremely difficult to master, and in one study of a 12-year-old who used this method (Weinberg and Westerhouse, 1973), half her speech was silent, and the rest was very noisy and difficult to understand. Only immediate family members could understand the speech effectively – others found it mostly incomprehensible.

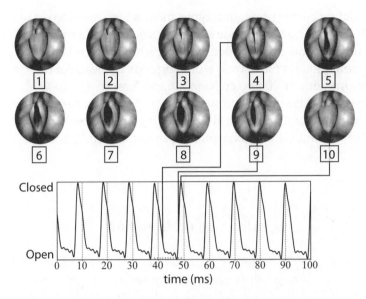

Figure 6.8 Breathy voice: one full cycle of vocal fold opening and closure, as seen via high-speed video. Note that the EGG image at the bottom does not come from the same person, and is added for illustrative purposes (image by D. Derrick, full video available on YouTube by tjduetsch).

6.2.1.1 Breathy voice Breathy *voice* is common in women's and children's speech. Breathy voice is characterized by the combination of phonation and the frication of air at the glottis, and it is easily recognized in the speech of Hollywood starlets from the 1950s. Marilyn Monroe's singing of "Happy Birthday Mr President" for John F. Kennedy is a classic example.

Breathy voice is typically produced in one of two ways. In one type of breathy voice, the LCA muscles are contracted less than in modal voice, leaving a longitudinal gap between the vocal folds that never entirely closes at any point in the cycle. This longitudinal gap can be very nearly closed, or it can be more open, as in the production of a voiceless glottal fricative [h], where a much higher ΔP is required to achieve phonation. In the second type of breathy voice, the IA muscles are not contracted enough to close the small posterior gap between the arytenoid cartilages. The vocal folds open and close during phonation, but there is always an opening at the back for air to escape (see Figure 6.8). This opening is sometimes referred to as a *glottal chink* in reference to the term for the unprotected openings between plates in a suit of armor.

Figure 6.8 shows endoscopic photographs of the vocal folds (images 1 through 10 in Figure 6.8 – see the end of this chapter for more information about endoscopy), with an EGG signal plotted below. As you can see from the sharp downward slope at point 4 and the sharp upward slope at point 9 in Figure 6.8, both the opening and closing phases in breathy voice happen quickly. Between the opening and the closure, the vocal folds stay open for a relatively long time – often more than half of their cycle.

Because the vocal folds do not fully close during breathy voice, they do not resonate as effectively and harmonics of the fundamental frequency decrease in amplitude rapidly. As a result, breathy voice is quieter than modal voice, and may be perceived as sexy or gentle. Also, since the space between the vocal folds is always partially open during breathy voice, more air escapes during production and breathy speech requires faster respiration or shorter phrases.

Unlike some of the other non-modal phonations described below, modal and breathy voice form a continuum. Nevertheless, individual speakers can usually produce a clearly perceivable contrast between modal and breathy voiced speech. As a result, breathy voice can be used in phonemic contrasts. This is the case for many languages and speech sounds, as in the vowels of Gujarati, the nasals of Hindi, and the stops in Hindi and some Bantu languages of southern Africa.

6.2.1.2 Creaky voice

Like breathy voice, *creaky voice* is also used as both a tool for age, gender, and social distinction, and for phonological contrast within some of the world's languages.

There is a minimum fundamental frequency below which modal voicing can no longer continue – usually about a quarter of the frequency of a person's average speaking fundamental. At this point the nature of phonation changes and the speaker begins to use creaky voice, also known as *laryngealization* or *vocal fry*. The term *stiff voice* has also been applied to a variety of phenomena that partially resemble creaky voice. In creaky voice, the vocal folds are very shortened and slackened to maximize their mass per unit length, and the IA muscles are contracted to draw the arytenoid cartilages together. This action allows the vocal folds to stay together for a much longer part of the phonation cycle than in modal voicing (see Figure 6.9), only allowing a tiny burst of air to escape between long closure periods. Multiple mechanisms have been described for producing creaky voice, including some that engage the aryepiglottic folds, as seen in Figure 6.9 (Edmondson and Esling, 2006) or the ventricular folds (Laver, 1980).

Figure 6.9 shows endoscopic photographs of the vocal folds above, and an EGG signal plotted below. During most of the long, gradual downward slope of the opening phase, the vocal folds remain closed until the very brief open period at the bottom of the graph (recall that the vocal folds open from the bottom upward, and that the glottis still appears closed from above during this gradual opening phase). In creaky voice, as soon as the glottis opens, it snaps shut again, as you can see from the sharp upward slope during the closing phase.

During creaky voice, the vocal ligaments often vibrate out of phase with the TA muscle. As a result, creaky voice phonation cycles alternate longer

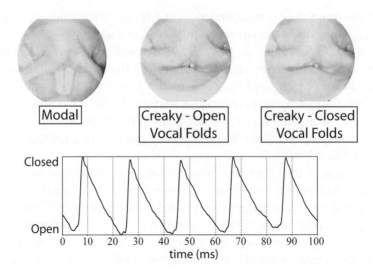

Figure 6.9 Creaky voice versus modal voice – as seen via a laryngoscope: top view. Note that this speaker's mechanism for producing creaky voice appears to engage the aryepiglottic folds. Note that the EGG image at the bottom does not come from the same person, and is added for illustrative purposes (image by D. Derrick, with data from Esling and Harris, 2005).

and shorter, resulting in higher acoustic *jitter* than in modal voicing. Similarly, phonation cycles alternate between higher and lower amplitudes (i.e., there is higher acoustic *shimmer*) than in modal voicing. The most extreme cases are nearly 180° out of phase, and can result in a perceived halving of the fundamental frequency (Ladefoged and Maddieson, 1996). Creaky voice is associated with a slightly damped fundamental frequency of vibration, and a more prominent acoustic second harmonic (h2), giving it a positive spectral tilt. Because the vocal folds stay together for a relatively long time, very little air escapes during the production of creaky voice, which is why people are more likely to use creaky voice when they are tired (and not wanting to expend energy breathing). Some populations are more likely than others to use creaky voice; older people often have creaky voice for clinical reasons and younger people often for sociolinguistic reasons. This is especially true at the ends of phrases. Some languages make phonemic distinctions between creaky and modal voice. In Central America, for example, a region rich with distinctive phonation types, Zapotecan Mayan contrasts modal and creaky vowels, Jalapa Mazatec contrasts modal and creaky nasals, and Cuzco Quechua contrasts creaky (glottalized) stops with non-glottalized stops.

6.2.1.3 Other subharmonic phonation Subharmonic phonation is a broad term that describes a variety of phonation patterns that generally give the effect of

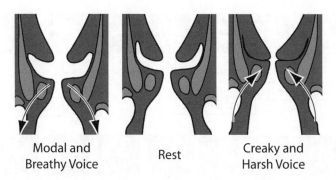

Modal and   Rest   Creaky and
Breathy Voice   Harsh Voice

Figure 6.10   Vertical compressing and stretching of the true and false vocal folds, as the larynx is raised and lowered (image by D. Derrick and W. Murphey).

lowered pitch, spanning across more than one glottal pulse. While creaky voice as described above can produce subharmonic phonation that uses only the vocal folds, subharmonic phonation types often involve vibration of other laryngeal structures as well.

During modal phonation, the true and false vocal folds usually vibrate at the same rate and phase, though not nearly as intensely, since the false vocal folds do not fully close. However, when the false vocal folds open and close at different rates or phases to the true folds, subharmonic phonation can occur. This mismatch is immediately perceivable auditorily, and shows up in high-speed imaging of the larynx. Taking one-dimensional slices of the high-speed images and stacking them beside each other produces *kymographs* (Greek, "wave" + "write"), graphical representations of the spatial position of an object over time (see the online assignment at the end of this chapter). Through these kymographs, it is easy to visualize subharmonic phonation caused by the false vocal folds (Lindestad *et al.*, 2004). The false vocal folds are commonly associated with laryngealization in the environment of a glottal stop, or with *harsh voice* (Edmondson and Esling, 2006). The true and false vocal folds can be compressed together vertically or stretched out as the larynx is raised or lowered (see Figure 6.10).

Similarly, subharmonic phonation may occur with mismatched oscillation of the aryepiglottic folds. During *growl* phonation, for example, the aryepiglottic folds are compressed anteroposteriorly, so that the *cuneiform tubercles* (fleshy surface) of the aryepiglottic folds make contact medially with the tubercle of the epiglottis (Sakakibara *et al.*, 2004). This compression in the middle of the airway folds the aryepiglottic folds in half, leaving a space on either side (see Figure 6.11). These two side cavities can oscillate in phase, out of phase, or sometimes in unstable patterns with relation to the vocal folds.

It is not clear what muscles are responsible for this anteroposterior folding constriction of the epiglottis. Contracting the aryepiglottic muscles,

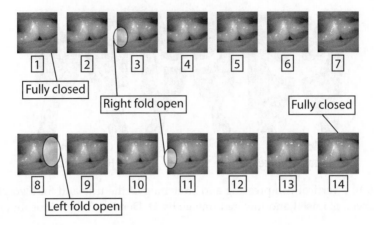

Figure 6.11 Voiceless aryepiglottic trill as seen via high-speed video (image by D. Derrick, with data from Moisik *et al.*, 2010).

which extend from the oblique interarytenoids upward along the sides of the epiglottis, can create a constriction of the aryepiglottic folds, but this would produce too much tension in the folds themselves to allow free vibration; alternatively, it has been suggested that fibers of the thyroarytenoids may be involved (Edmondson and Esling, 2006), or that perhaps a retracted tongue root could press downward on the epiglottis, causing it to buckle. English speakers often use the aryepiglottic folds for growl voice while singing: this type of singing can be heard from performers ranging from Louis Armstrong to death metal bands.

The aryepiglottic folds are also used linguistically for trilling (see Figure 6.11). *Aryepiglottic trilling* uses essentially the same mechanism as growl voice, except that the former term is usually associated with a trill consonant while the latter term more often applies to the vocalic phonation type. The large size and irregular shape of the aryepiglottic folds result in increased acoustic jitter and frication during these trills. Some languages such as Bai, spoken in China, have been described as using aryepiglottic trills phonemically (Edmondson *et al.*, 2001).

Acoustically, subharmonic phonation types can includes period doubling, amplitude modulation, and vocal fry, which are all perceptually distinguishable from each other (Gerratt and Kreiman, 2001). While vocal fry is usually identified with creak-like phonation in a clinical setting, the other two are characteristic of many phenomena, including creaky voice, growl voice, or "diplophonia," a minor condition that typically makes a person's voice sound deeper than their fundamental frequency.

These subharmonic phonation types all have one thing in common – non-linearity. In any system, if you can relate the passage of time to changes in the system either directly or through some kind of a mathematical transform, be it a sinusoidal pattern or a quadratic formula, then the system is linear. Linearity may sometimes work for certain types of true vocal fold phonation, but not when the vocal folds are coupled with other vibrating structures in the rest of the larynx or vocal tract. These interactions are too complex, and too random. This non-linearity makes relating acoustics to articulator motion extremely difficult, and in some cases impossible without extra information.

Register vs. voice

The term *register*, often used in describing singing, refers to "the voice quality produced by a specific physiological constitution of the larynx" (Crystal, 2003). As such, sung registers are similar to different *voices* or *phonation types*. The lowest register, often called vocal fry register, is equivalent to creaky voice. The middle registers, modal and falsetto, are equivalent to modal and falsetto *voice*, respectively. The fourth and highest register, the *whistle register*, is poorly understood. Some consider it just an extension of falsetto, but this is hard to confirm because it involves a constriction of the epiglottis that makes the phonation patterns very hard to see with a laryngoscope. Also, since whistle tones can be as high as 4000 Hz or higher, the motion of the glottis is difficult to film with conventional camera equipment. In traditional choral training, there is a distinction between different types of "voice": *chest voice* and *head voice*, and sometimes *pharyngeal voice*. Chest and head voice were traditionally considered distinct registers, but laryngoscopic analysis indicates that both involve modal voicing, with the distinction involving resonance properties, giving the physical effect of "feeling" the voice predominantly in the chest or in the head. Pharyngeal voice, a translation of the Italian *voce faringea*, is a quality described of Italian tenors several centuries ago, but it is not clear what it actually describes. It is certainly the case that speaking while contracting the pharynx produces a distinctive voice quality, but it's not clear whether what is traditionally called "pharyngeal voice" actually had much to do with the pharynx.

6.2.1.4 Falsetto Falsetto may be thought of as the opposite extreme from creaky voice, in that it is phonation at fundamental frequencies too high for modal voicing. As the CT muscles stretch the vocal folds to the limits of their elasticity, the TA muscles are no longer used to provide resistance. With the TA muscles relaxed, the vocal ligaments are placed under even greater tension. The TA muscles droop to the sides and the vocal ligaments

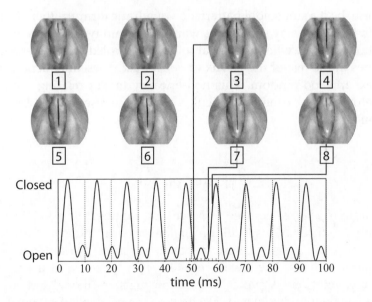

Figure 6.12 Falsetto: one full cycle of vocal fold opening and closure, as seen via high-speed video. Note that the EGG image at the bottom does not come from the same person, and is added for illustrative purposes (image by D. Derrick, full video available on YouTube by tjduetsch).

thin out, eliminating the multiple masses and complex vibration phases associated with modal voice (see Figure 6.12). The vocal ligaments then vibrate not like modal phonation, but instead more like the strings on a guitar, ironically much like some of the earliest theories of modal phonation would have them do.

For most people, the vocal ligaments do not make contact at all during falsetto. However, trained singers often have more control and can force contact between the mucous membranes of the vocal folds during falsetto. This contact produces a louder and clearer falsetto. Because of the abrupt change in TA muscle tension, it is difficult to transition between modal voicing and falsetto smoothly, but singers can be trained to do so, as in yodeling.

6.2.2 The glottalic airstream mechanism

We now know about the great variety of vibrations the larynx can produce in response to a pulmonic airstream – an airstream produced by the lungs. We also know the larynx can do more than just vibrate: it can also move up and down (among other things). By moving up and down, it can change the sub- and supralaryngeal volumes and so can cause air to move, just like the lungs do. In this way, the larynx can create its own airstream – the *glottalic airstream* – which many languages use to produce linguistically contrastive sounds.

We have described the muscles used to raise and lower the larynx. Here we will focus on two types of sounds that employ these changes in larynx height: ingressives and ejectives.

Laryngeal valves

Jerold Edmondson and John Esling (2006) have described the larynx and laryngopharynx in terms of a complex system of semi-independent "valves" that control the many laryngeal actions used in speech and non-speech:

Valve 1 – True vocal fold abduction and adduction
Valve 2 – Ventricular fold incursion (and possibly abduction/ adduction)
Valve 3 – Compression of the arytenoids and aryepiglottic folds
Valve 4 – Retraction of tongue and epiglottis back and down
Valve 5 – Laryngeal raising/lowering
Valve 6 – Pharyngeal narrowing/constriction

In this analysis, modal voice involves the constriction of the true vocal folds (valve 1), with breathy voice representing only their partial constriction. Creaky voice involves lax compression of the true vocal folds, and compression of the arytenoids and aryepiglottic folds (valves 1 and 3). The addition of compression of the ventricular folds (valve 2) generates harsh voice. Falsetto involves laryngeal raising (valve 5), while a yawny or "faucalized" voice involves, instead, laryngeal lowering (valve 5). In this way, the phonation types, as well as tone in speech and the distinction between tense and lax vowels, can be accounted for through the complex interactions of laryngeal/ pharyngeal valves.

6.2.2.1 Implosives/glottalic ingressives Glottalic ingressives, often called *implosives*, often combine two airstreams: a *glottalic ingressive airstream* (air flowing inward from the direction of the mouth) combined with a *pulmonic egressive airstream* (air flowing out from the lungs). These stops (and, less often, affricates) involve closing off the upper vocal tract and (usually) drawing the larynx downward using the infrahyoid muscles. Air in the vocal tract rarefies or reduces in pressure (see Figure 6.13). When the stop

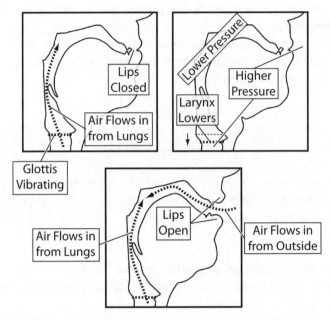

Figure 6.13 Timing of airflow and articulator motion for ingressive sounds: mid-sagittal cross-section (image by D. Derrick).

is released, air either does not move appreciably, or if there has been enough change in pressure, it rushes into the vocal tract. In addition to lowering the larynx to expand the upper vocal tract, you can also lower the tongue, lower the jaw, etc. (see Clements and Osu, 2002). Implosive consonants are usually voiced, meaning that air must flow into the vocal tract from the lungs at the same time. Because it is easier for both airflow processes to be salient if the space in the vocal tract is larger, with more room to change volume, it is easier to produce implosives with a closure farther forward in the mouth, such as a bilabial closure, than one farther back, such as a velar closure. As a result, bilabial implosives are the most common in the world's languages, and velar implosives are the least common. The opposite holds for ejective consonants. Implosives occur in many Sub-Saharan African languages, in some Southeast Asian languages, and elsewhere.

6.2.2.2 Ejectives/glottalic egressives Unlike glottalic ingressives, the *glottalic egressive* (also known as *ejective*) airstream requires the larynx to be raised. To make a glottalic egressive, first, close the larynx as if to form a glottal stop; second, make an oral constriction or stop (like a /t/) in the upper

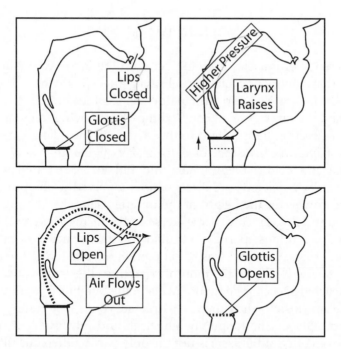

Figure 6.14 Timing of airflow and articulator motion for ejective sounds: midsagittal cross-section (image by D. Derrick).

vocal tract; third, raise the larynx, so that you feel the air inside your mouth is very pressurized; and lastly, release the oral constriction. If you do this right, you should hear a "popping" sound (in the case of an *ejective* stop) when this air is released through the mouth (see Figure 6.14). This mechanism moves enough air to produce ejective fricatives and affricates as well as stops. The basic raising of the larynx in this mechanism is produced using the suprahyoid and pharyngeal elevator muscles. If only a small amount of raising is used, *lenis* or weak ejectives are produced, sometimes with very little change in air pressure, making them difficult to distinguish from unaspirated stops. There are, however, many other muscles (e.g., the pharyngeal constrictors, tongue, and cheeks) that can assist in compressing the space behind the oral constriction, producing very strong, or *fortis*, ejectives. Despite their phonetic differences, weak and strong ejectives have not been shown to be contrastive in any languages. As a result of the relatively small space in the vocal tract from which air is released, ejectives are characterized by the sudden change in air pressure after the release of the stop. In addition, because the glottis must be tightly closed during their production, ejectives are necessarily voiceless.

Intrinsic f_0

The complex of muscles that interact with the larynx virtually guarantees that contracting one muscle will affect with the position of neighboring muscles and articulators. Since the tongue, the hyoid bone, and the larynx are all coupled together, moving the tongue can have an effect on the position of the larynx. In most languages, high vowels have an *intrinsic f_0* of 4 to 24 Hz higher than low vowels (Whalen and Levitt, 1995). Ohala and Eukel (1987) tested whether intrinsic f_0 was related to the resonances involved in the production of these vowels, or the height of the tongue itself.

Ohala and Eukel recorded speakers producing high and low vowels. In some conditions, participants had an unobstructed vocal tract, while in others, their jaw was held open with a bite block, forcing the tongue to rise higher in the mouth to produce the same vowels as in unobstructed speech. The high vowels in the bite-block condition had a higher intrinsic f_0 than the unobstructed vowel, suggesting a relationship between the tongue height itself and intrinsic f_0. It may be that the cricothyroid muscle is not the only way to affect the tilt of the laryngeal cartilages, and that a high tongue position can pull on the larynx and change the tilt. Such interdependence is common between the muscles and articulators of the vocal tract. New computer simulation techniques will help researchers uncover some of these interdependencies.

6.3   Measuring Laryngeal Articulations: Endoscopy

Because laryngeal structures are hard to get to and vibrate so quickly, it can be difficult to measure their movements. Nevertheless, several methods have been developed, each of which provides slightly different information about laryngeal movements. We described one method, EGG, in Chapter 5, and we'll describe another family of methods now.

Directly filming the larynx from above using an *endoscope* can provide much information not available through EGG. However, as with all tools, there is always a tradeoff. For example, while the exact locations of vocal fold contact and opening may be seen from above with endoscopy, in reducing the folds to a two-dimensional image, vertical variation in degree of closure cannot be observed.

Several types of endoscope are used in articulatory phonetics research. A *rigid endoscope*, which is a metal tube with mirrors and a camera, can be

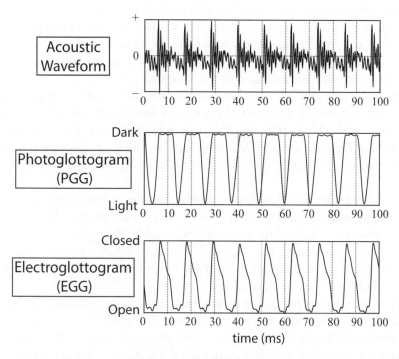

Figure 6.15 Comparison of glottal waveforms from acoustics, PGG, and EGG. Note that the acoustic waveform and EGG data come from the same person but the PGG data were constructed for illustrative purposes (image by D. Derrick).

inserted into the mouth to film laryngeal structures, but this makes speech difficult because the tube interferes with the oral articulators. On the other hand, inserting a flexible nasal endoscope containing a fiber-optic tube camera (*fibroscope*) through the nose will not interfere with phonation. Unfortunately, this highly invasive process normally requires anesthetization of parts of the nasal passage and medical supervision.

Historically, endoscopy has been used to record the larynx with low-speed cameras that operate at 24 or 30 Hz. As a result, it was impossible to see individual vocal fold vibrations. This limitation was originally overcome through the use of *stroboscopy*. By flashing a strobe light slightly slower or faster than the rate of phonation, it was possible to film many vocal fold vibrations in a row and catch slightly different parts of similar phonation cycles until the entire cycle could be characterized with some accuracy. Of course now it is possible to attach high-speed cameras to the end of fibroscopes or rigid endoscopes and film at thousands or even up to a million Hz.

Transillumination, also called *photoglottography* (PGG), is another tool that uses endoscopy – in this case, an endoscopic light source – to measure the glottal aperture over time. PGG involves inserting a bright fiber-optic light through the mouth or nose and shining it downward onto the glottis. The light that passes through the vocal folds is then picked up by a sensor placed on the outside of the neck just below the larynx. PGG data, along with the acoustic waveform and EGG data, are shown in Figure 6.15. Using PGG, one can observe variation in the size of the glottal opening, but not in degrees of closure (i.e., once the folds are closed, almost no light passes through the glottis until the next time it opens). Thus, it is similar in both its limitations and invasiveness to video endoscopy. However, newer non-invasive methods of PGG have been investigated (Honda *et al.*, 2012).

We must point out that for measuring glottal sounds, endoscopy and PGG have the disadvantage that if any structure above the glottis is physically in the way – including the ventricular folds, the epiglottis, the aryepiglottic folds, the tongue root or the pharyngeal walls – that structure will obscure the vocal folds. With these types of challenges, it is no surprise that there is still so much to learn about the larynx!

Direct measurements of non-modal phonation have only recently become possible, and even now the techniques are limited by the visibility of the structures, and the speed with which they move. Because of these historical limitations, much of the research into these types of phonation is just beginning to come together. The opportunities to learn new things about laryngeal mechanisms make this an exciting field of research.

In order to study all of the sounds in this chapter, in addition to measuring the vibrating parts of the larynx, it would be useful to have tools that could track the height and angle of the larynx as well. The tools we have talked about so far are not suited to measuring these aspects of larynx movements. Larynx height and angle can of course be extracted using techniques that image the entire head and neck, such as x-ray (see Chapter 7), and more recent work (Moisik *et al.*, 2011) suggests that optical flow analysis of ultrasound imaging (see Chapter 8) may show promise in measuring larynx height. To date, however, there has been little consensus in the field around how best to measure larynx height.

Now that we have finished with the larynx and laryngeal mechanisms, we will move upward in the vocal tract to cover velic sounds in the next chapter.

Exercises

Sufficient jargon

Define the following terms: styloid processes, mastoid processes, hyoid bone, body of hyoid bone, greater horns (cornu), lesser horns (cornu), extrinsic laryngeal muscles, pharynx, pharyngeal constrictor muscles, inferior pharyngeal constrictor, median raphe, laryngopharynx, middle pharyngeal constrictor, infrahyoid (strap) muscles, sternothyroid muscle, sternohyoid muscle, thyrohyoid muscle, omohyoid muscle, suprahyoid muscles, anterior belly of the digastric (ABD), posterior belly of the digastric (PBD), stylohyoid muscle, mylohyoid muscle, mylohyoid line, geniohyoid muscle, stylopharyngeus muscle, palatopharyngeus muscle, salpingopharyngeus muscle, non-modal phonation, breathy voice, glottal chink, creaky voice (laryngealization/vocal fry), stiff voice, jitter, shimmer, subharmonic phonation, kymograph, harsh voice, growl, cuneiform tubercles, aryepiglottic trill, vocal fry register, modal register, falsetto register, whistle register, chest voice, head voice, pharyngeal voice, falsetto, alaryngeal phonation, tracheostoma, esophageal speech, buccal, glottalic airstream, implosives, glottalic ingressive airstream, pulmonic egressive airstream, ejectives, lenis, fortis, intrinsic f_0, endoscope, rigid endoscope, fibroscope, stroboscopy, transillumination/photoglottography (PGG).

Short-answer questions

1 a) Which glottalic airstream mechanism – ingressive or egressive – would be more impaired by damage to cervical nerves C1–C3? Why?
   b) If cervical nerves C1–C3 were damaged, what other nerves could compensate in providing superior support for the hyoid?
2 Rank the length of the vocal folds (from longest to shortest) during the following phonation types: modal voice, creaky voice, and falsetto.
3 For each of the following measurement techniques, find and cite one speech research paper not mentioned in this book in which the following techniques are used: rigid endoscopy, fibroscopy, photoglottography (PGG). Follow the reference formatting used in the references section at the end of each chapter.

Practical assignment

For each chapter, this text has online assignments (at www.wiley.com/go/articulatoryphonetics) that either provide research data for analysis, or practical tools for understanding vocal tract anatomy. For Chapter 6, you will look at a set of images of a trill, converting them to a *kymograph*, or series of one-dimensional slices. This assignment will teach you how to use a specialized computer tool to analyze and interpret speech production data. Computer tools and techniques are often required in order to conduct research in articulatory phonetics. The assignment and the related images can be found in the online materials for this textbook under *Chapter 6*.

References

Clements, G. N. and Osu, S. (2002). Explosives, implosives, and nonexplosives: the linguistic function of air pressure differences in stops. In C. Gussenhoven and Natasha Warner (eds), *Laboratory Phonology 7*. Berlin: Mouton de Gruyter, 299–350.

Crystal, D. (2003). *A Dictionary of Linguistics and Phonetics* (5th edition). Malden, MA: Blackwell Publishing.

Edmondson, J. A., Esling, J. H., Lama, Z., Harris, J. G., and Shaoni, L. (2001). The aryepiglottic folds and voice quality in the Yi and Bai languages: laryngoscopic case studies. *Mon-Khmer Studies*, 31, 83–100.

Edmondson, J. A. and Esling, J. H. (2006). The valves of the throat and their functioning in tone, vocal register and stress: laryngoscopic case studies. *Phonology*, 23, 157–191.

Esling, J. H. and Harris, J. G. (2005). States of the glottis: an articulatory phonetic model based on laryngoscopic observations. In W. J. Hardcastle and J. M. Beck (eds), *A Figure of Speech: a Festschrift for John Laver*. Mahwah, NJ: Erlbaum, 347–383.

Gerratt, B. R. and Kreiman, J. (2001). Toward a taxonomy of nonmodal phonation. *Journal of Phonetics*, 29, 365–381.

Honda, K., Maeda, S., and Kitamura, T. (2012). Noninvasive photoglottography for measuring glottal aperture changes during speech. *Proceedings of the 2012 Autumn Meeting of the Acoustical Society of Japan*, pp. 303–304.

Isshiki, N. (1964). Regulatory mechanism of voice intensity variation. *Journal of Speech and Hearing Research*, 7, 17–29.

Ladefoged, P. and Maddieson, I. (1996). *The Sounds of the World's Languages*. Oxford, UK: Blackwell.

Laver, J. (1980). *The phonetic description of voice quality*. Cambridge: Cambridge University Press.

Lindestad, P. A., Blixt, V., Pahlberg-Olson, J., and Hammarberg, B. (2004). Ventricular fold vibration in voice production: a high-speed imaging study with kymographic, acoustic and perceptual analyses of a voice patient and a vocally healthy subject. *Logopedics, Phoniatrics, Vocology*, 29, 162–170.

Moisik, S. R., Esling, J. H., and Crevier-Buchman, L. (2010). A high-speed laryngoscopic investigation of aryepiglottic trilling. *Journal of the Acoustical Society of America*, 127, 1548–1558.

Moisik, S. R., Esling, J. H., Bird, S., and Lin, H. (2011). Evaluating laryngeal ultrasound to study larynx state and height. *Proceedings of the 17th International Congress of Phonetic Sciences (ICPhS XVII)*, 136–139.

Ohala, J. J. and Eukel, B. W. (1987). Explaining the intrinsic pitch of vowels. In R. Channon and L. Shockey (eds), *In Honour of Ilse Lehiste*. Dordrecht: Foris, 207–215.

Sakakibara, K.-I., Fuks, L., Imagawa, H., and Tayama, N. (2004). Growl voice in ethnic and pop styles. In *Proceedings of the Intl. Symposium on Musical Acoustics (ISMA)*, Nara, Japan.

Weinberg, B. and Westerhouse, J. (1971). A study of buccal speech. *Journal of Speech and Hearing Research*, 14, 652–658.

Weinberg, B. and Westerhouse, J. (1973). A study of pharyngeal speech. *Journal of Speech and Hearing Disorders*, 38, 111–118.

Whalen, D. H. and Levitt, A. G. (1995). The universality of intrinsic F0 of vowels. *Journal of Phonetics*, 23, 349–366.

Chapter 7

Articulating Velic Sounds

In Chapter 6, we discussed some of the many sounds you can produce using your larynx. As we move upward from there, the range of contrastive sounds you can make becomes ever greater. This is partly because the upper vocal tract can be divided into several large and distinct cavities. One major split is between the oral and nasal cavities; another is between the posterior oral cavity (the pharynx), and anterior oral cavity (the "mouth"). Both of these splits are defined by the same structure: the velum.

If you run your tongue from your front teeth backward along your palate (try this!), you will eventually feel that the palate softens. This pliable portion of the palate is called the soft palate, or *velum* (Latin, "veil"). This chapter will focus on understanding the function of the velum as a speech articulator. The velum plays a key role in making a variety of very different kinds of speech sounds: the oral-nasal distinction, velar and uvular consonant and vowel constrictions, and the lingual airstream used to make clicks (though clicks are somewhat more complicated, so we'll get to these later, in Chapter 11).

7.1 Anatomy of the Velum

Once the airstream has moved above the laryngopharynx into the *oropharynx* (the airspace behind the tongue), it can go one of two ways: to make oral sounds, air can flow forward into the oral cavity via an arch-shaped

Articulatory Phonetics, First Edition. Bryan Gick, Ian Wilson, and Donald Derrick.
© 2013 Bryan Gick, Ian Wilson, and Donald Derrick. Published 2013 by Blackwell Publishing Ltd.

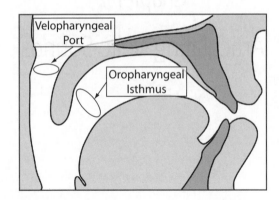

Figure 7.1   Velopharyngeal port (VPP) and the oropharyngeal isthmus (OPI): right view (see Kuehn and Azzam, 1978) (image by D. Derrick).

opening called the *oropharyngeal isthmus* (OPI), a causeway defined by the palatine arches. You can see this arch-shaped opening if you look in the back of your mouth with a mirror – try this! To make nasal sounds, air can flow upward into the *nasopharynx* (the area behind the velum) – and from there into the nasal passages – via the opening separating the mouth from the nose, called the *velopharyngeal port* (VPP). Figure 7.1 shows the location of both the VPP and the OPI.

Opening and closing the OPI and the VPP involves the coordination of a number of muscles, many of which are anchored to bones of the skull. We'll begin, therefore, by learning more about the anatomy of the skull.

7.1.1   The hard parts

We've already mentioned a few hard structures of the head in Chapter 6: the hyoid bone, the styloid process, and the mastoid process. These were introduced before the rest of the bones of the head because they provide important attachment points for some of the extrinsic laryngeal muscles. Now we'll describe the skull in fuller detail (see Figure 7.2).

The skull may look like one big bone, but it's actually made up of 22 bones. Except for the lower jaw (which we'll discuss in Chapter 8), all of these bones are firmly fixed together by fibrous *sutures* that lend the skull enough strength to protect the brain, while still allowing the skull the flexibility to accommodate the brain's rapid growth throughout childhood.

The part of the skull that holds the brain is called the *cranium* (Greek, "skull"). The five main bones of the cranium are the *frontal*, *parietal*, *occipital*, *temporal*, and *sphenoid* bones. Note that the first four of these terms will sound familiar, as they were used in Chapter 2 to describe the lobes of the brain! The spinal cord exits the skull through a large opening at the base of

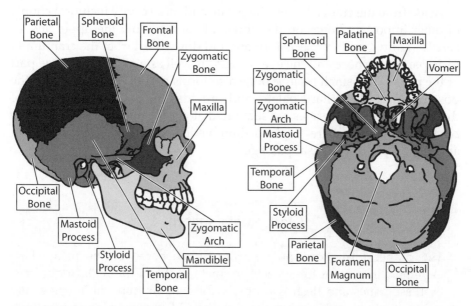

Figure 7.2 Skull: right side view (left), bottom view (right) (image by W. Murphey and A. Yeung).

the occipital bone called the *foramen magnum* (Latin, "large bore-hole"). Of the cranial bones, the temporal and sphenoid bones hold the lower front part of the brain, and their bottom surface provides many important attachment points for the speech muscles below.

The *temporal* bone is quite complex, being composed of three parts: the *squamous* (Latin, "scaly") part towards the front, the *petrous* (Latin, "rocky") part medially, and the *mastoid* part laterally. Now that you know about these, you can see where the styloid and mastoid processes emerge: the styloid process projects from the petrous part of the temporal bone, just below and medial to the ear, while the larger mastoid process is located farther back and lateral to the styloid process, projecting from the mastoid part (naturally!) of the temporal bone. The squamous part of the temporal bone is also important in that it forms part of the *zygomatic* (Greek, "yoke") *arch*, or cheekbone. The next time you're holding a model skull, you'll find that you can hook a finger right through the thin, bridge-like zygomatic arch (try this!). The posterior half of the zygomatic arch projects forward from the squamous part of the temporal bone. In the middle of the arch, it meets a thin projection from the *zygomatic bone*, a smaller bone that also forms the outer side of the eye socket.

The *sphenoid* (Latin, "wedge-shaped") bone is a smaller cranial bone that lies between the temporal bone and the frontal bone. This strangely shaped bone holds the lower front part of the brain, forms part of the sinuses, and provides the posterior bony wall of the VPP.

Aside from the cranial bones, the palate and nasal cavity include a couple of other important bones on the underside of the skull: the upper jaw, or *maxilla* (Latin, "jaw") projects forward and downward from the cranium to form part of the nose and the eye sockets, as well as making up a large part of the palate. The small *palatine* bone also forms part of the sinuses and the posterior part of the hard palate, and provides the anterior bony wall of the VPP. The nasal passages are separated along the midsagittal line by the *vomer* (Latin, "plowshare"), a razor-thin medial bone that separates the left and right sides of the nasal passage.

Cleft palate speech

The proper formation and suturing of the bones of the palate is extremely important for speech production. When the seal produced by these bones and flesh is properly formed, air from the lungs can only enter the nasal passage through the VPP. Failure of the bones to join properly during gestation will lead to *cleft palate*, a condition whereby the two sides of the maxilla or palatine bone do not join completely.

There are several types of cleft palate (see Figure 7.3), including *incomplete cleft palate*, in which posterior portions of the palatine bone and/or maxilla do not join, *unilateral complete cleft palate*, in which both the bone and lip are fissured anteriorly beneath the left or right nostril, and *bilateral complete cleft palate*, in which the fissure is divided, such that the lip has two divisions, one underneath each nostril.

Any cleft palate that results in a *fistula* (Latin, "pipe"), or hole, connecting the nasal passages to the oral passage, or that interferes with the function of the velopharyngeal port, can result in a *velopharyngeal insufficiency* (VPI), in which air leaks between the oral and nasal cavities. A VPI can be diagnosed by examining the hard palate for a fistula, or by holding an oral mirror underneath the nose during the production of sentences with no nasals. If the mirror fogs at the wrong times, there may be evidence of a VPI. Also, direct examination with a nasoendoscope can be effective for identifying fistulas or other VPIs, as can the use of a nasal airflow meter.

Untreated cleft-palate speech is characterized by *hypernasality*, in which nasals are produced in the place of oral sounds. Hypernasality is often also associated with other speech impairments, including deaf and hard of hearing (DHH) speech (see, e.g., Hudgins and Numbers 1942, Nickerson, 1975).

(Continued)

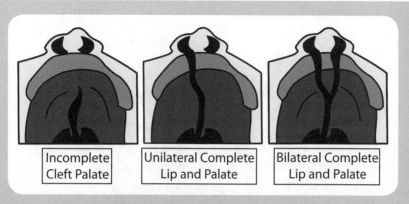

Figure 7.3 Three types of cleft palate (incomplete, unilateral complete, and bilateral complete): bottom view (image from public domain: Felsir).

Cleft palate is best treated with surgery to seal up fistulas in the lip or hard palate when a child is less than one year of age. Surgery to change the shape of the VPP may also be necessary. If these surgeries are not performed early enough, children often develop compensatory strategies in their speech, which can be very hard to unlearn, even if the physical impairments are later fixed.

One compensatory strategy used to counteract the problems created by a cleft palate is, for example, for a child to replace all oral stops with glottal stops to avoid unwanted nasal airflow during the oral stops. Once someone has learned to speak using compensatory strategies, surgery must be followed by speech therapy to eliminate the use of compensations and encourage the use and strengthening of the velopharyngeal mechanisms during speech (see, e.g., Peterson-Falzone *et al.*, 2006; see also Kuehn and Moon, 2000; Kuehn and Henne, 2003).

7.1.2 Muscles of the velum

According to traditional phonetic descriptions, the velum has only one main purpose: to open and close the VPP like a simple trapdoor. In this account, the velum is lowered to allow air to flow through for nasal sounds, but is otherwise kept raised and out of the way during speech.

While this may be partially true, at least for some speakers, a more complete story of the velum's function in speech is more complicated – but also much more revealing – and will require understanding a number of muscles. One complication is that the velum is actually part of multiple *sphincters*, or rings of muscles, that constrict a tube in the body. The VPP contains one set of sphincters, while the OPI contains another.

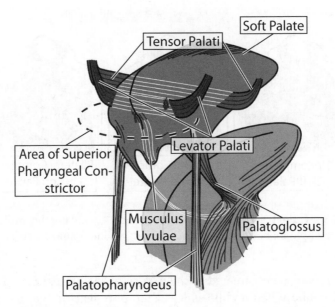

Figure 7.4 Muscles of the VPP: posterior isometric view (image by D. Derrick and N. Francis).

Before we get into the more complicated stuff, let's start with the muscles (see Figure 7.4) and how they help with the traditional "trapdoor" method of closing and opening the VPP.

7.1.2.1 Closing the VPP: trapdoor method Slightly more than half of people with normal velar function use the *trapdoor* method of closing the VPP (see Biavati *et al.*, 2009). This method is more properly known as the *coronal* method of VPP closure (because the main closing surfaces – the velum and the rear pharyngeal wall – meet in the coronal plane). For people who use this method, the velum does all the work, rising to form a complete seal against the rear pharyngeal wall. This method works best if the velum is sufficiently large to form a complete seal, or if the *adenoid pad*, a fleshy mass on the rear pharyngeal wall, is large enough to help provide a surface for sealing off nasal airflow. While several muscles are involved in the trapdoor method of closing the VPP, only one – *levator palati* – is generally thought to be absolutely necessary.

Levator palati (or *levator veli palatini*) is widely considered the most important muscle for opening and closing the VPP. When it contracts, it pulls the velum up to close the VPP, and when it relaxes, it allows the velum to lower, opening the VPP. This muscle originates from two structures: the petrous part of the temporal bone and the Eustachian tube, or auditory tube. From here, it courses downward, medially, and forward to enter the velum, meeting in the middle to form a U-shaped muscular sling. Innervated by the pharyngeal plexus via the vagus nerve (CN X) and the glossopharyngeal nerve (CN IX), the levator palati pulls the velum back and up, like a trapdoor.

The *palatoglossus* (PG) muscle is unusual in that it attaches only soft structures to other soft structures. In this case, it links the velum to the tongue below, so that it can either actively lower the velum, or possibly raise the tongue, or both (more on the PG when we discuss the OPI in Section 7.2.2). The PG muscle originates in the anterior surface of the soft palate and runs forward and downward to insert into the sides of the tongue. Some fibers of the PG meet in the middle of the velum, while others run all the way to the center line of the tongue, so that the PG forms a complete ring (almost a sphincter!) all on its own. The PG is innervated by the pharyngeal plexus.

It's sphincters all the way down!

In describing how constrictions in the vocal tract work, the word "sphincter" will come up a number of times in this book. In fact, almost any speech movement can be thought of in terms of sphincter actions. This isn't surprising, as the vocal tract also doubles as the upper end of the respiratory and digestive systems, which require constrictions at various points along the way. The human body actually has dozens of different types of sphincters, with the total number of individual sphincters numbering in the millions! Some sphincters in the body are "anatomical," meaning they are made of simple, complete rings of muscle, while others are "functional" or "physiological," indicating that they have a more complex anatomical structure, but still function to form constrictions. Also, some sphincters in the body are under voluntary control, while others are involuntary.

All of the sphincters in the vocal tract are physiological (not anatomical), and all are voluntarily controlled during speech, though their behavior can be automatic during some respiratory and digestive functions (this is what happens with the pharyngeal constrictors, the aryepiglottic folds, and other structures during the pharyngeal phase of swallowing, hence the term "swallowing reflex"; Goyal and Mashimo, 2006).

Some places in the vocal tract that have been described as containing physiological sphincters are shown in Figure 7.5.

Sphincters have special properties that are important for speech, including their ability to constrict a tube at a relatively fixed location,

(Continued)

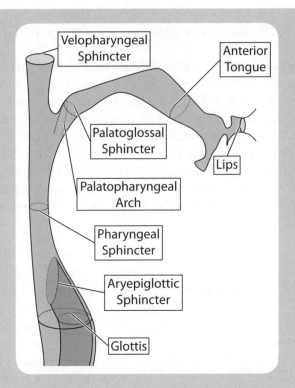

Figure 7.5 Some locations where sphincters have been described in the vocal tract (image by D. Derrick and B. Gick).

and to constrict from multiple sides. Thinking of the vocal tract in this way helps in understanding how different speech articulators act and interact, as well as giving insight into how best to measure and model speech articulations.

Another muscle that can actively pull down on the velum is the palat-opharyngeus muscle, a muscle we discussed in Chapter 6 along with the other pharyngeal elevators. Unlike palatoglossus, which pulls the velum down and forward, palatopharyngeus pulls down and back.

When considering the description of the velum as a "trapdoor," it's important to remember that the velum is not hard like a door, but soft, more like your lips. Insofar as the velum can be raised and lowered in trapdoor fashion, it is because it has been stiffened by tensing intrinsic muscles. The *musculus uvulae* and the aptly named *tensor palati* help in this way.

The *uvula* (Latin, "little grape") is a fleshy bulb that hangs off the end of the velum. Anyone who has watched original Warner Brothers cartoons has seen the uvula waggle around when the cartoon characters scream. If you look in the mirror (try this!), you can see your own uvula dangling down from the top of the arch at the back of your throat (the OPI – see Section 7.2.2). Although it may seem like a passive participant, the uvula does contribute to VPP closure: the *musculus uvulae*, a small muscle that arises from the soft palate and inserts into the uvula itself, stiffens the uvula, helping to tighten the VPP closure. The musculus uvulae is innervated by the pharyngeal plexus.

The *tensor palati* (or *tensor veli palatini*), as its name indicates, tenses the palate. This ribbon-like muscle originates from the sphenoid bone and the Eustachian tube, and wraps under the velum to insert into a tendon underneath. The tensor palati muscle is innervated by the mandibular branch of the trigeminal nerve (CN V), and contracts to tense the velum and open the Eustachian tubes. This tension in the palate is useful during swallowing. Some anatomy books also report that the tensor aids in raising the velum, but the evidence for this function is less clear.

Finally, the *superior pharyngeal constrictor* determines the shape and stiffness of the side walls of the pharynx. It may be possible for some people to close the VPP successfully without engaging the superior constrictor (using the trapdoor method), but this muscle is crucial in all other methods of VPP closure (see Section 7.2.1). This muscle originates mainly at the sphenoid bone and along a ligament linking the sphenoid bone to the lower jaw, and inserts posteriorly into the median raphe, briefly described in Chapter 6. The superior constrictor is innervated by the pharyngeal plexus.

Popping your ears

Have you ever felt an uncomfortable pressure in your ears as you descended in an airplane, or heard the "pop" as this pressure was released? This "pop" is the sound of air being allowed into your middle ear through your Eustachian tubes.

When the pressure around your head changes, it's important for the pressure inside your ears to equalize. This is one important function of the Eustachian tubes. If the Eustachian tubes fail to open, air cannot get from the nasopharynx up and back into the middle ear, and the external pressure can cause *middle ear barotrauma*, in which the pressure difference causes tissue damage in the eardrum.

Some people, such as dive-bombers, miners or scuba divers, are exposed to large changes in air pressure every day. For such people, it is vital that they learn reliable techniques for opening the Eustachian tubes to equalize pressure. Yawning and swallowing are both commonly used techniques, as they engage muscles attached to the Eustachian tubes, such as the salpingopharyngeus or the tensor palati.

(Continued)

More sophisticated methods have been developed for popping the ears, most of which involve some combination of contracting muscles attached to the Eustachian tubes and forcing the tubes open by increasing pressure in the nasopharynx. Examples of these methods include the *Frenzel maneuver*, which combines raising the larynx and compressing the pharynx while pinching the nostrils shut, thereby reducing the volume of the pharynx and increasing pressure (remember Boyle's Law!); and the *Valsalva maneuver*, which requires closing the nostrils, then pushing pulmonically as if trying to exhale through the nose (Roydhouse, 1993). If these don't work, there's even a medical procedure called *Politzerization* that involves mechanically blowing air up the nose during a swallow (Silman and Arick, 1999).

7.2 Sounds

In this chapter we'll look at two aspects of speech that use the velum: the oral-nasal distinction and uvular constrictions.

7.2.1 The oral-nasal distinction: more on the VPP

The state of the VPP – closed vs. open – determines the distinction between oral and nasal sounds. In Section 7.1.2.1 we described the trapdoor, or coronal, method of closing and opening the VPP to produce this distinction. People who don't use the trapdoor method for VPP closure may use a different method, taking advantage of the flexibility of the velopharyngeal sphincter mechanisms. Three other attested methods used to close the VPP include: the circular method, the circular with Passavant's ridge (CPR) method, or the sagittal method (Biavati *et al.*, 2009). These mechanisms are illustrated in Figures 7.6a and 7.6b.

The *circular* method, used by about 20% of people, involves contracting levator palati and the intrinsic muscles of the soft palate in "trapdoor" style, as well as using the superior pharyngeal constrictor to narrow the lateral pharyngeal walls, squeezing the trapdoor medially.

Another 15–20% of people use the *circular with Passavant's ridge* (CPR) mechanism. This is the same as the circular method, but it is combined with advancement of the *Passavant's ridge*, a prominence on the posterior pharyngeal wall, just below the adenoid pad. Most people seem not to have a prominent Passavant's ridge, and those who do probably use it in this way. Both of the "circular" methods are also sometimes called "drawstring" methods, as they close the VPP from multiple sides, like pulling the drawstrings on a purse.

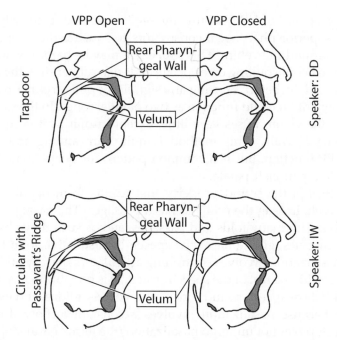

Figure 7.6a Various VPP closure mechanisms: midsagittal view (image by D. Derrick).

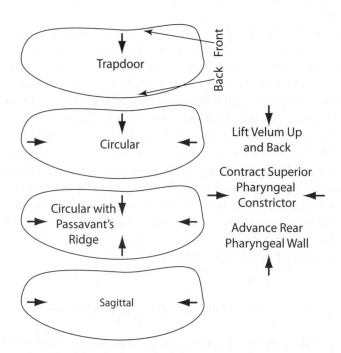

Figure 7.6b Various VPP closure mechanisms, superimposed on a transverse cross-section through the VPP (image by D. Derrick, inspired by Biavati *et al.*, 2009).

The last method of VPP closure, the *sagittal* method, primarily involves using the superior pharyngeal constrictors to squeeze the lateral pharyngeal walls around the velum. This squeezing may be hard to visualize, but imagine two people pulling on opposite ends of a rubber ring: the first thing the ring would do, before exerting any significant pull on either participant, is to narrow until it could function as two parallel ropes. In the sagittal type of closure, the velum raises very little, except insofar as it is squeezed by the pharyngeal walls. This method is quite rare among speakers with normal VPP function, but is a common pattern for people who have had surgeries to repair cleft palate.

Nasalization is the sound property that results from opening the VPP during speech, linking the oral and nasal passages. The nasal passages are large spaces with many folds and passages, and as such they absorb some sound frequencies, giving nasalized speech its distinctive sound qualities. Because nasalization involves controlling articulators that, by and large, do not interact with the rest of the speech system, it is possible to nasalize many different kinds of speech sounds, including vowels, glides, and even clicks. However, because nasalization involves a constant airflow through the nose, oral stops cannot undergo nasalization (the term "nasal stop" is often used for nasal consonants [m], [n], and so on, to indicate the complete oral closure). Although nasals are almost always voiced sounds, some languages such as Icelandic and Welsh have voiceless nasals, and Romanian can have devoiced nasals.

Because of the direct link between the tongue and the velum via the palatoglossus, velum position can interact with tongue position in subtle ways that may affect synchronic or diachronic phonological patterns. For example, an active constriction of the palatoglossus produced as part of a uvular constriction may pull down and forward on the velum, resulting in slight nasalization or nasal leakage – an effect that, over time, can lead to sound change. The passive action of the palatoglossus can also affect VPP closure, such that when the tongue is low in the mouth, the velum may be passively pulled down by the palatoglossus, and when the velum is raised, it can passively raise the tongue body. Because of these interactions, languages differ in the vowels that are more often nasalized (Hajek, 1997); in Thai, low vowels are nasalization targets, but in Chamorro, high vowels are targeted. The palatoglossus will be discussed further along with other extrinsic muscles of the tongue in Chapter 8.

7.2.2   Uvular constrictions: the oropharyngeal isthmus

The arching pillars peaked by the uvula at the back of your throat create a narrowing in the airway called the oropharyngeal isthmus (OPI), also

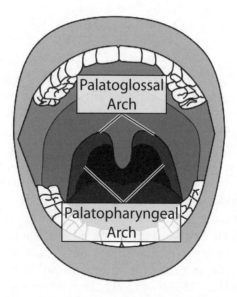

Figure 7.7   The double archway of the OPI (image by D. Derrick).

known as the *faucal* or *faucial isthmus* (Latin *fauces*, "throat"). These pillars are known variously as the *palatine arches,* or the *faucal* (or *faucial) pillars.* Note that the plural "arches" here is not an accident – if you look carefully in a mirror, open your mouth wide and move your tongue into different positions (try this!), you'll see that the OPI actually has a double archway. The more posterior archway is the *palatopharyngeal arch,* formed by the palatopharyngeus muscle reaching from the sides of the palate down and back into the pharynx, all the way to the thyroid cartilage; the more anterior archway is the *palatoglossal arch,* formed by the palatoglossus muscle linking the sides of the palate down and forward to the sides of the tongue (see Figure 7.7).

   The OPI is thus made up of a number of structures: the tongue on the bottom, the velum and uvula on the top, and the two pairs of faucal pillars on the sides. When this ring of muscle – which we'll call the *palatoglossal sphincter* – contracts, the result is a constriction between the tongue and the velum at the *uvular* place of articulation.

   Uvular constrictions such as that for French [ʁ] are actions of the whole palatoglossal sphincter, often bringing the top, bottom, and sides of the OPI closer together. The tongue of course plays an important role in these constrictions, but by no means an exclusive one. Chapters 8 and 9 will discuss articulations of the tongue in more detail.

Only one way out

One of the things that our bodies are set up to do very quickly is something called *pharyngeal peristalsis* – a wave-like movement of the pharyngeal constrictors that happens automatically when we swallow. Since we need to keep our airway clear to breathe and speak, any food that is in the pharynx gets quickly shot down to the esophagus in less than a second (at a speed of up to 40 cm/s). Once it reaches the esophagus, it slows to a tenth of its speed, to a leisurely 3–4 cm/s.

Swallowing, also called *deglutition*, has three phases: the oral, pharyngeal, and esophageal phase, with the oral phase being voluntary, and the other two reflexive. During the oral phase, we use our tongue, teeth, and cheeks to break up the food and shape it into a lump called a bolus. When the bolus reaches the palatoglossal arch at the end of the oral cavity, reflexes take over and the pharyngeal phase starts.

Normally, there are four ways out of the pharynx – upward through the nose (via the VPP) or the mouth (via the OPI), or downward through either the trachea (via the aryepiglottic folds and the glottis) or the esophagus. When you swallow, three of these four exits are sphinctered shut, so that the food gets shot down the only opening left – the esophagus. If one of the other doors doesn't close fast enough or tightly enough, food or liquid can end up where you probably don't want it to be.

When you think about the phases of swallowing, including the doors that must be closed, you soon realize that many of the same nerves and muscles that are used in chewing and swallowing are also used in speaking! Because of this, swallowing problems in the elderly (e.g., after a stroke) may be positively affected by speech therapy, and vice-versa.

7.3   Measuring the Velum: X-ray Video

It's notoriously difficult to observe or measure actions of the velum directly. One tool that has been used to do this is *x-ray video*, also called *cineradiography, cinefluorography*, or *cineroentgenography* (the latter after Wilhelm Conrad Röntgen, who named this kind of radiation "x-rays"). This imaging technique allows a researcher to film movements happening inside a person's body. Figure 7.8 shows x-ray images for two French speakers.

X-rays are a kind of electromagnetic radiation that is able to pass through many materials that are opaque to normal light. X-rays are absorbed by

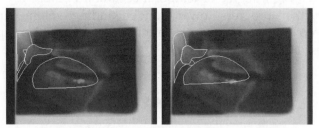

Different French speakers produce /ʁ/ differently

Rear Pharyngeal Wall | Lighter muscle is thicker

Velum | Teeth are light

Tongue | Fillings very light

Speaker 1: Velum moves down and thickens

Speaker 2: Velum thickens, but does not move

Figure 7.8 X-ray film of two French speakers each producing a uvular "r" in a different way: right side view; note that the tongue, velum, and rear pharyngeal wall have been traced in these images (image by D. Derrick and N. Francis, with data from Munhall *et al.*, 1995).

high-density tissues because the radiation cannot completely penetrate them. Because of this, different types of tissue in the body can be inferred based on their degree of x-ray absorption. Bone, being the most dense, absorbs the most x-rays and appears to be white, while muscle and fat, being less dense, absorb less and appear in shades of gray. Air, being the least dense, is completely penetrated by x-rays and so appears black.

Because x-ray video images the whole head with a relatively high temporal resolution (a standard video rate of 30 Hz is common), and because it is a real-time imaging technique (meaning you can see things as they are happening), it is particularly useful for diagnosing velopharyngeal insufficiency and swallowing disorders, where things are moving fast. It is also useful for tracking velum motion in speech (see Munhall *et al.*, 1995).

An x-ray video scanner takes an image through the entire head, flattening all the 3-dimensional information into a 2-dimensional picture. As such, every structure the x-rays pass through casts a "shadow." These overlapping shadows can be difficult to decipher, so that properly interpreting an x-ray image requires very good knowledge of 3-dimensional anatomical structures in the vocal tract. X-ray film also exposes subjects to ionizing radiation, and thus for research it is only used today in tandem with medical diagnoses, or in a few countries where special dispensation is granted for academic research. However, it is possible to find many x-ray videos of speech that were made in previous decades that are still useful for research today (see, e.g., Munhall *et al.*, 1995).

Since it is so difficult to measure the velum directly, electromyography (see Chapter 3) has often been used to study the activity of muscles in the velum, and nasalization is often measured through other indirect means such as nasal airflow (see Chapter 4). By making an audio recording along with nasal airflow it is possible to track the timing and flow rate of nasal airflow with a high degree of temporal accuracy. Because it is so hard to measure, further progress toward understanding velum function will depend on novel measurement techniques and advanced computer modeling of these structures.

Exercises

Sufficient jargon

Define the following terms: velum (soft palate), oropharynx, oropharyngeal isthmus (OPI), nasopharynx, velopharyngeal port (VPP), sutures, cranium, frontal bone, parietal bone, occipital bone, temporal bone, sphenoid bone, foramen magnum, squamous part of temporal bone, petrous part of temporal bone, mastoid part of temporal bone, zygomatic arch (cheekbone), zygomatic bone, maxilla, palatine bone, vomer, incomplete cleft palate, unilateral complete cleft palate, bilateral complete cleft palate, fistula, velopharyngeal insufficiency (VPI), hypernasality, sphincter, coronal (trapdoor) method of VPP closure, adenoid pad, levator palati (levator veli palatini) muscle, superior pharyngeal constrictor muscle, palatoglossus (PG) muscle, uvula, musculus uvulae, tensor palati (tensor veli palatini), middle ear barotrauma, Frenzel maneuver, Valsalva maneuver, Politzerization, circular method of VPP closure, circular with Passavant's ridge (CPR) technique for VPP closure, Passavant's ridge, sagittal method of VPP closure, nasalization, faucal isthmus, palatine arches (faucal pillars), palatopharyngeal arch, palatoglossal arch, palatoglossal sphincter, uvular place, pharyngeal peristalsis, deglutition, x-ray video (cineradiography, cinefluorography or cineroentgenography).

Short-answer questions

1 In Chapters 8 and 9, we will see that there are many different muscles and mechanisms available for moving the tongue. If someone has

damage to their pharyngeal plexus, what structure of the OPI would be responsible for closing OPI for French [ʁ]?

2 Arabic pharyngeals are produced using multiple mechanisms to reduce the volume of the lower pharynx. It has often been observed that these pharyngeals are associated with nasalization in many Arabic dialects.

(1) What muscle directly links the two relevant structures in this case (you may want to recall what you learned about this muscle from Chapter 6)?

(2) Considering the use of this muscle, what is a likely mechanism used by Arabic speakers to reduce the volume of the lower pharynx?

3 For the following measurement technique, find and cite two speech research papers not mentioned in this book in which the technique is used: x-ray video. Follow the reference formatting used in the references section at the end of each chapter.

Practical assignment

For each chapter, this text has online assignments (at www.wiley.com/go/articulatoryphonetics) that either provide research data for analysis, or practical tools for understanding vocal tract anatomy. For Chapter 7, you will look at a set of x-ray frames extracted from cinefluorographic recordings of different speakers producing the French uvular fricative [ʁ]. The assignment and the related assignment images can be found in the online materials for this textbook under *Chapter 7*.

References

Biavati, M. J., Sie, K., Wiet, G. J., and Rocha-Worley, G. (2009). Velopharyngeal insufficiency. *eMedicine: Otolaryngology and Facial Plastic Surgery*, 1–21.

Goyal, R. K. and Mashimo, H. (2006). Physiology of oral, pharyngeal, and esophageal motility. *GI Motility online*, May 16th, 2006.

Hajek, J. (1997). *Universals of Sound Change in Nasalisation*. Oxford, UK: Blackwell.

Hudgins, C. V. and Numbers, F. C. (1942). An investigation of the intelligibility of the speech of the deaf. *Genetic Psychology Monographs*, 25, 289–392.

Kuehn, D. P. and Azzam, N. A. (1978). Anatomical characteristics of palatoglossus and anterior faucial pillar. *Cleft Palate Journal*, 15, 349–359.

Kuehn, D. P. and Henne, L. J. (2003). Speech evaluation and treatment for patients with cleft palate. *American Journal of Speech-Language Pathology*, 12, 103–109.

Kuehn, D. P. and Moon, J. B. (2000). Induced fatigued effects on velopharyngeal closure force. *Journal of Speech, Language, and Hearing Research*, 43, 486–500.

Munhall, K. G., Vatikiotis-Bateson, E., and Tohkura, Y. (1995). X-ray film database for speech research. *Journal of the Acoustical Society of America*, 98, 1222–1224.

Nickerson, R. S. (1975). Characteristics of the speech of deaf persons. *Volta Review*, 77, 342–362.

Peterson-Falzone, S. J., Trost-Cardamone, J. E., Karnell, M. P., and Hardin-Jones, M. A. (2006). *The Clinician's Guide to Treating Cleft Palate Speech*. St Louis, Missouri: Mosby.

Roydhouse, N. (1993). *Underwater Ear and Nose Care* (2nd edition). Flagstaff, Arizona: Best Publishing Company.

Silman, S. and Arick, D. S. (1999). Efficacy of a modified Politzer apparatus in management of Eustachian tube dysfunction in adults. *Journal of the American Academy of Audiology*, 10, 496–501.

Chapter 8

Articulating Vowels

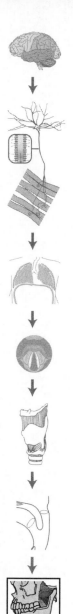

Your tongue is one of the most flexible parts of your body, capable of taking on an incredible range of different shapes. In view of this, it seems surprising that phonologists have managed to describe the vowel systems of most languages using only two dimensions of tongue position: height (high vs. low) and anteriority (front vs. back), as shown in the traditional *vowel quadrilateral* in Figure 8.1 and the circular tongue diagram in Figure 8.2. Similarly, speech scientists have observed that tongue shapes for most English vowel sounds can be described using as few as two principal components (Harshman *et al.*, 1977; Stone *et al.*, 1997). Because of the relative simplicity of vowel shapes, many models of speech production have been able to treat the tongue itself as a simple, undifferentiated mass of flesh that gets pulled around by forces outside of the tongue itself.

While the tongue's inner workings are anything but simple (we'll discuss this more in Chapter 9), many of its gross movements – particularly those we use to make vowels – can indeed be described using a more simplified model that focuses largely on extrinsic forces. For the present chapter, we will maintain this simplified view of tongue function, focusing on the structures that hold the tongue in place – the jaw and the extrinsic muscles of the tongue – and their operation during vowels.

Articulatory Phonetics, First Edition. Bryan Gick, Ian Wilson, and Donald Derrick.
© 2013 Bryan Gick, Ian Wilson, and Donald Derrick. Published 2013 by Blackwell Publishing Ltd.

Tongues, tentacles, and degrees of freedom

When something is able to move freely in some particular direction or around some rotational axis, it is said to have a *degree of freedom* (DoF). For example, a sliding door has one DoF (side-to-side), as does a hinged door (rotation from the hinge). The more degrees of freedom an object has, the more complex movements it can perform. In principle, a flexible structure like a tongue could have unlimited degrees of freedom. But, as they say, freedom isn't free: for every DoF there needs to be some mechanism in place to control it. In humans, this means that higher-DoF systems use more brainpower.

Bernstein (1967) notes that one of the key challenges in motor control is to reduce the degrees of freedom, so as to reduce cognitive load. Nature provides us with many examples of creatures making use of this kind of strategy. Two examples of this are how babies reach for an object and how octopuses use their tentacles.

If you've ever seen a baby reach for an object, you may have noticed large, sweeping movements hinging at the shoulder rather than the more complex, adult-like movements integrating all of the available degrees of freedom in the human arm, wrist, and hand. This is because infants simplify their reaching tasks by locking joints, such as their wrists and elbows, thereby reducing degrees of freedom (Spencer and Thelen, 2000; Berthier and Keen, 2006).

Similarly, Sumbre *et al.* (2006), in their work on tentacle movement in octopuses, observe that an octopus could in theory move a tentacle in an unlimited number of ways to reach for food and get it into its mouth – by curving or bending the tentacle at any point along its length. In reality, however, octopuses use highly consistent movements: they create three "pseudo" joints (proximal, medial, and distal) in each tentacle, creating an articulated structure that is strikingly similar to a human arm (proximal joint = shoulder; medial joint = elbow; distal joint = wrist). By using only three joints, the octopus' motor task of putting food into its mouth is greatly simplified.

Returning to the human tongue, it's easy to see the DoF problem, but the solution is not so clear. Most theories of speech articulation treat the tongue – and the rest of the vocal tract – as a 2D structure in the midsagittal plane (as in Figure 8.2). This is one way of reducing the degrees of freedom, but it is almost certainly not the actual mechanism humans use to handle DoF reduction in their vocal tracts. More research will be needed to tell how human tongues lick the DoF problem.

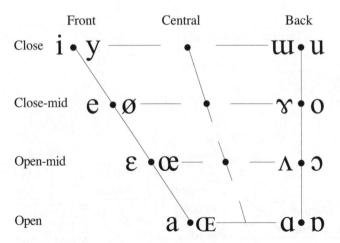

Figure 8.1 Traditional vowel quadrilateral (image from Creative Commons, Kwamikagami, based on International Phonetic Association, 1999).

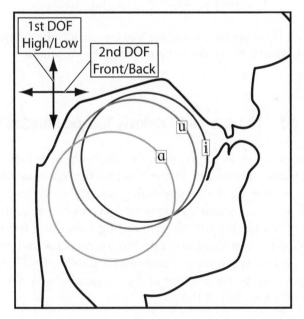

Figure 8.2 A midsagittal circular tongue model with two degrees of freedom (image by D. Derrick).

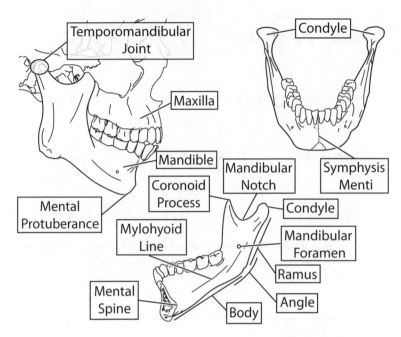

Figure 8.3   Full jaw (top left); mandible anterior view (top right); right half of mandible – side view from inside (bottom) (image by W. Murphey).

8.1   The Jaw and Extrinsic Tongue Muscles

In some models of vowel production, the tongue moves rather like a ball, making one main constriction in the mouth. Vertical movements can be accomplished mainly by the tongue riding up and down on the jaw, while both vertical and horizontal movements may enlist the *extrinsic tongue muscles*, which link the tongue to surrounding bones and tissues. We have already described one of these extrinsic tongue muscles (the palatoglossus) in Chapter 7, and we will introduce the rest in this chapter. Since any movement of the jaw affects the position of the tongue, let's first have a look at the anatomy and function of the jaw.

8.1.1   The hard parts

The human jaw is made up of two main parts: the upper jaw, or maxilla (which we discussed as part of the skull in Chapter 7), and the lower jaw, or *mandible* (Latin, "chew"). Because this chapter is concerned with the movements of the tongue, we will mainly be concerned with the moving part of the jaw – the mandible (see Figure 8.3).

There are some useful identifying landmarks on the mandible: the *body* of the mandible is the horseshoe-shaped lower part that holds the lower teeth and forms the lower jawline and chin. The *ramus* (Greek, "branch") is the vertical part of the mandible that connects up to the skull, and the *angle* is the bend in the mandible where the body connects to the ramus. At the top of the ramus are two protrusions: the larger, more posterior one is the *condyle* (Greek, "knuckle"), while the smaller, more anterior one is the *coronoid* (Greek, "crow's beak-shaped") *process*. The depression between the condyle and the coronoid process is called the *mandibular notch.*

The mandible is actually made up of two separate bones that meet in the middle early in development along a line called the *mental symphysis* (Latin, from Greek, "conjunction"). This word "mental," from Latin *mentum* "chin," is totally unrelated to the word "mental" referring to the mind; it is, though, related to the first part of the word "mandible," and possibly loosely related to the word "munch" as well. At the bottom of the symphysis is a lump of bone that makes up the point of the chin, called the *mental protuberance*. On the inside of the jaw at this same point are bony lumps called the *mental spine*. The mental spine provides the origin point for the geniohyoid (a suprahyoid muscle we discussed in Chapter 6) as well as the genioglossus, a tongue muscle we'll discuss in Section 8.1.3.

The mandible connects to the temporal bone of the skull at a joint called the *temporomandibular joint* (TMJ). The TMJ is where the ball-shaped condyle of the mandible fits into the concave *mandibular fossa* of the temporal bone. This joint is cushioned by a fibrous *articulator disk* that protects the jaw from rough impact during chewing.

Six degrees of freedom (6DoF) and the tenacious badger

Physicists know that when you say "6DoF" you're talking about a rigid object. That's because any freely moving rigid object can have exactly six degrees of freedom (see Figure 8.4). There are three *translations* or "slide" directions: 1) up-down, 2) forward-backward, and 3) side-to-side. There are also three *rotations*: 1) *yaw* (turning like a top, around an up-down axis), 2) *roll* (turning like a doorknob, around a forward-backward axis), and 3) *pitch* (turning like a wheel on a bicycle you're riding, around a side-to-side axis). All possible movements of a solid object in space can be described in terms of these six degrees of freedom.

While it may be tempting to think of the mandible as only having one degree of freedom (rotating open and shut at the TMJ, like a trap-door), the human mandible actually uses all six degrees of freedom.

(Continued)

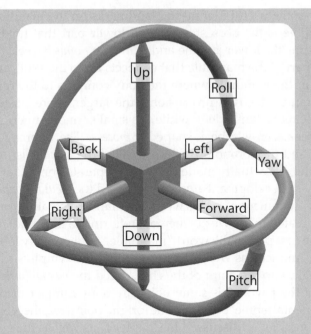

Figure 8.4 The six degrees of freedom of a rigid body in 3D space (image by D. Derrick).

This is because the TMJ is not a fixed joint, but allows the mandible to be freely *dislocated*, or slid out of the joint, in any direction. These degrees of freedom are particularly useful for grinding food during chewing.

Although many mammals have 6DoF jaws like humans, the badger is a notable exception. A badger's condyles are locked into horizontal grooves on the skull, giving the badger's mandible only two degrees of freedom: rotation open and shut, and translation side-to-side. Because of this, a badger can clamp its jaws down on prey with the utmost tenacity, and dislocating its jaw is impossible without fracturing the skull. Fortunately, humans are not on the badger's menu!

In Section 8.1.2, we will first describe how you raise, or *elevate*, the mandible, and then will go on to see how you lower, or *depress*, the mandible. We'll start with the strong, shallow muscles, mainly used for biting and chewing, and will go on to look at the smaller deep muscles, which tend to be more important for making the finer movements needed for speech.

8.1.2   Jaw muscles

The *masseter* (Greek, "chewer") is the main lifter, or *elevator*, of the mandible, and the strongest jaw muscle. It does most of the heavy work of

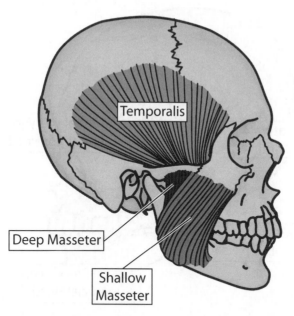

Figure 8.5 Shallow muscles of the jaw: right side view (image by E. Komova and A. Yeung).

the jaw needed for *mastication*, or chewing. Being a large, shallow muscle, it's easy to feel the masseter working: just press your hands to your cheeks, just below and in front of your ears, and clench and relax your jaw a few times (try this!) – you can't miss it. The masseter has two parts, or *heads*: a deep head and a shallow head, both of which originate at the zygomatic arch (see Figure 8.5). The *deep head* inserts into the upper half of the ramus and the coronoid process. The larger, *shallow head* of the masseter inserts into the lateral surface of the ramus and the angle. Because of these muscle vectors, the masseter elevates but also protrudes the mandible. It is innervated by the mandibular nerve, a branch of the trigeminal nerve (CN V).

While the masseter is the jaw's powerful chewing muscle, the *temporalis* (also called "temporal") muscle, is the fast muscle used to snap the jaw shut for biting. The temporalis originates in a fan-like shape in the large grooved ring on the temporal bone of the skull, passes through the zygomatic arch and inserts into the coronoid process of the mandible. Find the soft "temples" on the side of your head, just above your cheekbones, and gently press with all four fingers of either hand. Now, while repeatedly clenching and relaxing your jaw, slide all four fingers slowly upward from your temples, fanning the fingers out slightly as they move up. You should feel an arc of muscles tensing and relaxing with each clench. This is the origin of the temporalis. Like the masseter, the temporalis muscle is innervated by the mandibular nerve, a branch of the trigeminal nerve (CN V).

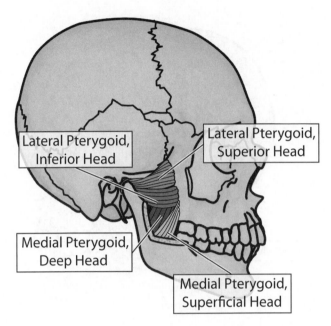

Figure 8.6a Deep muscles of the jaw: left side view (image by E. Komova and A. Yeung).

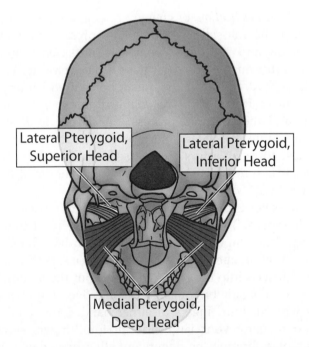

Figure 8.6b Deep muscles of the jaw: bottom view (image by E. Komova and A. Yeung).

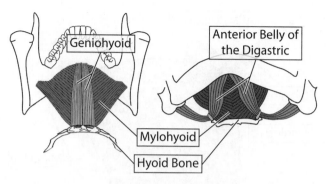

Figure 8.7 Mandible depressors (posterior view on left; anterior view on right) (image by W. Murphey).

Both of the shallow jaw muscles are used in the strong raising, or *elevation*, motions needed for biting or chewing. However, the jaw is also capable of very subtle movements, such as those needed for speech production, and the deep muscles that attach on the inside of the jaw are the ones that largely control these movements. These muscles include the lateral and medial *pterygoid* (Greek, "wing-like") muscles (see Figures 8.6a and 8.6b). Both of the pterygoid muscles are innervated by the trigeminal nerve (CN V).

The *medial (internal) pterygoid* muscle is like a smaller, internal mirror image of the masseter. Like the masseter, it has two portions or heads. The larger, deep head originates on the side of the sphenoid bone and the smaller, superficial head originates from the palatine bone and maxilla. The fibers of both heads pass downward, outward and back to insert into the lower interior surface of the ramus and angle of the mandible. Together, the medial pterygoid on the inside of the mandible and the masseter on the outside form a muscular sling that elevates the jaw.

The *lateral (external) pterygoid* muscle also has two heads. Unlike the other "two-headed" jaw muscles, the two heads of the lateral pterygoid have quite different vectors, and have traditionally been thought to have different functions. Later findings, however, suggest that the two heads work together, functioning as a single muscle (Murray *et al.*, 2007). The superior head originates just behind the cheekbone on the greater wing of the sphenoid bone, and inserts into the articulator disk of the TMJ. The inferior head originates behind the back teeth on the maxilla, and inserts into the front of the condyle. Working in concert, the two heads of the lateral pterygoid control side-to-side translation of the mandible, and are also active during protrusion. Because it is not used for raising or lowering the jaw, the lateral pterygoid is not usually thought to be of primary importance for speech.

Three main muscles are responsible for depressing, or lowering, the mandible (see Figure 8.7). These lie below the mandible, and also act to

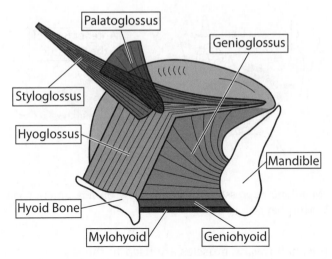

Figure 8.8 Extrinsic tongue muscles: right side view. Geniohyoid and mylohyoid are included for context only (image by D. Derrick).

raise and stabilize the hyoid bone and floor of the mouth, and as such are among the suprahyoid muscles that were described in detail in Chapter 6. The most superficial of these jaw-lowering muscles is the anterior belly of the digastric (ABD) muscle. The next most superficial depressor muscle is the mylohyoid. Finally, the deepest of these muscles is the geniohyoid, which connects the inside of the chin to the hyoid bone.

Because they can tense the floor of the mouth on which the tongue rests, all of these jaw depressor muscles also contribute more directly to controlling the raising and lowering of the tongue body.

8.1.3   Extrinsic tongue muscles

While actions of the jaw and tongue floor can account for much of the gross up-and-down movement of the tongue for vowels, jaw motion alone cannot account for the distinction between front and back vowels. For that, we'll need the extrinsic muscles of the tongue (see Figure 8.8). The extrinsic tongue muscles are those muscles that attach the tongue directly to surrounding structures: the genioglossus, palatoglossus, hyoglossus, and styloglossus. As you can tell from their names, these muscles all have their origins outside of the tongue, and insert into the meat of the tongue (hence the *-glossus* "tongue" ending).

The *genioglossus* (GG; Greek, "chin-tongue") muscle originates at the mental spine of the mandible (just above the origin of the geniohyoid) and

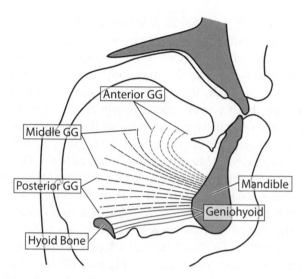

Figure 8.9 Regions of control of the genioglossus (GG) muscle: right midsagittal view (image by D. Derrick).

spreads out posteriorly and vertically in a fan-like shape to insert into the substance of the tongue. Even though it's an extrinsic muscle, the GG muscle often acts like an intrinsic muscle, as it makes up more of the bulk of the tongue than any other single muscle. The GG is innervated by the hypoglossal nerve (CN XII).

The GG muscle protracts and depresses the tongue, and can help to create a midline groove in the tongue. However, this description does not do the muscle justice since the GG has several distinct regions that can be independently controlled (see Figure 8.9). In fact, every muscle of the tongue is known to have regions of relatively independent control (see Dang and Honda, 2002; Gérard *et al.*, 2003; Stone *et al.*, 2004; Vogt *et al.*, 2006). In the GG muscle, there are at least three major separate regions of control that produce very different actions: the *anterior genioglossus* (GGa) inserts into the tongue tip and blade, and functions to lower and retract the front of the tongue. The *middle genioglossus* (GGm) inserts into the body of the tongue; contracting the GGm lowers the tongue body and pulls it forward, and because the whole GG muscle is concentrated medially in the tongue, it also aids in midline tongue grooving. The *posterior genioglossus* (GGp) inserts into the dorsum and root of the tongue; contracting it pulls the tongue root forward, helping in the production of high vowels, and in enlarging the oropharynx during inspiration.

The palatoglossus (PG) muscle, a thin muscle that arches over the palate and inserts laterally into the sides of the tongue body, was described in Chapter 7 along with other muscles of the palate. When the velum is held in place by other muscles, the PG may help to elevate and, to a degree, retract the tongue. As such, the PG may aid the jaw and the GG in the production of some high vowels. Note, however, that the PG is a very thin muscle and would exert very little effective pull on the much more massive tongue, and research supporting the role of the PG in speech has been highly variable and inconclusive. One important function of the PG is in constricting the OPI for uvular constrictions, at least partly by bringing the anterior faucial pillars closer together. Being a part of the nasopharynx as well as the oral cavity, the PG is the only tongue muscle innervated by the accessory (CN XI) and vagus (CN X) nerves via the pharyngeal plexus.

The *hyoglossus* (HG) is a quadrilateral-shaped muscle that attaches the sides of the tongue to the hyoid bone (see Figure 8.8). The muscle originates at the superior border of the greater horn of the hyoid bone and inserts vertically into the sides of the tongue. In many speakers, a small set of HG muscle fibers turns forward to run along the sides of the tongue, for some people extending nearly all the way to the tongue tip. Like all the rest of the tongue muscles (except the PG), the HG is innervated by the hypoglossal nerve (CN XII). The HG pulls the tongue down and back, especially the back of the tongue, and so contributes to lowering the tongue for low vowels.

Lastly, the *styloglossus* (SG) muscle originates from the tips of the styloid processes and courses downward and forward, dividing into two parts. The longitudinal part weaves together, or *interdigitates*, with the inferior longitudinal muscle (an intrinsic tongue muscle we will discuss in Chapter 9), and the oblique part overlaps the HG and enters into the substance of the tongue. Although traditional accounts of the SG muscle maintain that its role is to raise and pull back the tongue, later evidence questions the extent of this function (more on this in Section 8.2.2). The SG is innervated by the hypoglossal nerve (CN XII).

8.2 Sounds: Vowels

The traditional vowel diagram, seen earlier in Figure 8.1, lays out the vowel space schematically in the form of a two-dimensional quadrilateral. This layout works because of the two gross articulatory dimensions of height (or "closeness") and anteriority we discussed above, with high vowels shown at the top of the quadrilateral, and anterior vowels at the left. Lip rounding isn't given a dimension of its own in the vowel quadrilateral, as it is considered redundant in many vowel systems (we will discuss rounding and other actions of the lips in Chapter 10).

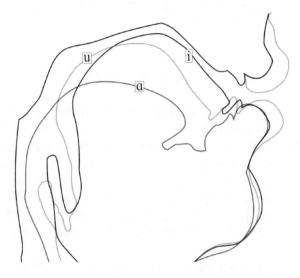

Figure 8.10   Overlay of tongue positions for three English vowels (high front [i], high back [u], and low back [ɑ]) from MRI data: right midsagittal view (image by D. Derrick).

Individual variation in vowels

As was true with VPP closure in Chapter 7, some of the mechanisms for producing vowel distinctions vary quite dramatically across individual speakers. For example, x-ray film studies have shown that some speakers use their jaw for changing vowel height, while others barely move their jaw and instead appear to change the shape of their tongue (Perkell, 1969; Chapter 9 will cover some of the ways the tongue can change shape). It's important for phoneticians to be aware of these kinds of individual differences, as they can often underlie and help to explain phonetic or phonological variation elsewhere in the system. Fortunately, though, there are some generalizations in vowel production that do seem to apply to most or all speakers.

When we described the extrinsic tongue muscles in Section 8.1.3, we pointed out some of the functions of these muscles in producing different vowels according to a rather traditional textbook view. A more up-to-date version of the story, while a bit more complex, will help you to think about vowel articulation a bit differently, and will give you a preview of the way we'll talk about the tongue in Chapter 9. Figure 8.10 shows tongue shapes and positions for [i], [u], and [ɑ], representing the three main types of vowels we describe in Sections 8.2.1, 8.2.2, and 8.2.3 – high front vowels, high back vowels, and low vowels.

8.2.1   High front vowels

If you think about where your tongue moves when you make a *high front vowel*, one problem becomes immediately obvious: there's no muscle in the front of the mouth that can contract to pull the tongue up and forward! In order to explain how sounds like this work, we need a different principle for tongue movement. Namely, we'll need to draw on the *hydrostatic* (Greek, "water-stable") properties of the tongue. A *hydrostat* is an object, like a water balloon for example, that has a fixed volume. If you squeeze one part of a hydrostat, some other part will bulge out, displacing the volume.

According to the traditional story, we produce high front vowels by contracting the GGp, which draws the root of the tongue forward, pushing the bulk of the tongue upward. This maneuver clearly makes use of the tongue's hydrostatic properties: squeeze the tongue root, and the tongue body squishes upward – after all, where else could it go? Well, in fact, it could easily end up going too far forward, even so far as to push right out of the mouth. To counteract this, we need an antagonist. The GGa contracts antagonistically in front vowels, as has been shown in both EMG and structural MRI studies (Fujimura and Kakita, 1979; Baer, Alfonso, and Honda, 1988; Honda, Takano, and Takemoto, 2010). When both the GGp and the GGa contract simultaneously, the tongue body is squeezed upward – rather than simply forward – in a controlled way.

8.2.2   High back vowels

High back vowels are traditionally thought of as being produced by contracting the styloglossus. However, MRI work by Takano and Honda (2007) reveals that the SG can't pull the tongue toward the styloid process because of a tendon that acts like a sling constraining the movement of the posterior SG. Takano and Honda show that the SG has a nearly identical length and orientation across all five Japanese vowels, including [ɯ] and [o]. Apparently, the SG most likely helps to stabilize the tongue and, where it interfaces with the sides of the tongue, helps to bunch the tongue dorsum to aid in making high back vowels. So, if the SG doesn't pull the tongue up and back for [u], how does it get there? Hydrostatics, of course! Rather than being "pulled" up and back, the tongue is squeezed up and back with the right balance of GGa and GGp, along with a bit of help from some of the intrinsic muscles of the tongue (which we'll talk about in Chapter 9).

As described above, it has sometimes been suggested that the palatoglossus may also contribute somewhat to tongue raising, though its function can vary both across and within speakers (Lubker and May, 1973).

8.2.3   Low vowels

The *low vowels* present another interesting case. Low vowels are characterized by an open oral space, and a relatively tight constriction in the pharynx. Thus, on the "height" or "closeness" scale, low vowels are "low" or "open." In fact, there is a fair degree of jaw lowering for low vowels, and since the tongue is riding on the mandible, the tongue usually lowers along with the jaw. However, another way of thinking about low vowels is in terms of the *constriction* they form in the pharynx. It's not clear whether the pharyngeal constriction for [ɑ] is the hydrostatic by-product of pushing the tongue body down, or whether the constriction itself is being controlled – or both.

On targets

When you make a vowel, are you making a movement or a sound? Well, clearly you're making both, but what is the main goal of your action? There has been much debate among speech researchers on this question. This is sometimes referred to as the "targets" debate.

When you reach your hand for an object, it's relatively clear that the "target" of the movement is in physical space. Nevertheless, there are still many ways you could describe that movement (e.g., in terms of end posture, muscle lengths, joint angles, etc.).

Speech complicates things even more by adding sound into the mix. When you make a speech movement, is the "target" of the movement in articulatory space (something like "move your tongue tip from position A to position B"), or is it in auditory space (something like "move your tongue so as to make sound C"), or something else?

Feedback perturbation studies have shown that both articulatory and auditory goals seem to be alive and well in speech. These kinds of studies cleverly use feedback to manipulate people's goals in speech.

In a study of auditory feedback perturbation, Houde and Jordan (1998) had participants produce many repetitions of vowels. The participants whispered, and were only able to hear their own speech through headphones. Instead of hearing their actual speech, however,

(Continued)

the researchers had altered (or "perturbed") the sounds to see whether participants' targets would shift. By the time the perturbations were removed, the participants had indeed shifted their vowel targets, showing that people do try to match certain sounds when they speak.

In a later study, Tremblay *et al.* (2003) showed that speech targets could similarly be changed by perturbing articulatory feedback. They used a robot to deliver tiny perturbations to participants' jaws while they were speaking. The robot's arm altered the movement path of the jaw, but not enough to change the acoustic output. As with Houde and Jordan's study, when the perturbations were removed, participants' speech targets had shifted.

Clearly, we need both sounds and movements – and probably more – to make speech work. As Houde (2009) puts it, "speech production creates associations between motor, somatosensory, and auditory representations, and [...] altering one of these representations affects the others."

This dichotomy between configurations and constrictions is one that runs throughout the speech-related disciplines, from phonology to speech motor control. We'll discuss theories more in Chapter 11, but for now let's think about what this means for low vowels.

Many phonologists have assigned the low vowels a feature (such as [low]), which refers to the height of the tongue body, suggesting that the pharyngeal constriction produced during low vowels is an incidental by-product of tongue hydrostatics. Others, meanwhile, have classed the low vowels together with pharyngeals, implying that there may be an *active* constriction in the pharynx. In terms of muscle activity, both of these components appear to be active.

GGa and GGm may be invoked to lower the front of the tongue for low vowels, as is HG, which pulls the tongue down and back. Interestingly, however, SG can also be involved in making low back vowels, bunching the tongue backward as it does for high back vowels (Takano and Honda, 2007). Further, the tongue retraction seen in low back vowels has been associated with constriction in the oropharynx created by the pharyngeal constrictors (Kokawa *et al.*, 2006). The middle, and to some extent, superior constrictors can pull the root of the tongue back, but can also narrow the pharynx. All of this suggests that constricting the pharynx – whether by retracting the tongue root or by narrowing the pharynx laterally – may be an important part of producing low vowels.

It is entirely possible that different languages or speaker populations – or even different individuals – categorize speech sounds according to different aspects of their physical production, such as, in this case, "low" versus "pharyngeal." This is one of the many questions in articulatory phonetics for which we need to collect more articulatory data across languages, dialects, and individuals in order to move forward.

Schwa and, uh . . . , filled pauses

Filled pauses, the sounds that arise when one is pausing to think (out loud) of what to say next, are often thought to resemble a language's neutral vowel or schwa. However, Clark and Fox Tree (2002) have shown that words that appear in filled pauses, such as *uh* and *um*, are not simply schwa-like noises, but are actually conventional English words that are planned for and chosen to fit the context.

Related to this, scholars have traditionally thought of schwa as a non-vowel (or a "neutral" vowel) with no place of articulation. Articulatory phonetics research has changed this view, showing that English schwa is articulated with a retracted tongue root (Gick, 2002a). This contrasts with schwa in other languages, such as French, where schwa has been described as having noticeably rounded lips (Price, 1991).

8.2.4   ATR and RTR

One additional dimension that is active in many vowel systems is *advanced tongue root* [ATR] vs. *retracted tongue root* [RTR], a distinction most often seen in languages of Africa. While many accounts have described ATR as operating independently of tongue height, there is often a correlation between the two. This is to be expected, given what we now know about the hydrostatic properties of the tongue.

As with the high vowels, the tongue root may be drawn forward for ATR vowels by constricting GGp, with a possible contribution from any of geniohyoid, mylohyoid, and ABD on the hyoid bone. Some research, however, has suggested that the ATR feature is not just about advancing the tongue root, but rather is a more general feature of pharyngeal expansion (Lindau, 1979; Tiede, 1996). If this is true, then ATR must also involve mechanisms for other movements such as widening of the lateral pharynx walls and larynx lowering (see Chapter 6).

For RTR, as with the low vowels, the tongue root may be retracted by the pharyngeal constrictors, or by hydrostatic forces elsewhere in the tongue.

Inverse problems, pseudoinverse solutions

What physical shape of the vocal tract provides us with a particular speech sound? What muscle actions result in a particular vocal tract shape? For many such questions, there are, or appear to be, many possible solutions. For example, the tongue can be raised and lowered by raising or lowering the jaw, or by contracting the palatoglossus, or by the actions of the GGp and GGa. Similarly, the tongue can be retracted by contracting the hyoglossus, or by contracting the middle pharyngeal constrictor. Nearly every motion of the vocal tract has similar redundancies.

Because of this redundancy, a phonetician looking at an acoustic signal may not know exactly how the tongue is shaped, and one looking at a tongue shape may not know exactly which muscles are active. Cases like this, with a single output but multiple possible inputs, are known to scientists as *inverse problems*.

Inverse problems have a certain appeal of their own. A famous inverse problem is featured in Douglas Adams' *The Hitchhiker's Guide to the Galaxy*, where the supercomputer Deep Thought determined that the Answer to the Ultimate Question of Life, the Universe, and Everything was "42" – but it didn't know the question. In Finland, the Finnish Inverse Problem Society (*Suomen inversioseura ry*) even organizes the annual national Inverse Problems Days.

Phonetics research is full of inverse problems. When scientists are faced with an inverse problem, they often employ a *pseudoinverse solution*, where one attempts to compute which solution requires the least "cost" (in terms of, say, energy consumed or distance moved) in order to achieve the observed output. A pseudoinverse solution will always be more accurate the better the whole system is understood.

8.3 Measuring Vowels: Ultrasound

When measuring vowels, it's important to be able to see broad changes in the shape of the entire tongue. It is relatively easy to image the tongue's surface shape, from epiglottis to tongue tip, with an *ultrasound* machine (see Stone, 2005).

Ultrasound machines use a medical imaging technique designed for soft-tissue analysis. An ultrasound probe, or *transducer*, is a hand-held device that can be held against the skin. The transducer uses piezoelectric crystals to produce high-frequency sound (ultra-high, in fact!) ranging from 3–16

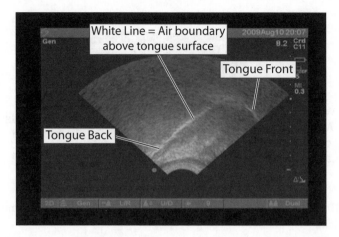

Figure 8.11a Ultrasound images of tongue: right midsagittal B mode (image by D. Derrick).

MHz, with lower frequencies penetrating deeper into flesh but providing less detail. Some of these sound waves penetrate skin, fat, and muscle (parts of the body that hold a lot of water), while some reflect back to the transducer. The sound waves get absorbed by bone and reflect sharply off of air boundaries, so that ultrasound doesn't image bone or air very well. The ultrasound machine calculates the length of time it takes for sound waves to travel back to the transducer, and calculates the distance based on time, producing a one- (M-mode) or two- (B-mode) dimensional image. Ultrasound machines can generate two-dimensional images at more than 120 Hz, but most machines output video at standard film speed, which is normally 24 Hz in Europe and about 30 Hz in the Americas.

Since there are no bones between the tongue floor and the upper surface of the tongue (except the tiny hyoid bone), you can hold an ultrasound transducer against your neck just behind your chin, and image the surface of your tongue. Because the sound is reflected off the air just above the surface of the tongue, the air above the surface appears as a white line. Imaging surfaces opposite the tongue, such as the palate and the rear pharyngeal wall, is only possible when there is no intervening airspace, as when swallowing or holding a mouthful of liquid (Epstein and Stone, 2005).

Although it is possible to get a limited three-dimensional tongue image with ultrasound, so far high-speed ultrasound imaging can only be achieved in two dimensions. Fortunately, midsagittal slices are often quite informative when studying the production of vowels – and most consonants as well. You can also turn the transducer 90 degrees to view a coronal or transverse cross-section of the tongue. Typical midsagittal ultrasound images of the tongue are shown in Figures 8.11a and 8.11b.

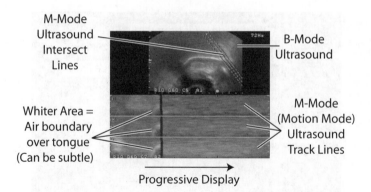

Figure 8.11b Ultrasound images of tongue: right midsagittal B/M mode (image by D. Derrick).

You can find many differently shaped transducers, each with its own specialized uses, though smaller ones with a tightly curved surface tend to work best for speech. Larger transducers may not fit well beneath the chin, may restrict jaw movement, or may fail to image the tongue tip because of the pocket of air under the tip called the *sublingual cavity*.

Ultrasound machines are also relatively easy to use, minimally requiring a processor, transducer (probe), and acoustic or video recording tools depending on the research project. Portable ultrasound machines can make ultrasound an ideal instrument for field phonetics research (Gick, 2002b). Ultrasound machines do not produce ionizing radiation, and so ultrasound is widely considered safe to use for research (see, e.g., Jia *et al.*, 2005). Because ultrasound gives quick and easy visual feedback about the position and shape of the tongue, it can also be a very useful tool for teaching people how to position the tongue to make sounds, whether in a clinical setting (Bernhardt *et al.*, 2005) or in language teaching (Gick *et al.*, 2008).

Despite its advantages, as with all tools, there are some challenges to using an ultrasound machine. Depending on the research question, it may be necessary to control or correct for head and/or transducer movement. This can be accomplished simply by having participants lean their head against a wall or headrest while seated, or by using a more elaborate restraint or tracking system (see Chapter 10 for an example of the latter). Older ultrasound machines will also interleave image data, so that the image on the screen can include information recorded up to 30 ms earlier. Lastly, ultrasound waves will reflect off any soft tissue, so that ultrasound images can sometimes look grainy, making it difficult to track the surface of the tongue automatically. Edge-tracking software and statistical tools (Davidson, 2006) have been developed to address this challenge (Li *et al.*, 2005).

Exercises

Sufficient jargon

Define the following terms: vowel quadrilateral, degree of freedom (DoF), extrinsic tongue muscles, mandible, body of the mandible, ramus, angle, condyle, coronoid process, mandibular notch, mental symphysis, mental protuberance, mental spine, temporomandibular joint (TMJ), mandibular fossa, articulator disk, 6DoF, translations, rotations, yaw, roll, pitch, dislocated mandible, elevate/elevator, depress/depressor, masseter, mastication, deep head of masseter, shallow head of masseter, temporalis muscle, medial (internal) pterygoid muscle, lateral (external) pterygoid muscle, anterior genioglossus (GGa) muscle, middle genioglossus (GGm) muscle, posterior genioglossus (GGp) muscle, hyoglossus (HG) muscle, styloglossus (SG) muscle, interdigitate, high front vowel, hydrostatic/hydrostat, high back vowel, low vowel, feedback perturbation, filled pauses, advanced tongue root (ATR), retracted tongue root (RTR), inverse problem, pseudoinverse solution, ultrasound, transducer (probe), sublingual cavity.

Short-answer questions

1   If the hypoglossal nerve were damaged, what are two possible alternative mechanisms available for retracting the tongue root for low back vowels?
2   Which jaw muscles are used mainly for mastication? Which are used mainly for speech?
3   Which two translations of the jaw are normally used in speech? Which rotation of the jaw is normally used in speech?
4   For the following measurement technique, find and cite two speech research papers not mentioned in this book in which that technique is used: ultrasound. Follow the reference formatting used in the references section at the end of each chapter.

Practical assignment

For each chapter, this text has online assignments (at www.wiley.com/go/articulatoryphonetics) that either provide research data for analysis, or practical tools for understanding vocal tract anatomy. For Chapter 8, you will look at a set of ultrasound frames extracted from ultrasound video recordings of the same speaker producing speech normally and with an obstruction in their mouth. The assignment and the related assignment images can be found in the online materials for this textbook under *Chapter 8*.

References

Baer, T., Alfonso, P., and Honda, K. (1988). *Electromyography* of the tongue muscle during vowels in /pVp/ environment. *Annual Bulletin of the Research Institute of Logopedics and Phoniatrics, 22*, 7–20.

Bernhardt, B. M., Gick, B., Bacsfalvi, P., and Adler-Bock, M. (2005). Ultrasound in speech therapy with adolescents and adults. *Clinical Linguistics and Phonetics, 19*, 605–617.

Bernstein, N. A. (1967). *The Coordination and Regulation of Movements*. London, UK: Pergamon.

Berthier, N. E. and Keen, R. (2006). The development of reaching in infancy. *Experimental Brain Research, 169*, 507–518.

Clark, H. H. and Fox Tree, J. E. (2002). Using *uh* and *um* in spontaneous speaking. *Cognition, 84*, 73–111.

Dang, J. and Honda, K. (2002). Estimation of vocal tract shapes from speech sounds with a physiological articulatory model. *Journal of Phonetics, 30*, 511–532.

Davidson, L. (2006). Comparing tongue shapes from ultrasound imaging using smoothing spline analysis of variance. *Journal of the Acoustical Society of America, 120*, 407–415.

Epstein, M. A. and Stone, M. (2005). The tongue stops here: ultrasound imaging of the palate. *Journal of the Acoustical Society of America, 118*, 2128–2131.

Fujimura, O. and Kakita, K. (1979). Remarks on quantitative description of the lingual articulation. In B. Lindblom and S. Öhman (eds), *Frontiers of Speech Communication Research*, New York: Academic Press, 17–24.

Ge'rard, J.-M., Wilhelms-Tricario, R., Perrier, P., and Payan, Y. (2003). A 3D dynamical biomechanical tongue model to study speech motor control. *Recent Research Developments in Biomechanics, 1*, 49–64.

Gick, B. (2002a). An X-ray investigation of pharyngeal constriction in American English schwa. *Phonetica, 59*, 38–48.

Gick, B. (2002b). The use of ultrasound for linguistic phonetic fieldwork. *Journal of the International Phonetic Association, 32*, 113–121.

Gick, B., Bernhardt, B. M., Bacsfalvi, P., and Wilson, I. (2008). Ultrasound imaging applications in second language acquisition. In J. Hansen and M. Zampini (eds), *Phonology and Second Language Acquisition*, Amsterdam: John Benjamins, 309–322.

Harshman, R., Ladefoged, P., and Goldstein, L. (1977). Factor analysis of tongue shapes. *Journal of the Acoustical Society of America, 62*, 693–707.

Honda, K., Takano, S., and Takemoto, H. (2010). Effects of side cavities and tongue stabilization: possible extensions of the quantal theory. *Journal of Phonetics, 38*, 33–43.

Houde, J. F. (2009). There's more to speech perception than meets the ear. *Proceedings of the National Academy of Sciences of the USA (PNAS), 106*, 20139–20140.

Houde, J. F., and Jordan, I. M. (1998). Sensorimotor adaptation in speech production. *Science, 279*, 1213–1216.

International Phonetic Association (1999). *Handbook of the International Phonetic Association: A Guide to the Use of the International Phonetic Alphabet*. Cambridge, UK: Cambridge University Press.

Jia, H., Duan, Y., Cao, T., Zhao, B., Lv, F., and Yuan, L. (2005). Immediate and long-term effects of color Doppler ultrasound on myocardial cell apoptosis of fetal rats. *Echocardiography: A Journal of Cardiovascular Ultrasound and Allied Techniques, 22,* 415–420.

Kokawa, T., Saigusa, H., Aino, I., Matsuoka, C., Nakamura, T., Tanuma, K., Yamashita, K., and Niimi, S. (2006). Physiological studies of retrusive movements of the human tongue. *Journal of Voice, 20,* 414–422.

Li, M., Kambhamettu, C., and Stone, M. (2005). Automatic contour tracking in ultrasound images. *Clinical Linguistics and Phonetics, 19,* 545–554.

Lindau, M. (1979). The feature expanded. *Journal of Phonetics, 7,* 163–176.

Lubker, J. F. and May, K. (1973). Palatoglossus function in normal speech production. *Papers from the Institute of Linguistics, 17,* 17–26. University of Stockholm.

Murray, G. M., Bhutada, M., Peck, C. C., Phanachet, I., Sae-Lee, D., and Whittle, T. (2007). The human lateral pterygoid muscle. *Archives of Oral Biology, 52,* 377–380.

Perkell, J. S. (1969). *Physiology of Speech Production: Results and Implications of a Quantitative Cineradiographic Study.* Research Monograph No. 53. Cambridge, Massachusetts: The MIT Press.

Price, G. (1991). *An Introduction to French Pronunciation.* Oxford: Blackwell.

Spencer, J. P. and Thelen, E. (2000). Spatially-specific changes in infants' muscle coactivity as they learn to reach. *Infancy, 1,* 275–302.

Stone, M. (2005). A guide to analysing tongue motion from ultrasound images. *Clinical Linguistics & Phonetics, 19,* 455–501.

Stone, M., Epstein, M. A., and Iskarous, K. (2004). Functional segments in tongue movement. *Clinical Linguistics & Phonetics, 18,* 507–521.

Stone, M., Goldstein, M. H., and Zhang, Y. (1997). Principal component analysis of cross sections of tongue shapes in vowel production. *Speech Communication, 22,* 173–184.

Sumbre, G., Fiorito, G., Flash, T., and Hochner, B. (2006). Octopuses use a human-like strategy to control precise point-to-point arm movements. *Current Biology, 16,* 767–772.

Takano, S. and Honda, K. (2007). An MRI analysis of the extrinsic tongue muscles during vowel production. *Speech Communication, 49,* 49–58.

Tiede, M. K. (1996). An MRI-based study of pharyngeal volume contrasts in Akan and English. *Journal of Phonetics, 24,* 399–421.

Tremblay, S., Shiller, D. M., and Ostry, D. J. (2003). Somatosensory basis of speech production. *Nature, 423,* 866–869.

Vogt, F., Lloyd, J. E., Buchaillard, S., Perrier, P., Chabanas, M., Payan, Y., and Fels, S. S. (2006). An efficient biomechanical tongue model for speech research. In H. C. Yehia, D. Demolin, and R. Laboissiere (eds), *Proceedings of ISSP 2006 – 7th International Seminar on Speech Production,* 51–58.

Chapter 9

Articulating Lingual Consonants

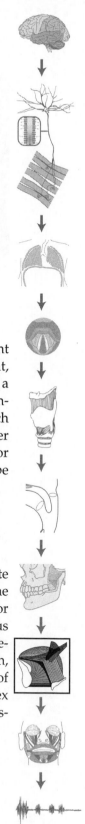

In this chapter we'll look at how the tongue moves to make consonant sounds. Chapter 8 described the tongue as an undifferentiated hydrostat, manipulated by the jaw and the extrinsic tongue muscles – kind of like a water balloon with strings attached. This simplified model worked reasonably well for describing basic vowel shapes. For consonants, however, such as approximants, fricatives, and stops, the tongue must take on a wider range of postures, requiring a more complex model of how it works. For this, we will need to consider how the muscles inside the tongue can be used to change its shape.

9.1 The Intrinsic Tongue Muscles

Much of the bulk of the tongue is made up of muscles that both originate and insert inside the tongue. These *intrinsic tongue muscles* do not pull the tongue toward hard structures, but rather work internally to squeeze or pull the tongue into different shapes. As we discussed in the previous chapter, the human tongue is a muscular hydrostat, and so works somewhat like an elephant's trunk or an octopus' tentacles (Kier and Smith, 1985). An example of a hydrostatic object is shown in the left column of Figure 9.1. Muscular hydrostats can produce an abundance of complex shapes, including extremely elongated ones, or shapes with multiple distinct regions of contraction or expansion.

Articulatory Phonetics, First Edition. Bryan Gick, Ian Wilson, and Donald Derrick.
© 2013 Bryan Gick, Ian Wilson, and Donald Derrick. Published 2013 by Blackwell Publishing Ltd.

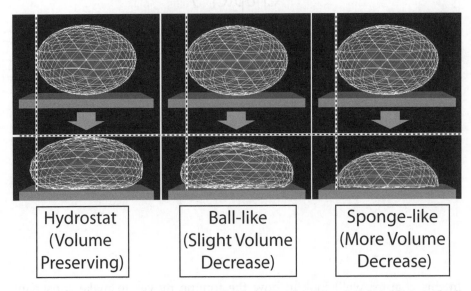

| Hydrostat (Volume Preserving) | Ball-like (Slight Volume Decrease) | Sponge-like (More Volume Decrease) |

Figure 9.1 Example of a hydrostat (left) dropped onto a hard surface – think "water balloon." The sponge on the right loses volume (i.e., there is no expansion to the sides as it loses volume vertically), while the hydrostat on the left bulges out to the sides. The ball in the middle is partially hydrostatic – it also bulges out to the sides, but loses some of its volume vertically (image by D. Derrick).

The human tongue has four intrinsic muscles that can squeeze in different directions. These four muscles can be thought of in pairs: The first pair consists of the tightly interwoven transversus and verticalis muscles, which run side-to-side and up-and-down within the tongue. The second pair consists of the superior longitudinal and inferior longitudinal muscles, which both run lengthwise front-to-back through the tongue (see Figure 9.2). All of the intrinsic tongue muscles are innervated by the hypoglossal nerve (CN XII).

9.1.1   The transversus and verticalis muscles

The fibers of the *transversus* or transverse lingual muscle run horizontally from the centerline of the tongue out to the sides, angling slightly upward. More precisely, the muscle originates at the *lingual septum*, a fibrous layer of tissue that defines the midsagittal plane of the tongue; from here, it passes laterally to insert into the *lingual margin*, or edge of the tongue. The

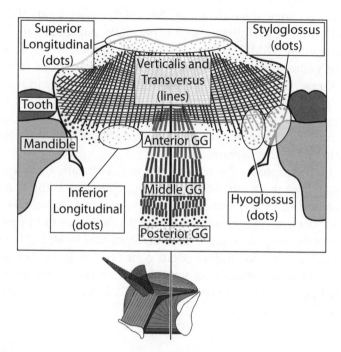

Figure 9.2 Tongue muscles: coronal cross-section through the mid-tongue; the location of the cross-section is indicated by the vertical line through the sagittal tongue image at the bottom (image by D. Derrick, inspired by Strong, 1956).

muscle fibers of the transversus are organized in layers that run all the way from the tongue tip to the tongue root. The sheets are stacked all along the length of the tongue, like slices of bread, so that they lie in the coronal plane in the front half of the tongue, and in the transverse plane in the back half. When the transversus muscle contracts, it narrows the tongue from side-to-side, which can also elongate and vertically thicken the tongue.

The *verticalis* or vertical lingual muscle is a layered set of muscle sheets interleaved between the transversus sheets, concentrated in the anterior part of the tongue. The individual fibers of the verticalis angle slightly inward and upward, passing laterally between the superior and inferior longitudinal muscles, making the verticalis muscle wider at the bottom than the top. Because of these vectors, contracting the verticalis pulls the upper surface of the tongue downward. This can lengthen the tongue and squeeze the sides of the tongue outward, flattening and widening the tongue (Abd-El-Malek, 1939; Takemoto, 2001).

As described above, the individual fibers of the transversus and verticalis muscles interdigitate so tightly that it is normally impossible to distinguish between them using EMG. However, one can simulate the actions of these muscles with computer modeling, or can infer their actions from changes in tongue shape. For example, low and high vowels differ in how the verticalis and transversus muscles are used: flattening and lateral expansion of the anterior tongue in low vowels indicates that the verticalis is being used, while narrowing and raising of the tongue in high vowels suggests involvement of the transversus.

One of the functions of the transversus and verticalis muscles is to seal the tongue against the teeth. Strong (1956) proposed that the superior portions of the verticalis and transversus muscles contract independently of the inferior portions of both muscles in order to bulge the upper portion of the sides of the tongue to form the seal. Since that time, further evidence has suggested a need for independent control of regions of the intrinsic tongue muscles. Some models of tongue motion now include this ability (Payan and Perrier, 1997; Napadow *et al.*, 2002; Fels *et al.*, 2003, 2006; Lloyd *et al.*, 2012).

9.1.2   The longitudinal muscles

The *superior longitudinal* (SL) muscle is a thin sheet of longitudinal muscle that forms a carpet-like surface over the top of the tongue. Contracting the SL curls the tip of the tongue upward and gives the tongue a concave shape. The SL muscle is thicker along the midline, with individual fibers that run from root to tip. Near the tip, some of the fibers run obliquely along the sides, so that the SL muscle can also curl the sides of the anterior tongue upward. Stone *et al.* (2004) argue that independent functional control of small, local portions of the superior longitudinal muscle is necessary for the proper formation of the curled tongue tip characteristic of retroflex sounds. As with the transversus and verticalis, biomechanical modeling is useful in demonstrating these fine distinctions in local activation of intrinsic tongue muscles.

The *inferior longitudinal* (IL) muscle is a narrow band of muscle that runs along either side of the genioglossus, just medial to the hyoglossus muscles. The fibers run from the tongue root to the tip, and some of the posterior fibers attach to the body of the hyoid bone. Along the bottom surface of the tongue body, some of the fibers of the IL muscle interdigitate with the styloglossus. The anterior portion of the IL runs parallel to the GGa and, like the GGa, contracts to turn the tongue tip downward. Generally, when the IL muscle is active, it helps give the tongue a convex shape.

Tongue shape and genetics

Exactly how the fibers of intrinsic tongue muscles are laid out is vital to the formation of many tongue shapes, and some of those vectors are the result of specific genetic mutations. For instance, the ability to twist the tongue to the right or left, to curl the lateral edges, to roll the edges of the tongue up and bend them over to produce the appearance of a split tongue, to form clover-leaf patterns with the tongue tip, and to fold the tip up on the base of the tongue have all been described as hereditary traits (Gahres, 1952). Usually, speech sounds do not require these specific genes, but forming the oft-described "retroflex" posture, with the tongue tip curled back, requires a minimum length, thinness, and muscle fiber orientation at the tongue tip. Fortunately, those of us who lack this combination of characteristics can either "bunch" our tongues toward the palate, or just tilt our tongue tips up, but do not produce the characteristic curl.

9.2 Sounds: Lingual Consonants

Most phoneticians tend to think of consonants in terms of constrictions of one variety or another. While there are different theories about exactly how constrictions work (see Chapter 11), one common way to describe consonantal constrictions is in terms of their *degree* (related to "*manner of articulation*") and *location* (related to "*place of articulation*"). It's possible to describe many of the lingual constrictions used in speech in terms of these two parameters.

9.2.1 Degrees of constriction and tongue bracing

As discussed in Chapter 8, the vocal tract typically is most open during vowel sounds. Stop consonants, at the other extreme, are the most closed sounds. The continuum between these open and closed sounds is known as *degree of constriction*. Degree of constriction (see Figure 9.3a) provides a descriptive tool that phoneticians can use to distinguish between different kinds of sounds such as vowels, approximants, fricatives and stops.

In addition to the primary constriction itself, lingual consonants (and probably most vowels as well) often involve an additional constriction known as bracing (Stone, 1990; McLeod, 2006; see Figure 9.3b). *Bracing* is when the tongue is held in contact with some surface (e.g., the molars) other than its target. Though bracing has been given relatively little attention in

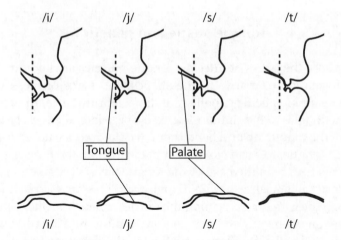

Figure 9.3a Degrees of anterior tongue constriction for vowel, approximant, frica-tive, and stop: midsagittal (top) and coronal (bottom) cross-sections are shown; dotted lines indicate location of the coronal cross-sections (image by D. Derrick, W. Murphey, and A. Yeung).

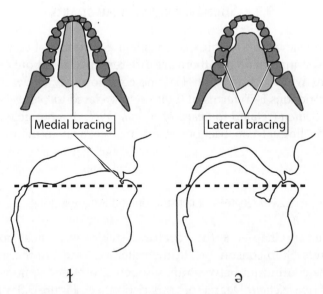

Figure 9.3b Lateral constrictions with medial bracing for a lateral fricative (on the left) and medial constrictions with lateral bracing for schwa (on the right): trans-verse (top) and midsagittal (bottom) cross-sections are shown; dotted lines indicate location of the transverse cross-sections (image by D. Derrick, W. Murphey, and A. Yeung).

the literature, it offers several apparent advantages when using the tongue to make constrictions, including: 1) it forces airflow through constriction locations, 2) it helps maintain stability and accuracy of the tongue, 3) it reduces degrees of freedom of the tongue, and 4) it gives the speaker somatosensory feedback about tongue position, as proprioception may be relatively limited in the tongue (on this last point, see Carleton, 1937; Adatia and Gehring, 1971).

Most of the time when we talk about lingual consonant constrictions, we are referring to *medial constrictions* (sometimes called *central* in phonetics). In medial constrictions, airflow is funneled along the midline of the tongue. This funneling of airflow works because of *lateral bracing*. In the case of medial constrictions, this means the tongue is touching the sides of the palate and/or the upper lateral teeth. Without bracing of the sides of the tongue, medial consonant sounds wouldn't work at all, as air would just move around the sides of the constriction! Thus, regardless of degree, *medial tongue constrictions are normally paired with lateral bracing*.

Lateral constrictions are much the same, except that airflow is directed along the sides of the tongue, and *medial bracing* is used. Thus, mirroring medial constrictions, regardless of degree, *lateral tongue constrictions are normally paired with medial bracing*.

9.2.1.1 Approximant constrictions

Consonants with lingual constrictions that are not so tight as to disrupt or block airflow are known as *approximants*. These sounds include examples such as [j] and [w] (among others) medially, and [l] and [ʎ] laterally. Approximants retain some vocalic qualities, but are often more tightly constricted and have different temporal properties from vowels at the same location.

9.2.1.2 Turbulent constrictions

A tighter constriction coupled with a tongue shape that facilitates accelerated airflow can result in air turbulence at a lingual constriction location. These kinds of sounds are often called *fricatives*. Disturbance of airflow becomes stronger as the constriction increases until an ideal, or "critical," degree of constriction is achieved, maximizing the turbulence for that constriction location (hence these kinds of constrictions are sometimes called *critical constrictions*).

Lingual fricatives make use of various tongue shapes to achieve turbulence. For example, while [ʃ] typically has a "domed" anterior tongue shape, distributing the airflow across the surface of the tongue, [s] often uses the genioglossus muscle to create a groove down the midline of the anterior tongue. This *medial grooving* creates a narrow passage that functions as a Venturi tube (see Chapter 5), accelerating airflow, which breaks against the teeth to produce the high-frequency turbulence associated with [s]. Lateral fricatives can be produced symmetrically (bilaterally), with both sides of the tongue lowered, or asymmetrically (unilaterally), with only one side fully lowered. Many speakers produce laterals asymmetrically, which is particularly helpful in focusing the airflow needed to create turbulence.

9.2.1.3 *Periodic constrictions*   Under just the right conditions, some lingual constrictions can result in periodic vibration, or *trill*, of the anterior tongue, similar to what we saw with phonation in Chapter 5. As with the vocal folds, trilling the tongue requires not just a narrow constriction, but also the right shape of the airway posterior to the constriction and the right degree of tenseness in the vibrating body. Periodic constrictions of the tongue itself only occur at the tongue tip, where the tongue vibrates against the hard palate. Trilling can also occur at the uvula, where the tongue remains relatively stationary while the uvula and velum vibrate against the lingual surface (see Chapter 7), or at the pharynx, where the aryepiglottic folds vibrate independently of the tongue (see Chapter 6). The velum can also vibrate during the pulmonic ingression associated with snoring. While it is physically possible for some people to achieve periodic vibration between the sides of the tongue and the buccal walls, no language has been reported as using lateral trills.

Trills are almost universally voiced, taking advantage of the physical and acoustical coupling of different vocal tract structures. There are a few notable exceptions, such as the Czech voiceless trill (Dankovičová, 1997), which contrasts with a voiced trill.

9.2.1.4 *Closure constrictions*   Often called *stops* or *plosives*, the narrowest degree of consonant constriction creates a complete closure that is tight enough to prevent oral airflow altogether. Because these constrictions must often withstand the air pressure increasing behind them, it is not enough for articulators merely to make contact – the tongue must actually compress against an opposing surface, creating a tight seal.

A useful way to think about these tight constrictions is in terms of *overshoot*, where the physical target of the movement is actually beyond the constriction, as if in an attempt to penetrate an opposing surface (see Figure 9.4a). You can see this compression in ultrasound or x-ray film images, where the tongue deforms as it squishes against the palate at the point of constriction. In addition to producing an airtight closure, overshoot has been described as requiring less careful control than producing some other degrees of constriction.

A *tap* is like a very quick or light stop – a closure or near-closure constriction that is produced with little or no overshoot. Overshoot can also occur tangentially to a surface (usually the alveolar ridge), resulting in a *flap* (see Figure 9.4b). In a flap sound, the articulator briefly touches – or almost touches – a surface then continues on in the same direction.

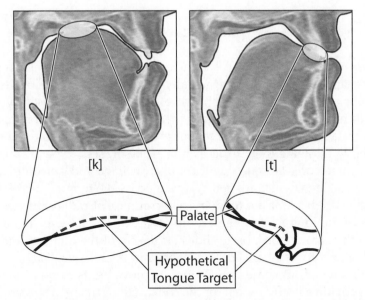

Figure 9.4a Overshoot in lingual stop production: right midsagittal view of vocal tract (image by D. Derrick).

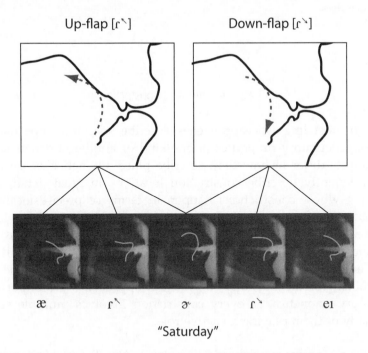

Figure 9.4b Overshoot in flap production: right midsagittal view of vocal tract; the up-arrow and down-arrow tap symbols indicate an upward vs. downward flap motion, after Derrick and Gick (2011) (image by D. Derrick, with x-ray data from Cooper and Abramson, 1960).

Ballistic tongues

Some animals take overshoot to the extreme, having specialized skeletal structures that are built to actually "launch" the tongue into action. Perhaps nature's most exceptional example of this *ballistic* type of tongue movement may be found in the chameleon. Chameleon tongues act as catapults, storing large amounts of energy slowly and releasing it rapidly, allowing them to accelerate at 500 m/s^2 to a speed of 6 m/s. The chameleon's tongue has a central cartilage rod surrounded by elastic collagen, which is itself surrounded by the tongue's accelerator muscle. The back of the tongue has a complex of radial muscles that squeeze the tongue, pushing the tip forward. The tongue "launches" when the accelerator muscle slides off the tip of the cartilaginous rod (Müller and Kranenbarg, 2004; Meyers and Nishikawa, 2000).

Thinking about some human tongue movements as quasi-ballistic may provide a useful model for the constrictions made in speech. That is, for many consonant constrictions, overshoot allows an articulator to move faster in exchange for reduced precision in degree of constriction.

9.2.2   Locations of constriction

Although most linguistic approaches describe speech sounds mainly in terms of articulatory properties of one kind or another, phoneticians and phonologists differ in how they describe place. Phoneticians, on the one hand, frequently describe constriction locations in great detail, usually specifying where constrictions happen in terms of precise locations on the *opposing surfaces*, or those surfaces in the vocal tract against which the tongue can constrict. Phonologists, on the other hand, often make reference to the moving parts of the anatomy, using features such as [coronal] for the tongue anterior, [dorsal] for the tongue body/dorsum, [ATR] for the tongue root, [labial] for the lips, and so on. Both approaches are important for articulatory phonetics, as every constriction involves multiple surfaces, with many of them playing an active role.

9.2.2.1   Tongue anterior constrictions   The anterior "free" part of the tongue is extremely flexible, and can make constrictions at many different locations. Sounds made using this part of the tongue, sometimes called *coronal* sounds, frequently pattern together phonologically in languages. Most anterior tongue constrictions require the use of the transversus and verticalis muscles both to elongate the tongue and to brace the tongue against the side or front teeth and palate, the SL muscle to raise the tongue front, and the IL muscle to stabilize the tongue, as an antagonist to the SL. Many different constrictions can be achieved by controlling these muscles, sometimes along with the genioglossus. This part of the tongue can constrict against the palate or the teeth – or even the lips.

Linguolabials and Britney Spears

Linguolabial consonants are made by protruding the tongue tip out of the mouth to make contact with the upper lip. They are very rare in the languages of the world, being mainly associated with a few island languages in Vanuatu. Linguolabials have received some attention in popular culture, as some female performers have developed the use of linguolabial variants of several English lingual consonants – including [l] and interdentals – while speaking or singing, a practice made famous by Britney Spears.

In the anterior tongue, subtle variations in shape can make a big difference in making distinctive sounds. For example, in contrast to the grooved tongue shape for the alveolar fricative [s] discussed above, other sounds such as the interdental fricative [θ] tend to be made with the tongue held relatively flat, so that airflow is distributed across the surface, then flows between the teeth, and bounces on the lips (Shadle, 1985; Stone and Lundberg, 1996).

The difference in grooving between sounds like [s] and [θ] is sometimes confounded with an "apical-laminal" distinction in anterior tongue shape. An *apical* constriction is one where the tongue tip (or "apex") is pointed upward or forward so that the constriction is made between the edge of the tongue and the palate or teeth, while a *laminal* constriction has the tongue tip pointed downward so that the constriction is made with the *blade*, or the flat part of the tongue just behind the tip. The consonant systems of several Australian languages are well known for maintaining multiple apical-laminal distinctions. Individual speakers of a language may vary quite a bit in producing apical vs. laminal variants of sounds. This is the case with /s/, where speaker populations are split between those who produce apical /s/ and those who produce laminal /s/ (Dart, 1991).

Finally, most anterior lingual constrictions are made using the tongue's upper surface. However, because the anterior portion of the tongue is extremely flexible, it is possible to make anterior constrictions using the underside of the tongue. *Retroflex* constrictions, as these are often called, are formed by raising and backing the tongue tip until the underside of the tongue faces the upper teeth and alveolar ridge. The shape of the oral cavity is quite distinctive in retroflexes, producing an auditory quality that is easily recognized. As noted earlier, contracting the anterior part of the superior longitudinal muscle is important in raising and curling the tongue tip for retroflexes.

Tongue-tied?

Usually when someone says they're *tongue-tied*, they are using the term figuratively to mean they can't find the words to express themselves. Some people, though, are quite literally tongue-tied.

The medical name for tongue-tie is *ankyloglossia* (Greek, "bent tongue"). Ankyloglossia is a congenital condition whereby the tongue is tethered to the floor of the mouth by an abnormally short *lingual frenulum* (Latin, "bridle"), the thin fold of mucous membrane attached to the inferior midline of the tongue.

Surprisingly, it's only in the most severe cases that ankyloglossia has a serious effect on speech. When it does interfere with speech, it has been observed to affect tongue anterior sounds such as [t, d, z, s, θ, ð, n, l] in children's speech (Messner and Lalakea, 2002), and has been reported to disrupt English /r/.

Tongue-tie can be treated with a *lingual frenectomy*, in which the frenulum is surgically removed. This procedure has unfortunately become popular among some non-English-speaking populations in the belief that it will improve normal children's ability to acquire English /r/. However, a lingual frenectomy will have no appreciable effect on the mobility of a normal tongue, and no studies have shown that the procedure has a positive effect on speech except in the most extreme clinical cases (in which there would be apparent problems with speech, regardless of the language).

9.2.2.2 Tongue body/dorsum constrictions   The *tongue body/dorsum* is the central mass of the tongue that lies behind the more flexible anterior part and above the tongue root. While still somewhat flexible, this part of the tongue is less "free" than the anterior part, partly because it is this part that remains braced against the teeth and palate during most speech constrictions. Some schools of thought have preferred to use the term "tongue body" for this part of the tongue, while others have endorsed the term "tongue dorsum." Still others have distinguished between the two, as they can sometimes serve different functions, the more anterior "body" being used for palatal constrictions and the more posterior "dorsum" being used for dorsal constrictions, such as uvulars. The tongue body/ dorsum can bulge upward or backward, can groove downward in the middle, can widen or narrow, and can stretch or compress longitudinally. These movements allow it to form constrictions at the hard palate, to interact with the soft palate or uvula, or to move backward into the upper pharynx.

The farthest forward tongue body constrictions are known variously as *palatals* or *postalveolars*, and include such sounds as the high front vowel [i], the palatal approximant [j], fricatives [ç , ʝ] and stops [c , ɟ]. These sounds are typically formed by hydrostatically doming the tongue body upward toward the hard palate.

The tongue body/dorsum shape for *velars* such as [k] and [g] and *uvulars* such as the fricative [χ] or the stop [q] are normally formed hydrostatically as well. In most languages, sounds that are called "velar" are actually constricted at the rear of the hard palate rather than at the velum, whereas "uvular" sounds are more likely to interact with the velum. In some cases, uvulars are still more retracted, interfacing with the rear (palatopharyngeal) faucial pillars, or even the rear pharyngeal wall. These might be more properly termed "upper pharyngeals." Constrictions that are truly velar or uvular are different from more anterior lingual constrictions in that the opposing surfaces can be actively involved in making the constriction as well as the tongue, as described in Chapter 7. This can be readily seen in x-ray films of French speakers (see Munhall *et al.*, 1995), where the velum lowers to meet the tongue body/dorsum during the uvular rhotic. This role-reversal between constrictor and opposing surface is perhaps at its extreme in uvular trills (as opposed to tongue anterior trills), where the uvula itself (along with much of the velum) is the primary vibrating body, with the tongue acting as the relatively passive "opposing surface."

9.2.2.3 Tongue root constrictions The *tongue root*, sometimes called the "anterior pharyngeal wall," is more constrained in its movements than the other parts of the tongue, mainly moving toward the rear pharyngeal wall as part of sphincteric constrictions in the pharynx. Constrictions using the tongue root are variously referred to as "radical," "pharyngeal," and "guttural" sounds, all of which may mean different things to different people. This variation in usage stems at least partly from the fact that, prior to relatively recent technological advances, little has been known about how the more posterior parts of the vocal apparatus work during speech.

The pharynx: the wellspring of language?

Esling *et al.* (2004) have proposed that the pharynx is the key to understanding the development of speech. They have collected evidence
showing that newborns from a range of language backgrounds produce
similar pharynx-generated sounds. Newborns first start to control
their pharyngeal and laryngeal articulators, testing and practicing
their phonetic production skills. This is most easily observed in the
pharyngeally constricted cries of babies that become more regularly
modal as the baby reaches one year of age.

It's not clear to what extent sounds traditionally described as pharyngeal
constrictions actually involve the tongue root. For example, pharyngeal
trills (discussed in Chapter 6) are not produced by vibrating the tongue root
(which, like the tongue body/dorsum, is far too massive to trill), but by
vibrating the aryepiglottic folds. Similarly, while the tongue root does
appear to be involved in the ATR/RTR distinction in vowels (discussed in
Chapter 8), this is only one of several ways to expand or contract the
pharynx. Indeed, to what extent the tongue root ever acts as a completely
independent articulator remains a topic of debate among researchers.

Whatever structure is responsible, constrictions in the pharynx are important not just for stops, fricatives, trills, approximants and vowels, but also
for distinctions in voice quality (see Chapter 6) and as a secondary feature.

9.3   Measuring Lingual Consonants: Palatography and Linguography

Some of the techniques we have covered in this book, such as ultrasound
imaging, allow researchers to measure the shape of the tongue for all sorts
of sounds. For some lingual consonant constrictions, however, it can be very
useful to be able to see the fine details of tongue-palate contact using
palatography.

The term *palatography* refers to several methods used to measure where
the tongue makes contact against the roof of the mouth. The traditional
technique, known as *static palatography*, had already been in use for some
time before Peter Ladefoged described it in detail in 1957, and is still used
by some researchers today. In this method, a mixture of charcoal and veg-
etable oil is "painted" onto the tongue of a speaker who then produces
a single token of a desired sound segment. An oral mirror is used to

allow the palate to be photographed. The resulting images are used to identify the place of contact between the tongue and palate for the segment in question. This same method can be applied in reverse, with the mixture being painted onto the palate, allowing the pattern of contact on the tongue to be observed, a method known as *linguography*. Static palatography and linguography are particularly useful for looking at more anterior consonant sounds such as stops, fricatives, and clicks, and can be applied in nearly any field situation. One story tells of Peter Ladefoged using local cooking oil and burnt toast for a palatography experiment because there was no activated charcoal on hand. Static palatography has the disadvantage of only being able to identify the constriction pattern in a single instance, after which the articulators must be cleaned and the mixture reapplied.

To address some of the limitations of static palatography, Shibata (1968) described the first practical attempt at dynamic palatography, more commonly known as *electropalatography* (EPG). The technique involves building a palatal insert, similar to a dental retainer, containing a grid of surface electrodes with more electrodes concentrated at the front of the palate to capture the finer tongue anterior distinctions (see Figure 9.5). The spatial

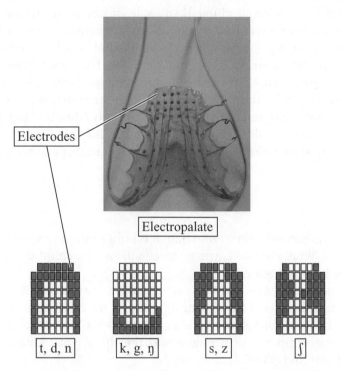

Figure 9.5 An electropalate (top) and electropalatography data (bottom); black cells indicate tongue contact on the electropalate (image by D. Derrick).

resolution of most EPG systems is relatively low, normally recording a grid of fewer than a hundred points, but this resolution is sufficient for most sounds. When the tongue touches the electrodes on the palatal insert, a machine records the points of contact between the tongue and the electrodes up to hundreds of times per second, giving EPG a high score for temporal resolution. One drawback of most systems is that the palatal inserts must be custom built and can be quite expensive and time consuming to produce.

EPG can be used in combination with other tools such as ultrasound (see Chapter 8) to provide greater detail about tongue-palate interaction. EPG allows the tracking of small changes in tongue contact position during rapid movements, and can be useful in treating disorders that affect speech articulation (Hardcastle *et al.*, 1991).

Exercises

Sufficient jargon

Define the following terms: intrinsic tongue muscles, transversus muscle, lingual septum, lingual margins, verticalis muscle, superior longitudinal (SL) muscle, inferior longitudinal (IL) muscle, degree of constriction, manner of articulation, location of constriction, place of articulation, medial constriction, lateral bracing, lateral constriction, medial bracing, approximants, fricatives, critical constrictions, medial grooving, trill, stops/plosives, overshoot, tap, flap, ballistic movement, opposing surfaces, coronal sounds, linguolabials, apical, laminal, blade, retroflexes, ankyloglossia (tongue-tie), lingual frenulum, lingual frenectomy, tongue body/dorsum, palatals, post-alveolars, velars, uvulars, tongue root, radicals/pharyngeals/gutturals, palatography, static palatography, linguography, electropalatography (EPG).

Short-answer questions

1 If the hypoglossal nerve were damaged (disabling many of the tongue muscles), what are two extrinsic mechanisms you could use to raise the tongue body for speech?

2 What mechanisms would you use to make an "apiconasal" constriction (i.e., one between the tip of your tongue and the tip of your nose)? What would have to change to make an "apicomental" constriction (i.e., one between the tip of your tongue and the tip of your chin), and what would stay the same?

3 For the following measurement technique, find and cite two speech research papers not mentioned in this book in which the technique is

used: electropalatography (EPG). Follow the reference formatting used in the references section at the end of each chapter.

Clay tongue assignment (see Figures 9.6a and 9.6b)

For each chapter, this text has online assignments (at www.wiley.com/go/articulatoryphonetics) that either provide research data for analysis, or practical tools for understanding vocal tract anatomy. For Chapter 9, you will build a tongue out of modeling clay. Printable versions of the assignment and the related assignment images can be found in the online materials for this textbook under *Chapter 9*.

Clay tongue instructions

You will need 8 colors of children's modeling clay obtainable at a dollar store. More malleable playing clay or Japanese paper-clay tends to be too soft for this assignment. You also need a short (10-cm) length of wire about as thick as a metal coat hanger, as shown in Figure 9.6b.

1 Take a ball of clay and flatten it out in a large oval, exactly the size of the one labeled "Superior Longitudinal" in Figure 9.6a; it should be the same thickness as in the coronal cross-section shown in Figures 9.6a and 9.6b.
2 Take a different color of clay and roll it into a ball – make it as spherical as possible – such that the diameter of the sphere exactly matches that of the circle labeled "Transversus & Verticalis" in Figure 9.6a.
3 Take a third color of clay and roll into a smaller ball – again making it as spherical as possible – such that the diameter of the sphere exactly matches that of the circle labeled "Genioglossus" in Figure 9.6a.
4 Take a fourth color of clay, and build two tapered cylinders that fit exactly into the shape labeled "Inferior Longitudinal" in Figure 9.6a.
5 Take a fifth color of clay, and build it into two long blocks that fit exactly into the shape labeled "Geniohyoid" in Figure 9.6a; make sure the thickness matches that of the coronal cross-section shown in Figure 9.6a.
6 Take a sixth color of clay, and build it into two tapered cylinders that fit exactly into the shape labeled "Styloglossus" in Figure 9.6b.
7 Take a seventh color of clay, and make it into two flat shapes that fit into the shape labeled "Hyoglossus" as seen in Figure 9.6b.
8 Take the eighth color of clay, and make it into two flat shapes that fit into the shape labeled "Mylohyoid" as seen in Figure 9.6b.

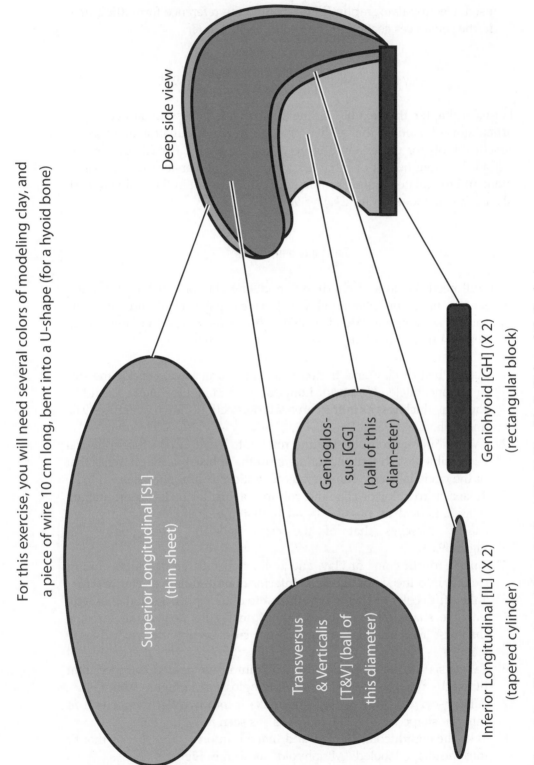

For this exercise, you will need several colors of modeling clay, and a piece of wire 10 cm long, bent into a U-shape (for a hyoid bone)

Deep side view

Superior Longitudinal [SL]
(thin sheet)

Genioglos-
sus [GG]
(ball of this
diam-eter)

Transversus
& Verticalis
[T&V] (ball of
this diameter)

Geniohyoid [GH] (X 2)
(rectangular block)

Inferior Longitudinal [IL] (X 2)
(tapered cylinder)

Figure 9.6a Clay tongue model exercise (image by D. Derrick, B. Gick, and G. Carden).

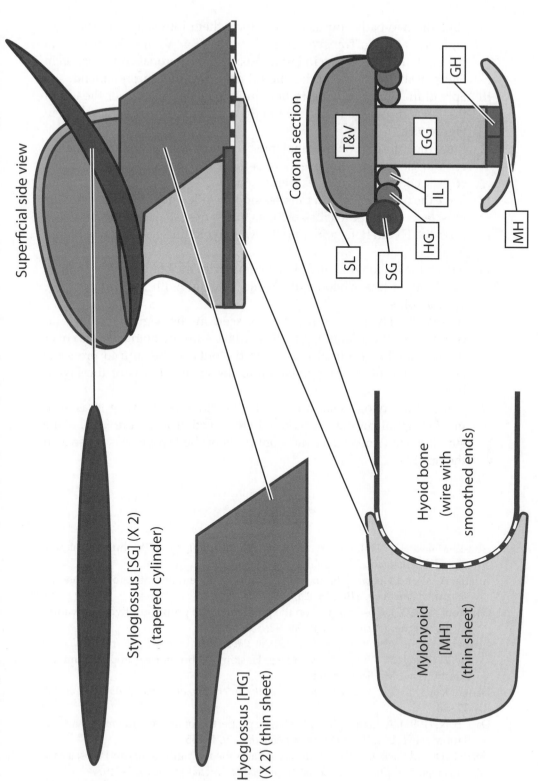

Figure 9.6b Clay tongue model exercise (image by D. Derrick, B. Gick, and G. Carden).

9 Take the two balls you made, and form them into shapes of the Genioglossus and the Transversus & Verticalis (T & V) muscles as seen in the sagittal cross-section in Figure 9.6a and the coronal cross-section in Figure 9.6b; the two muscles should press together but not blend.

10 Spread the Superior Longitudinal muscle like a carpet over the top of the T & V muscles as suggested in the midsagittal cross-section seen in Figure 9.6a.

11 Press the Inferior Longitudinal muscles into the sides of the Genioglossus muscle where it intersects with the T & V muscles, as seen in the cross-sections in Figures 9.6a and 9.6b.

12 Place the two Geniohyoid muscles side-by-side under the Genioglossus muscle as seen in the cross-sections in Figures 9.6a and 9.6b.

13 Push the Hyoid bone wire into the Mylohyoid muscle as seen in Figure 9.6b.

14 Attach the Mylohyoid and Hyoid complex to the bottom of the tongue; the front of the Mylohyoid should line up with the front of the Geniohyoids.

15 Attach the Hyoglossus muscles as seen in the sagittal profile and coronal cross-section in Figure 9.6b. Make sure the pointed ends cover the inferior longitudinal muscle on the outside; be sure to press the bottom edge of the Hyoglossus into the greater horns of the Hyoid bone.

16 Attach the Styloglossus muscles to the sides of the tongue as seen in the sagittal profile and coronal cross-section in Figure 9.6b. Make sure the front ends cover the front parts of the Hyoglossus muscle on the outside.

References

Abd-El-Malek, S. (1939). Observations on the morphology of the human tongue. *Journal of Anatomy, 73*, 201–212.

Adatia, A. K. and Gehring, E. N. (1971). Proprioceptive innervation of the tongue. *Journal of Anatomy, 110*, 215–220.

Carleton, A. (1937). Observations on the problem of the proprioceptive innervation of the tongue. *Journal of Anatomy, 72*, 502–507.

Cooper, F. S. and Abramson, A. S. (1960). *A Pilot X-ray Film of English Articulations with Stretched Sound*. New York: Haskins Laboratories and Columbia-Presbyterian Medical Center.

Dankovičová, J. (1997). Czech. *Journal of the International Phonetic Association, 27*, 77–80.

Dart, S. N. (1991). Articulatory and acoustic properties of apical and laminal articulations. *UCLA Working Papers in Phonetics, 79*, 1–155.

Derrick, D. and Gick, B. (2011). Individual variation in English flaps and taps: a case of categorical phonetics. *Canadian Journal of Linguistics, 56*, 307–319.

Esling, J. H., Benner, A., Bettany, L., and Zeroual, C. (2004). Le contrôle articulatoire phonétique dans le prébabillage. In B. Bel and I. Marlien (eds), *Actes des XXVes Journées d'Étude sur la Parole*. Fés, Morocco: AFCP, 205–208.

Fels, S. S., Vogt, F., Gick, B., Jaeger, C., and Wilson, I. (2003). User-centered design for an open source 3D articulatory synthesizer. In *Proceedings of the 15th International Congress of Phonetic Science (ICPhS 15)*, 179–182.

Fels, S., Vogt, F., van den Doel, K., Lloyd, J., Stavness, I., and Vatikiotis-Bateson, E. (2006). ArtiSynth: A Biomechanical Simulation Platform for the Vocal Tract and Upper Airway. Technical report TR-2006-10, Computer Science Dept., University of British Columbia.

Gahres, E. E. (1952). Tongue rolling and tongue folding and other hereditary movements of the tongue. *The Journal of Heredity*, 43, 221–225.

Hardcastle, W. J., Gibbon, F. E., and Jones, W. (1991). Visual display of tongue-palate contact: electropalatography in the assessment and remediation of speech disorders. *International Journal of Language & Communication Disorders*, 26, 41–74.

Kier, W. and Smith, K. (1985). Tongues, tentacles and trunks: the biomechanics of movement in muscular-hydrostats. *Zoological Journal of the Linnean Society*, 83, 307–324.

Lloyd, J. E., Stavness, I., and Fels, S. (2012). ArtiSynth: A fast interactive biomechanical modeling toolkit combining multibody and finite element simulation. In Payan, Y. (ed), *Soft Tissue Biomechanical Modeling for Computer Assisted Surgery* (pp. 355–394), Studies in Mechanobiology, Tissue Engineering and Biomaterials 11. Berlin: Springer-Verlag.

McLeod, S. (2006). Australian adults' production of /n/: an EPG investigation. *Clinical Linguistics & Phonetics*, 20, 99–107.

Messner, A. H. and Lalakea, M. L. (2002). The effect of ankyloglossia on speech in children. *Otolaryngology–head and neck surgery*, 127, 539–545.

Meyers, J. J., and Nishikawa, K. C. (2000). Comparative study of tongue protrusion in three iguanian lizards, Sceloporus undulatus, Pseudotrapelus sinaitus and Chamaeleo jacksonii. *Journal of Experimental Biology*, 203, 2833–2849.

Müller, U. K. and Kranenbarg, S. (2004). Power at the tip of the tongue. *Science*, 304, 217–219.

Munhall, K. G., Vatikiotis-Bateson, E., and Tohkura, Y. (1995). X-ray film database for speech research. *Journal of the Acoustical Society of America*, 98, 1222–1224.

Napadow, V. J., Kamm, R. D., and Gilbert, R. J. (2002). A biomechanical model of sagittal tongue bending. *Journal of Biomechanical Engineering*, 124, 547–556.

Payan, Y. and Perrier, P. (1997). Synthesis of VV sequences with a 2D biomechanical tongue model controlled by the Equilibrium Point Hypothesis. *Speech Communication*, 22, 185–205.

Saito, H. and Itoh, I. (2003). Three-dimensional architecture of the intrinsic tongue muscles, particularly the longitudinal muscle, by the chemical-maceration method. *Anatomical Science International*, 78, 168–176.

Shadle, C. H. (1985). The acoustics of fricative consonants. In *Research Laboratory of Electronics, Technical Report 506*. Cambridge, MA: MIT.

Shibata, S. (1968). A study of dynamic palatography. *Annual Bulletin of the Research Institute of Logopedics and Phoniatrics, University of Tokyo*, 2, 28–36.

Stone, M. (1990). A three-dimensional model of tongue movement based on ultrasound and x-ray microbeam data. *Journal of the Acoustical Society of America, 81,* 2207–2218.

Stone, M., Epstein, M., and Iskarous, K. (2004). Functional segments in tongue movement. *Clinical Linguistics & Phonetics, 18,* 507–521.

Stone, M. and Lundberg, A. (1996). Three-dimensional tongue surface shapes of English consonants and vowels. *Journal of the Acoustical Society of America, 99,* 3728–3737.

Strong, L. H. (1956). Muscle fibers of the tongue functional in consonant production. *The Anatomical Record, 126,* 61–79.

Takemoto, H. (2001). Morphological analyses of the human tongue musculature for three-dimensional modeling. *Journal of Speech, Language, and Hearing Research, 44,* 95–107.

Chapter 10

Articulating Labial Sounds

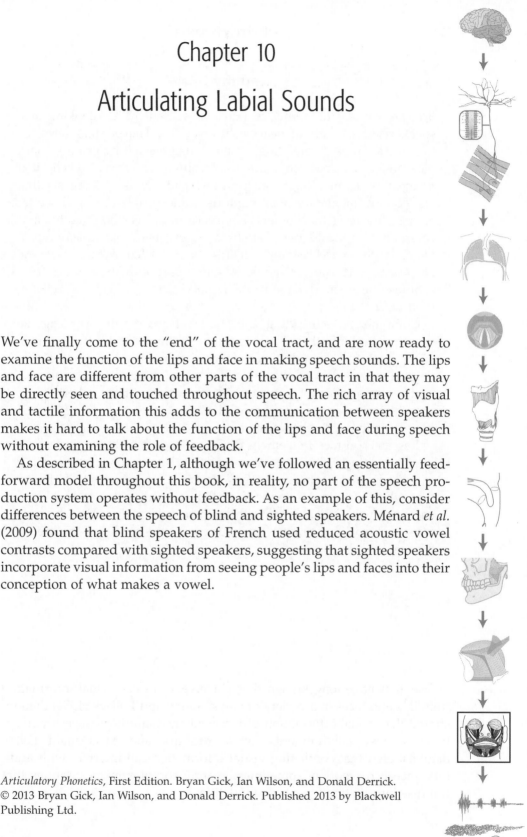

We've finally come to the "end" of the vocal tract, and are now ready to examine the function of the lips and face in making speech sounds. The lips and face are different from other parts of the vocal tract in that they may be directly seen and touched throughout speech. The rich array of visual and tactile information this adds to the communication between speakers makes it hard to talk about the function of the lips and face during speech without examining the role of feedback.

As described in Chapter 1, although we've followed an essentially feed-forward model throughout this book, in reality, no part of the speech production system operates without feedback. As an example of this, consider differences between the speech of blind and sighted speakers. Ménard *et al.* (2009) found that blind speakers of French used reduced acoustic vowel contrasts compared with sighted speakers, suggesting that sighted speakers incorporate visual information from seeing people's lips and faces into their conception of what makes a vowel.

Articulatory Phonetics, First Edition. Bryan Gick, Ian Wilson, and Donald Derrick.
© 2013 Bryan Gick, Ian Wilson, and Donald Derrick. Published 2013 by Blackwell Publishing Ltd.

Read my lips!

Speechreading is the ability to perceive speech by just looking at a speaker's face (without hearing any sound). The popular term for this is, of course, "lipreading," a term dispreferred by professionals, who prefer to acknowledge that the "reading" is by no means limited to the lips. Even though the phrase "read my lips" suggests that visible movements are unambiguous, some people are much better at speechreading than others. Henry Kisor, a deaf book editor and columnist for the *Chicago Sun-Times*, gives many examples of problems with speechreading, in his book called *What's that Pig Outdoors?: A Memoir of Deafness*. The first part of the title comes from a phrase he misunderstood when speechreading: "What's that big loud noise?"

Computer speechreading, the ability of a computer to recognize speech using only the visual signal, has attracted many researchers. Computers that could do voice recognition in noisy environments, or voice recognition from only the video signal, would be valuable in a number of applications, such as defense applications where silent speech is necessary, video surveillance/monitoring, and enhanced pronunciation evaluation systems.

Research on face movement during speech has shown that much of what's going on inside the vocal tract can be recovered from looking at a moving face (Yehia *et al.*, 1998). In fact, Calvert *et al.* (1997) found that when we see a moving face the auditory parts of our brain become active – but only if we think the face is talking. That is, when we speechread, our brain actually uses our eyes to "hear" the speech we see.

Scientists have long known that perceivers can use visual information from lips and faces in a variety of ways. Sunby and Pollack (1954) demonstrated that visual information of faces enhances auditory speech perception in noisy environments, while McGurk and MacDonald (1976) demonstrated that conflicting visual information can interfere with auditory speech perception, sometimes creating complex misperceptions that can fuse information from both modalities.

The uncanny valley

When you see a human-like robot, puppet or doll, you're likely to feel more empathy toward it the more it looks like a real human – but only up to a point. Mori (1970) famously noticed that there's a certain point, when a representation is almost perfectly human-like (but not quite), at which people react in revulsion to it, almost as if the still representation were a corpse and the moving representation a zombie. This phenomenon (a sudden steep drop in perceived familiarity when human likeness is very high) has been called the *uncanny valley* (Mori, 1970).

Related to this, have you ever noticed that the speech of a puppet or cartoon character seems fine even though the mouth is just waggling open and shut? Imagine if you saw a human face with the mouth moving the same way. Would you find it as convincing? The upshot: perceivers seem to have very low expectations of poor representations of humans, but very high expectations as the representations approach reality. When those high expectations are not met, perceivers reject the representations.

This is important for speech researchers to know, and its effect is not limited to the visual modality: we can forgive even the most bizarre speech sounds and unnatural responses coming from a really bad robot voice, but as speech synthesis improves and the voice approaches a more human-like quality, the listener expects nearly perfect speech sounds and responses. Anyone who has had to interact with automated phone answering systems knows just how unreal – and uncomfortable – the experience can be when there is a mismatch between one's expectations and reality.

In addition to sight and sound, speech information from the face and lips can also be picked up through touch. Alcorn (1932) developed the *Tadoma* speech training method for the blind and deaf to take advantage of this, as a way to enhance auditory speech perception. In this method, the perceiver places his or her thumb on the lips of a speaker, with the index finger above the line of the mandible, and the other fingers fanned across the neck (see Figure 10.1). It is now well known that this direct sensation of face motion and airflow from the mouth can enhance perceivers' accuracy in hearing speech sounds, even with no prior training.

Let's look at how the lip and face muscles act to make these audible, visible, touchable speech movements work.

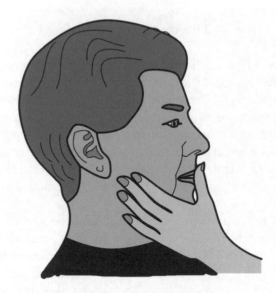

Figure 10.1 The Tadoma method (image by D. Derrick).

10.1   Muscles of the Lips and Face

The lips, a complex organ at the upper end of the vocal tract, are soft and extremely flexible, and can take on a variety of shapes, from rounded and protruded to spread to pinched shut. As with the intrinsic muscles of the tongue, many lip and face muscles are so intertwined that it is impossible to know for certain the functions of individual muscles based on direct measurement by EMG (Blair and Smith, 1986). What we do know about these muscles comes from a combination of indirect sources, such as suggestive EMG studies, anatomical studies, and computer modeling. All of the muscles of the lips and face we discuss in this book are innervated by the facial nerve (CN VII). Muscles of the lips and face are shown in Figure 10.2.

10.1.1   The amazing OO

The *orbicularis oris* (OO; Latin, "ring-shaped mouth") muscle performs sphincter-like actions and makes up much of the substance of the lips. It is a complex muscle made up of a network of fibers, arranged into several layers from superficial to deep, each of which exerts a slightly different kind of pull on the lips (see Figure 10.3). The OO is also organized in concentric rings, creating an important distinction between the *marginal* part of the orbicularis oris (OOm; the inner rings, closest to the center of the lip opening) and the *peripheral* part of the orbicularis oris (OOp; the outer rings, farthest from the center of the lip opening).

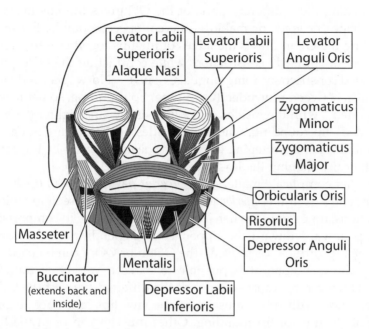

Figure 10.2 Muscles of the lips and face: anterior coronal view (image by W. Murphey).

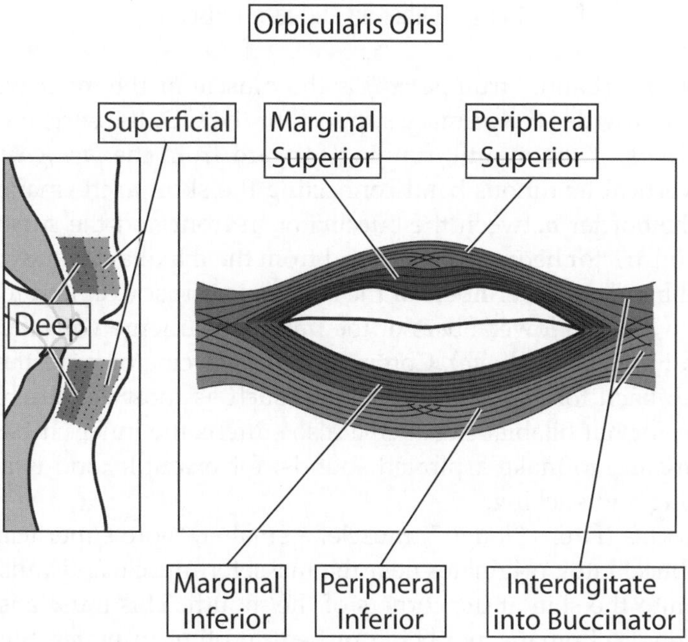

Orbicularis Oris

Figure 10.3 Orbicularis oris muscle: right midsagittal cross-section (left), coronal view (right) (image by D. Derrick).

Contracting these different parts of the OO gives the lips many of the varied shapes needed for making different speech sounds. For example, contracting the OOm draws the edges of the lips together into a rounded, unprotruded, "pursed" constriction, while contracting the OOp produces a protruded constriction. Some languages, such as Norwegian and Swedish, distinguish between protruded (OOp-type) lip rounding, sometimes called "outrounded," with the insides of the lips visible, and tighter (OOm-type) "inrounded" lip rounding, where the insides of the lips are not as visible (Traunmüller, 1979). Stiffening the lips has been shown to be important for hydrostatically shaping the lips (Nazari *et al.*, 2011).

To further complicate matters, the *superior* part of the OO (OOs) can act independently from the *inferior* part (OOi) – as can be seen in labiodental constrictions, for example, where only the OOi is active in compressing the lower lip upward toward the upper teeth. Depending on the variety of labiodental (protruded or pursed), the OOmi or OOpi can be used.

Using the OO alone, it is possible to make a variety of rounded lip shapes. However, for most sounds, all the different parts of the OO work in cooperation with other muscles of the jaw, lips, and face to produce either flat closures or lip rounding. Other muscles can open the lips, act as synergists or antagonists to the OO, or simply allow local variations in lip shape.

10.1.2   Other lip and face muscles

The *buccinator* (Latin, "trumpeter") is the muscle of the inner wall of the cheek, and provides the primary support for the OO. It inserts into the OO at the corners of the mouth, running forward from the *pterygomandibular raphe* (a vertical tendinous band connecting the skull to the mandible that defines the border between the buccinator in front and the superior pharyngeal constrictor behind), downward from the maxilla, and upward from the mandible. The upper fibers of the buccinator cross over and merge into the OOi, while the lower fibers of the buccinator merge with the OOs (as shown in Figure 10.3 above). Contracting the buccinator pulls the sides of the mouth back for "spread" lip shapes, such as those for the high front vowels or for flat bilabial closures; it also stiffens the inner cheeks to hold in air pressure, to make aspirated sounds, for example, and is important for chewing and sucking.

The *risorius* (Latin, "laugh") muscle, a smaller, more superficial muscle than the buccinator, originates near the masseter muscle and runs forward to insert into the skin at the corners of the mouth. This muscle is thought to be unique to humans, not being present in other primates. Similarly to the buccinator, the risorius contracts laterally to draw the sides of the mouth taut and spread the lips, producing an "insincere" smile.

The small *mentalis* muscle, sometimes aptly called the "pouting" muscle, originates at the front of the mandible just below the incisors, and inserts into the skin of the chin. This muscle pulls the chin upward toward the lower teeth into a pout, and in so doing pushes the base of the bottom lip upward. The mentalis can be used to strengthen any upward movement of the lower lip.

The *levator labii superioris* (LLS) muscle is a broad sheet of paired muscles that originates along the lower orbit of the eyes from the nose to the zygomatic arch, and inserts into the upper lip. The LLS raises the upper lip.

As with the LLS, the *zygomaticus* major and minor raise the upper lip. Contracting the zygomaticus major, also known as the "sincere" smile muscle, simultaneously raises the corners of the mouth and causes "crow's feet" at the corners of the eyes. The zygomaticus minor raises the upper lip to aid in lip opening. Both muscles originate at the zygomatic arch (near the corners of the eye) and insert into the skin at the corners of the mouth.

And the longest muscle name is . . .

Levator labii superioris alaeque nasi (Latin, "Lifter of the upper lip and the wing of the nose"), also known as the "snarl" or "Elvis" muscle, has been famously used to raise the upper lip by snarlers from Billy Idol to Dave Mustaine. While it's not all that important for speech, tiny LLSAN, which originates at the bridge of the nose and inserts into the superior orbicularis oris, has its own claim to fame: it bears the longest name of any muscle in the animal kingdom!

The *depressor anguli oris* muscle, also known as the *triangularis menti*, is a small triangular muscle that originates along the lower edge of the mandible, and inserts into the angle or sides of the mouth. Some fibers also insert into the upper lip. It lowers the corners of the mouth, such as when you frown, and may aid in lip constrictions by pulling downward on the upper lip.

The *depressor labii inferioris* muscle consists of a pair of small, quadrilateral muscles that originate along the lower edge of the mandible and insert into the skin of the lower lip. This muscle is used in lowering and spreading the lower lip.

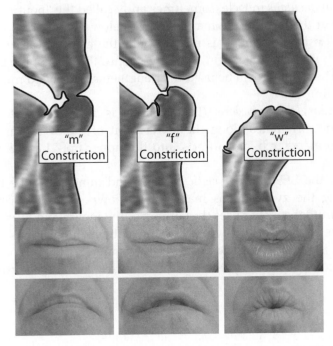

Figure 10.4   Labial constrictions by type (stop, fricative, approximant). Midsagittal MRI images are shown above, and frontal video images below (image by D. Derrick).

10.2   Sounds: Making Sense of [labial]

While the lips may take on a potentially limitless range of shapes, there are three broad classes of postures that are by far the most widely attested cross-linguistically. These three shapes can be seen in the three different types of lip constrictions in English (see Figure 10.4): bilabials (e.g., [b, p]), labiodentals (e.g., [f, v]) and rounding (e.g., [o, w]). In *bilabial* constrictions, the lips are relatively spread, and the upper and lower lips close together flat; in *labiodental* constrictions (usually fricatives), the lips are again spread, with the lower lip pulled back and raised to constrict against the upper teeth; and in *rounded* constrictions (usually vowels or approximants), the lips typically take on a protruded "O" shape.

Phonologists' research on labial sounds supports the idea that these three very different lip shapes may correspond to a single category in the minds of speakers. Clements (1991) expresses this idea by describing the single feature [labial] as having multiple "expressions": in consonants, [labial] takes the form of a relatively spread lip constriction (applying to both bilabial and labiodental sounds), while in vocalic sounds, the same feature is realized with substantial lip rounding.

How can three such different articulations correspond to a single mental category? While these three common types of lip constrictions may seem very different at first glance, a good understanding of articulatory phonetics suggests a simpler story.

In Chapter 9, we described the principle of overshoot. Overshoot is a desirable feature for any constriction, as it allows us to produce constrictions without having to provide fine control. It's easy to see how overshoot is useful in producing labial stops: an overshot bilabial closure pushes the lips together, sealing the lips tightly. Compressing the lips beyond the point of initial closure simply allows more air pressure to build up during the stop closure, which helps to enable more explosive release bursts.

For creating turbulence, however, a bilabial constriction doesn't work so well. A bilabial fricative requires bringing the spread lips close enough together to initiate turbulence without allowing a complete closure. A much easier way of creating a turbulent near-closure is to allow the bottom lip to constrict quasi-ballistically against the upper teeth, forming an imperfect seal through which it is easy for air to escape. It is difficult – or, depending on your dentition, impossible – to push the lower lip into the upper teeth tightly enough to stop airflow entirely, making this a very effective way to produce reliable labial fricatives while still allowing overshoot.

Finally, for vowels and approximants, the most common constriction typically involves rounding and protruding of the lips, extending the length of the vocal tract and lowering its resonances. Because rounding and protrusion are produced using a sphincter mechanism made up of the peripheral ring of OO, it would require extreme, dedicated force to constrict this outer ring so tightly that a fricative or stop could result. Again, as with bilabial and labiodental constrictions, rounding provides a mechanism for making a lip constriction of the desired degree (approximant) while allowing a great deal of freedom in terms of accuracy.

To be sure, there are languages with more nuanced distinctions in labialization than these three types alone. For example, Heffner (1950), among others, described a distinction between *vertical lip rounding* (a decrease in vertical lip aperture) and *horizontal lip rounding* (a decrease in horizontal lip aperture). Likewise, Japanese and other languages use *lateral compression*, or pinching the corners of the mouth together tightly, for labial fricatives and vowels. This mechanism "braces" the lips, much like the tongue braces against the teeth and palate for lingual constrictions. Other types of bilabial fricatives can occur occasionally, usually as reduced allophones of bilabial stops (as in Spanish and related languages), and often in transition to the much more historically stable labiodentals.

Admiralty Island raspberries

Although *bilabial trills* are extremely rare sounds in the languages of the world, they crop up in widely scattered places, from Cameroon to Brazil to the Admiralty Islands in Papua New Guinea (Ladefoged and Maddieson, 1996). In many other languages, a voiceless bilabial trill is used as a metalinguistic interjection to show disdain, disapproval or uncertainty. A famous variation on this vibrates the lower lip against the protruded tongue, giving a sound more commonly known as a *raspberry* or a *Bronx cheer*.

Interestingly, the frequency rate of vibration of the lips is almost the same for bilabial trills as it is for the tongue in lingual trills, even though the lips have more mass. Perhaps the frequency of vibration is affected by the fact that bilabial trills are almost always followed by a high rounded vowel, so the lips are slightly stiffened when creating the constriction.

10.3   Measuring the Lips and Face: Point Tracking and Video

Because the lips and face are externally visible, they are relatively easy to measure compared to other parts of the vocal tract. Methods for measuring the lips and face fall into two broad categories: *video imaging* and *point tracking*. First, we'll talk briefly about video imaging techniques, then we'll cover two methods for *optical point tracking* (tracking points attached to the outside of the body), and finally we'll discuss two point-tracking methods that can be used both outside and inside the body.

Video imaging is one of the cheapest and easiest ways to get started with analyzing the lips and face during speech. Figure 10.5 shows video frames of different types of lip constrictions in Norwegian. Video provides not positional coordinates of specific points, but rather a whole image changing over time. Use of film in speech research began soon after filmmakers realized that synchronizing audio and video in film was critical for enjoying movies, an observation made when sound was first introduced in movies (described by Dixon and Spitz, 1980). Standard video can provide plenty of spatial data about the face and tends to have high spatial resolution. Standard frame rates vary from country to country, but tend to fall between about 24 and 30 frames per second (fps, or Hz), an adequate temporal resolution to observe most gross movements of the lips and face. For more advanced analysis methods, the lips may be painted with contrasting lipstick and filmed, after which measures such as lip aperture may be automatically calculated. Optical flow techniques can also be applied as a way

[i]   [y]   [ʉ]

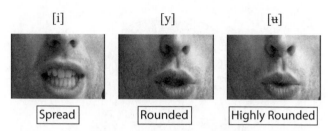

Spread   Rounded   Highly Rounded

Figure 10.5   Video images of lip constrictions in Norwegian (speaker: S. S. Johnsen).

of automatically extracting quantitative information from video of the moving face. Alternatively, measures such as lip aperture, lip shape, and face shape may be computed from regular video using changes in color density to recompute two- and three-dimensional information. The results can be used to understand the relationship between lip motion and the rest of a speech act, or for designing talking heads that mimic lip motion. In addition to standard video imaging, *high-speed video imaging* may be used to observe movements of the lips or face in cases where higher temporal resolution is needed, for example, during labial trills or the release of plosives. High-speed cameras can film at frame rates of thousands or even millions of fps, giving them an almost limitless temporal resolution. The biggest problem with the boundless frame rate is that filming at such a high temporal and spatial resolution can fill up a mammoth hard drive in seconds. There is definitely such a thing as too much data! Researchers have also combined the use of high-speed video and visible smoke for studying airflow out of the vocal tract during speech (Derrick *et al.*, 2009).

For those who have more time, money, and lab space dedicated to measuring the talking face, point-tracking techniques are available. *Optotrak* is a 3D optical point-tracking system that uses 3 single-axis cameras to track 3D movements of *infrared-emitting diodes* attached to the face and lips, as seen in Figure 10.6. These diodes are connected to the Optotrak system by wires or wireless remote to allow freedom of motion for experiment participants. Optotrak has excellent spatial resolution, at approximately 0.15 mm in 3D, and excellent temporal resolution. Temporal resolution is serially shared among all of the diodes so that sampling rate decreases with the number of sensors used in an experiment. So, for example, tracking 10 points at a total sampling rate of 4600 Hz would capture information at 460 Hz each. Optotrak is relatively straightforward to set up, calibrates automatically, and stores data in a format that is easily understood by many computer programs. While Optotrak markers can theoretically heat up significantly over time, experiments do not normally last long enough for this to be an issue, and safeguard settings can be maintained in the software to prevent this from happening.

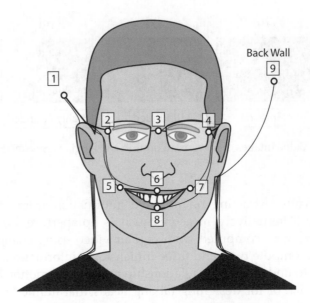

Figure 10.6 Optotrak: example placement of nine infrared markers (image by D. Derrick).

Vicon MX is another infrared motion capture system, but Vicon MX tracks 3D movements of reflective markers by shining infrared light on them. Like Optotrak, the number of points you track limits Vicon's temporal resolution, but the spatial resolution is somewhat less accurate, at about 0.5 mm in 3D. Like Optotrak, Vicon has software for creating raw data and motion capture movies. The Vicon system uses very light-weight markers, and since the system tracks reflected infrared light emitted from the source camera, no wires are required. Unlike Optotrak, the marker positions can get confused by the tracker, as the system has no way to identify which point is being tracked apart from motion proximity. Reflective clothing and glasses can also get interpreted as infrared markers, and the Vicon system is sensitive to ambient lighting conditions.

The above optical point-tracking tools can record the movements of multiple external flesh points at high temporal resolution, allowing researchers to make detailed kinematic measurements. *Kinematics* is the study of movement (not to be confused with *dynamics*, which is the study not just of movements themselves, but also of the forces that underlie them). Now, we discuss two point-tracking technologies that can track movements not only outside, but also inside the body: x-ray microbeam and electromagnetic articulography.

X-ray microbeam uses narrowly focused x-ray beams to track the location of metal spheres attached to the vocal tract along the midsagittal plane. This method exposes participants to considerably less radiation than standard

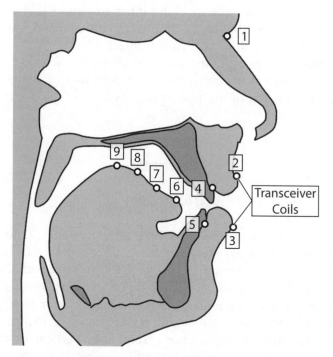

Figure 10.7 Electromagnetic Articulometer (EMA) marker placement: right mid-sagittal cross-section (image by D. Derrick).

x-ray, and it allows for tracking of the metal spheres at a very high spatial and temporal resolution. Unfortunately, because of the size and cost of the apparatus, only one x-ray microbeam facility has ever been fully developed for speech research (at the University of Wisconsin), and that system is no longer in operation. Nevertheless, a large and excellent x-ray microbeam database exists, from which the data are still used in research today.

Electromagnetic articulometer (EMA) systems use alternating current magnetic fields and electromagnetic detectors for tracking the positions of small metal transceiver coils attached to the articulators, as seen in Figure 10.7. Older systems tracked points only along the midsagittal plane (Perkell *et al.*, 1992), and could only record information about spatial location (x, y, z). Later systems are able to track points anywhere within the field range (i.e., off mid-line), and can record information about 5 degrees of freedom – three translations and two rotations (see Chapter 8). EMA offers excellent spatial and temporal resolution for tracking speech articulators. The biggest disadvantages of EMA are that the system is expensive, it can be sensitive to changes in temperature, air movement, and local magnetic fields, markers can come loose during data collection, and some systems can be difficult and time consuming to set up and calibrate. EMA also requires attaching a lot of equipment to research participants, and markers cannot normally be attached to the velum, tongue root, and other structures that may cause a gag reflex. Despite its drawbacks, improvements in EMA systems have made this a valuable tool for academic research.

Because these last two point-tracking systems are able to track points both inside and outside the body, they have been used in many studies to look at the coordination of multiple speech events, a topic we'll look at in the next chapter.

Exercises

Sufficient jargon

Define the following terms: speechreading, uncanny valley, Tadoma speech training method, orbicularis oris (OO), marginal part of OO (OOm), peripheral part of OO (OOp), superior part of OO (OOs), inferior part of OO (OOi), buccinator muscle, pterygomandibular raphe, risorius, mentalis, levator labii superioris (LLS), zygomaticus major/minor, levator labii superioris alaeque nasi (LLSAN), depressor anguli oris (triangularis menti), depressor labii inferioris, bilabials, labiodentals, rounding, vertical/horizontal lip rounding, lateral compression, bilabial trill, raspberry/Bronx cheer, point tracking, video imaging, Optotrak, infrared-emitting diodes, Vicon MX, high-speed video imaging, kinematics, dynamics, x-ray microbeam, electromagnetic articulometer (EMA).

Short-answer questions

1 List eight English speech sounds that would be affected if the facial nerve (CN VII) were damaged.
2 What lip muscles function as primary agonists in producing the lip shape for the vowel /i/? How about /u/?
3 For each of the following measurement techniques, find and cite one speech research paper not mentioned in this book in which that technique is used: optical tracking, video, and EMA. Follow the reference formatting used in the references section at the end of each chapter.

Practical assignment

For each chapter, this text has online assignments (at www.wiley.com/go/ articulatoryphonetics) that either provide research data for analysis, or practical tools for understanding vocal tract anatomy. For Chapter 10, you will look at a set of image frames extracted from video recordings of a speaker of the Oneida (Iroquois) language. In this assignment you will use a computer tool to compare lip apertures in different conditions. The assignment and the related images can be found in the online materials for this textbook under *Chapter 10*.

References

Alcorn, S. (1932). The Tadoma method. *Volta Review, 34*, 195–198.

Blair, C. and Smith, A. (1986). EMG recording in human lip muscles: can single muscles be isolated? *Journal of Speech and Hearing Research, 29*, 256–266.

Calvert, G. A., Bullmore, E. T., Brammer, M. J., Campbell, R., Williams, S. C. R., McGuire, P. K., Woodruff, P. W. R., Iversen, S. D., and David, A. S. (1997). Activation of auditory cortex during silent lipreading. *Science, 276*, 593–596.

Clements, G. N. (1991). Place of articulation in consonants and vowels: a unified theory. *Working Papers of the Cornell Phonetics Laboratory, 5*, 77–123.

Derrick, D., Anderson, P., Gick, B., and Green, S. (2009). Characteristics of air puffs produced in English "pa": Experiments and simulations. *Journal of the Acoustical Society of America, 125*, 2272–2281.

Dixon, N. and Spitz, L. (1980). The detection of audiovisual desynchrony. *Perception, 9*, 719–721.

Heffner, R-M. S. (1950). *General Phonetics*. Madison, WI: The University of Wisconsin Press.

Ladefoged, P. and Maddieson, I. (1996). *The Sounds of the World's Languages*. Oxford, UK: Blackwell.

McGurk, H. and MacDonald, J. (1976). Hearing lips and seeing voices. *Nature, 264*, 746–748.

Ménard, L., Dupont, S., Baum, S. R., and Aubin, J. (2009). Production and perception of French vowels by congenitally blind adults and sighted adults. *Journal of the Acoustical Society of America, 126*, 1406–1414.

Mori, M. (1970). Bukimi no tani [The uncanny valley]. *Energy, 7*, 33–35.

Nazari, M. A., Perrier, P., Chabanas, M., and Payan, Y. (2011). Shaping by stiffening: a modeling study for lips. *Motor Control, 15*, 141–168.

Perkell, J. S., Cohen, M., Svirsky, M., Matthies, M., Garabieta, I., and Jackson, M. (1992). Electro-magnetic midsagittal articulometer (EMMA) systems for transducing speech articulatory movements. *Journal of the Acoustical Society of America, 92*, 3078–3096.

Sunby, W. H. and Pollack, I. (1954). Visual contribution to speech intelligibility in noise. *Journal of the Acoustical Society of America, 26*, 212–215.

Traunmüller, H. (1979). Lippenrundung bei schwedischen vokalen. *Phonetica, 36*, 44–56.

Yehia, H., Rubin, P., and Vatikiotis-Bateson, E. (1998). Quantitative association of vocal-tract and facial behavior. *Speech Communication, 26*, 23–43.

Chapter 11

Putting Articulations Together

Throughout this textbook we have focused on describing constrictions at a single location within the vocal tract. However, in actual speech, even the simplest sounds may require the coordination of multiple different articulators. For example, seemingly simple labial sounds like [p] or [b] involve coordination of the upper and lower lips, jaw, glottis, and lungs, each of which involve the actions of many individual muscles.

This chapter will begin by looking at some different ideas about how this kind of basic coordination works. Once we have the tools in place for handling basic coordination, we'll turn our attention to more complex sounds that involve coordinating multiple oral events. Finally, we'll look at what happens to articulation when you combine sounds together into even larger "chunks" such as syllables, words, and phrases.

11.1 Coordinating Movements

Given the range of possible movements of all the vocal tract articulators, how do we control the timing of each tiny movement that goes into making a speech sound? Researchers have long tried to understand and model how humans coordinate vocal tract motion during speech. The two most common types of models are context-sensitive models and context-invariant models. In *context-sensitive models* (or *look-ahead models*), the model is "sensitive" to the upcoming "context"; this ability to look ahead means the details of movements can be planned out ahead of time, anticipating

Articulatory Phonetics, First Edition. Bryan Gick, Ian Wilson, and Donald Derrick.
© 2013 Bryan Gick, Ian Wilson, and Donald Derrick. Published 2013 by Blackwell Publishing Ltd.

what movements are coming up next. In *context-invariant models*, there is no looking ahead; in these models, the motor system has built-in mechanisms for averaging together adjacent movements automatically, regardless of context (see Munhall *et al.*, 2000 for a discussion of these two kinds of approaches).

The big question in context-sensitive models is: "How do my articulators usually coordinate the upcoming sequence?" The big question in context-invariant models is: "What's the fastest way to get my articulators from here to there?"

Pirates vs. ninjas

The infamous German pirate Klaus Störtebeker (c. 1360–1401) led a colorful life, but was best known for his death. Upon being sentenced to death by beheading, Störtebeker made one final request: after his head was removed, he would walk along the line of his pirate brothers, and all those he passed before falling would be spared the axe. According to legend, he passed between 5 and 12 of his comrades before being tripped by the executioner. Like a chicken running with its head cut off, Störtebeker's legendary feat is a testament to the idea that frequent movement routines – such as those we use for walking (or talking!) – may draw on *pre-planned motor programs* that can be carried out without involving the central nervous system at all.

Ninja warriors, in contrast, sought to master action without pre-planning. *Ninjutsu*, the fighting art of the ninja, held as one ideal the notion of de-voidness, or the "absence of any pre-determined shape or character" (Miller, 1996). In this state of consciousness, combat movements are resolved *online* in response to changing circumstances, without preconception or prejudice about what might happen next.

These cases illustrate two different ways of thinking about speech movements. Research – and common sense – suggests that we use both of these approaches to make speech work. Warriors practice fighting, memorize moves, and develop their skills so that they can draw upon their vast array of planned movement routines in combat; but these movements can be varied, combined and recombined in unexpected ways during combat, and our motor systems have on-line mechanisms that allow us to transition smoothly between maneuvers, and to create new ones. Similarly, speech needs to combine both pre-planning and online mechanisms to meet the real-time needs of communication.

11.1.1   Context-sensitive models

Henke (1966) proposed an early context-sensitive model for speech. This kind of model typically uses *motor plans*, or prepared patterns of motion that we store in our minds, to explain how speech is coordinated. Motor planning theories generally assume that we have a finite set of *motor primitives*, the smallest units of motor planning, stored in our memories. Motor primitives provide the commands the motor system needs to initiate a basic movement (Throughman and Shadmehr, 2000), and they are the building blocks of more complex *motor programs* (Mussa-Ivaldi and Bizzi, 2000). Motor programs are defined either in terms of larger combinations of commands that structure an entire movement sequence (Keele, 1968), or as a more abstract memory structure that guides the selection of possible movements (Schmidt, 1975; Keele, 1981). The latter definition allows flexibility of motion that's not restricted to specific muscle contractions. Finally, motor programs combine to form larger *motor plans*.

To bring this into the realm of speech, motor primitives are individual movements of specific articulators; motor programs are combinations of motor primitives fixed into frequently used memorized "chunks," such as phones or short strings of phones such as syllables or possibly even frequent words; and motor plans are larger structures made up of motor programs, including anything from less frequent words to new phrases and sentences. One way you can tell which kind of structure you're dealing with is that there are a limited number of motor primitives and motor programs, but an unlimited number of possible motor plans (Allott, 2003). In this kind of theory, speakers coordinate speech by working out in advance the movements they will use in an utterance.

11.1.2   Context-invariant models

Öhman (1967) was one of the first to propose a context-invariant model for how speech gets coordinated. The most popular context-invariant approach for speech has been task dynamics (e.g., Turvey *et al.*, 1982; Kelso *et al.*, 1986; Saltzman and Byrd, 2000). In *task dynamics*, a typical "task" represents the movement of some part or parts of the body toward a point in space. In contrast to motor planning theories, task dynamics models achieve these goals on the fly, by first defining a physical target (the "task") for an articulator, and then modeling the underlying mechanical forces (the "dynamics") needed to get there from wherever it started. In this way, instead of using a memorized plan, a pseudoinverse solution is used to determine the most economical path between targets.

Let's think about how task dynamics can work specifically for coordinating speech. A task dynamics model shows how a single articulator can be directed toward a goal, like closing the lips. However, closing the lips actually requires several articulators – the two lips and the jaw – to work together. This happens all the time when we are speaking: the actions of different speech articulators are coordinated together to achieve a common goal. Drawing on the task dynamics model, coordinated efforts come together to produce *articulatory gestures* (Browman and Goldstein, 1992). In this view, gestures can be combined to form linguistic structures of any size (phones, syllables, words, etc.), and serve many of the same functions as phonological features.

The big jerk

In task dynamics, articulators move in coordination to achieve the goals, or tasks, of the whole system. To show how this works, researchers have devised clever *mechanical perturbation* experiments.

What would happen if someone jerked down on your lower lip just as you were about to make a bilabial stop? Would each lip do its own thing and fail to make the closure, or would the upper lip compensate so you could make the closure anyway? Abbs and Gracco (1984) found that the upper lip always compensates for the lower lip, and that this happens from the very first trial where force is applied. This experiment suggests that the goal of the system is to get the lips closed – not simply to get each articulator to some position in space – and the lips cooperate with each other to accomplish that goal.

Another example of articulators working together to achieve a goal is coordination between the jaw and tongue. Kelso *et al.* (1984) showed that if an unexpected force keeps the jaw from rising, the tongue stretches higher to make up the difference. This cooperation between articulators under perturbation shows us that simple actions can be coordinated into a system for achieving speech goals.

Here's an exercise to demonstrate how different parts of your body can work together in a complex task. We call this "window washing" (try this!): Place your hands together in front of you in "prayer" position. Now separate your hands slightly. Pretend there's a large pane of glass between your hands, and it's your job to polish the glass. Now, start your washing by polishing in a circle, with both hands staying together. Easy! Try polishing in the opposite direction. No problem, right? Now separate your hands so that one is farther away from your chest and keep polishing, with a motion like pedalling a bike forward. Try pedalling the bike backward as well. Still easy! Okay. Now, try

(Continued)

polishing "forward" with one hand and "backward" with the other. Switch directions (for both hands). What do you think? If you're like most people, you can see from this demonstration that even though we think different parts of our body are independent, our motor systems treat them as if they are linked. This kind of link is at the root of how a task dynamics model treats coordinated action.

11.1.3   Unifying theories

Formal attempts to unify these two approaches have proposed distinct levels within the brain, a *motor program level* that governs motor planning and a *motor system level* that handles dynamics. The motor program level generates motor plans that are combined by the motor system level to produce speech (Semjen, 1992; Shaffer, 1992; see Summers and Anson, 2009).

In many respects, these different approaches fit together well. For example, both theories tend to focus on motor behavior aimed at reaching specified goals in physical space, and neither theory directly controls other aspects of the system such as, say, vocal tract shapes, vocal tract cavities, aerodynamics, or acoustic output (though it is certainly possible to map some of these aspects of speech together; for a neural model of how this can work, see Guenther, 2006). Also, both motor planning and task dynamics theories predict (though for different reasons) that articulator motions should be consistent (i.e., largely the same for the same speaker uttering the same sentence in the same prosodic context). Since these motions are not always consistent, this means there's still lots of room for new and improved models that can incorporate the many dimensions of speech, as well as the wide range of variation in how different people articulate speech, both within and across speakers and languages.

Learning coordination

While lip and jaw motion are not coordinated during early childhood development, by 6 years of age children learn to do this, at least during the production of labial stops (Green *et al.*, 2000). That is, a baby will produce "baba" by opening and closing the jaw and letting the lips passively smack together. However, by 6 years of age, a child will coordinate the closing of the jaw with lowering the upper lip and raising the lower lip to make labial closures, distributing the job across all of the available articulators.

11.2 Coordinating Complex Sounds

Now that we have some pieces in place to understand how basic speech movements work, we can apply these principles to larger, more complex structures. In particular, in the rest of this chapter, we'll be talking about sounds that involve coordinating multiple distinct events (such as constrictions or openings) in the vocal tract.

Tick, tick, tick . . .

Nearly all speech acts involve the coordination, or timing, of more than one movement, but how this timing works isn't so clear. Suppose we'd like to describe two articulator movements collaborating to produce a constriction. In order for this to work, there must be some mechanism that governs exactly when each movement will happen.

Some models have suggested that our bodies contain something like a "clock" ticking all the time (see Munhall *et al.*, 2000). With such a device, it would be easy to specify the timing of two movements, for example: "start moving the tongue tip, then wait 20 ms, then start lowering the velum." This kind of coordination is called *extrinsic timing*. The problem is that it's very hard to find independent evidence to suggest that such a clock exists (Fowler, 1980).

Task dynamics provides an *intrinsic timing* mechanism for coordinating gestures. Kelso *et al.* (1986) argued that the brain stores not actual times, but rather relationships between the movement cycles of different gestures. This kind of relative timing has been called *phase alignment*. Researchers have observed that the same patterns of relative timing occur again and again within a language, cutting across sounds, suggesting that languages may have global preferences for particular phase alignments.

As we've seen throughout this book, every moving part of the vocal tract is connected to other parts. However, some parts are very tightly connected to one another while others are free to move quite independently. Two articulators that are strongly interconnected are said to be *anatomically coupled*. Importantly, it's easier to coordinate articulators that aren't tightly coupled. This is simply because *independent articulators don't interfere with each other's goals* (this kind of interference is discussed in more detail in Section 11.3). The traditional "three-legged race" operates on this principle:

two people may run very fast side by side, but if you tie one person's right leg to the other person's left leg, much of their energy is lost to interference. Because of this principle, sounds that combine relatively independent articulators are much more common in the world's languages.

One case of this we've already seen in this book is that of nasal sounds (Chapter 7): because the velum is anatomically relatively independent of other articulators, just about any movement can be freely combined with nasalization. Likewise, the relative independence of the larynx allows nearly any speech sound to have voiced or voiceless (or creaky, breathy, etc.) variants. Coordination in this case simply means a certain laryngeal setting starts at or near the same time as some other articulation at a different location in the vocal tract.

The following sections discuss speech sounds that require coordination between different parts of the vocal tract.

11.2.1   Lingual-lingual sounds

As we discussed in Chapters 8 and 9, the tongue is a jointless muscular hydrostat made up of many different muscles. Therefore, a movement anywhere in the tongue can have complex implications for any other part of the tongue. Even within the tongue, however, there are regions of somewhat independent control that allow it to form more than one constriction at the same time – and some sounds make use of multiple lingual constrictions.

Because of the tight anatomical coupling between different parts of the tongue, *lingual-lingual* sounds (i.e., sounds with two independent lingual constrictions) can be difficult for first or second language learners to master, and they tend to be relatively rare in the world's languages. We'll focus on two classes of sounds in particular that can require strict coordination between multiple regions of the tongue: liquids and clicks.

11.2.1.1   Liquids   Liquids are a class of sounds that include lateral consonants and rhotics. For some liquid sounds, different parts of the tongue must act independently, with the movements carefully coordinated in time.

The lateral approximant /l/ is an example of this kind of liquid sound. In many languages, including English, /l/ is often described as coming in two main varieties: *light l* [l] and *dark l* [ɫ] (see Figure 11.1). Some languages, such as Albanian, even phonemically contrast these two types of /l/ sounds. Most variants of /l/ share two properties: an anterior medial constriction (normally a closure) and lateral airflow. What distinguishes the two variants is that the "darker" varieties have an additional tongue body/dorsum constriction, either up and back toward the velum or uvula, or backward into the upper pharynx. As such, it is only the darker variants of /l/ that

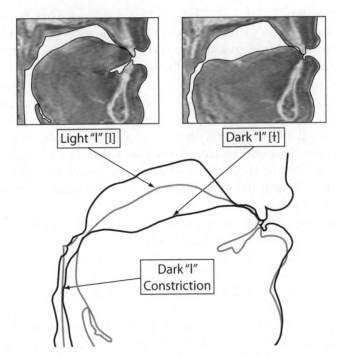

Figure 11.1 Light and dark English /l/ based on MRI images: right midsagittal cross-section; tracings are overlaid in lower image (image by D. Derrick).

require coordination of two lingual events. Not surprisingly, light l appears much more commonly in the world's languages.

It's worth noting here that, given the minimal requirements for producing a lateral approximant (i.e., anterior medial bracing and wide lateral openings), one might expect the tongue body to protrude dorsally automatically, simply to make up for the volume displaced by narrowing the tongue. While this dorsal protrusion may remain a purely hydrostatic by-product in some languages, cross-linguistic evidence suggests that it may become its own, independently controlled constriction in others (e.g., by losing its bracing or lateral quality, phonologically grouping with other dorsal sounds, etc.). It is thus important to consider an array of observable factors – kinematic, historical, and phonological – when describing a particular sound.

Rhotics make up another category of liquid approximant sounds. Some of the world's rhotics are known to be particularly complex in terms of lingual constrictions. English "r," for example, is famously complex (see Figure 11.2), with variants in many dialects having two constrictions involving lingual articulators (the tongue anterior and the tongue root) as well as a third constriction at the lips (Tiede *et al.*, 2004; Zhou *et al.*, 2008). In all variants, the anterior tongue makes a constriction in the palatal

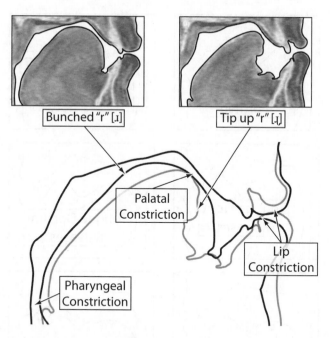

Figure 11.2 Bunched vs. tip-up English "r": right midsagittal cross-section; tracings are overlaid in lower image (image by D. Derrick).

region, and as with other medial sounds, all English /r/ variants use lateral bracing of the tongue. However, the shape of the anterior tongue can vary substantially across dialects, across individuals, or even across phonetic environments within an individual (Mielke *et al.*, 2010): for example, the tongue tip can be bunched low in the mouth with the blade providing most of the constriction, or it can be bunched high, or it can be curled back in a retroflex position.

To make matters more complex for these sounds, the relative timing and magnitude of each of the constrictions varies depending on a number of factors, such as syllable position and prosodic boundary (e.g., Sproat and Fujimura, 1993).

11.2.1.2 Clicks Clicks are speech sounds that use the tongue to produce airflow, using the *lingual airstream* (Miller *et al.*, 2009). This airstream is almost always used ingressively, hence the term *lingual ingressive* (often called "velaric ingressive"). In lingual clicks, the front of the tongue is used to form an anterior closure while the back of the tongue forms a seal against either the soft palate or the back of the hard palate (see Figures 11.3a, 11.3b, and 11.3c). In this way, a small "pocket" of air is formed between the front and back constrictions. The middle of the tongue body is then pulled down to enlarge the pocket and *rarefy*, or reduce the air pressure in, the cavity

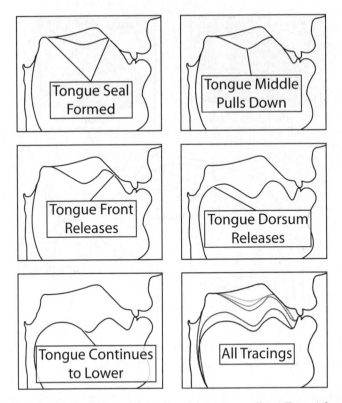

Figure 11.3a Schematic of a click produced by Jenggu Rooi Fransisko, a speaker of Mangetti Dune !Xung: right midsagittal cross-section (image by D. Derrick, with data supplied by A. Miller).

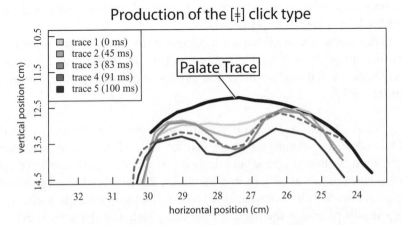

Figure 11.3b Tracings of the tongue during a palatal click [ǂ] produced by Jenggu Rooi Fransisko, a speaker of Mangetti Dune !Xung: right midsagittal cross-section (image by D. Derrick, with data supplied by A. Miller).

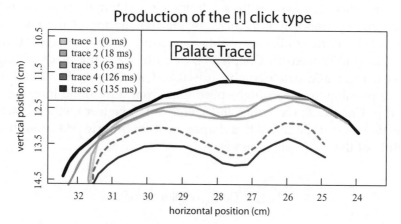

Figure 11.3c Tracings of the tongue during an alveolar click [!] produced by Jenggu Rooi Fransisko, a speaker of Mangetti Dune !Xung: right midsagittal cross-section (image by D. Derrick, with data supplied by A. Miller).

(remember Boyle's Law?). Once this vacuum is created, the front constriction releases first, either medially at the teeth or hard palate, or laterally. The result is a rapid inflow of air accompanied by a short and sometimes very loud transient burst that, though brief, still contains enough information to make the place of articulation easy to identify. The back constriction then releases a few milliseconds later.

The click, as described here, creates an ingressive lingual airstream, though it's possible to reverse the process to produce lingual egressives (these are not known to be contrastive in any language, but do occasionally appear as an alternative mechanism, as in Damin, an extinct Australian ceremonial speech style). Also, it's important to remember that not all clicks are lingual-lingual sounds – there are also labial clicks (in fact, this is how you make a "kissing" sound!). Despite the difficulty of controlling two tongue constrictions, lingual clicks are more common linguistically than labial clicks for aerodynamic reasons: it's simply much easier to create a vacuum in the tiny space created between the two tongue constrictions than in the larger space between the tongue and lips.

Because the lingual airstream does not block the airway, clicks can be combined with other airstream mechanisms. In one extreme example, N|uu, a language spoken in South Africa, combines lingual and glottalic airstream mechanisms during the production of ejective affricate clicks. This combination involves the near-simultaneous inflow of air from the lingual airstream combined with outflow of air from the glottal airstream. Clicks can also be either oral or nasal, as the uvular constriction does not require the velum to close off the nasopharynx, and the lingual airstream is not compromised by nasal airflow.

Because clicks involve multiple extremely rapid tongue movements, it is still effectively impossible to measure the full motion of the vocal tract during clicks. Early studies were able to measure tongue movements using x-ray video (discussed in Chapter 7), or to observe the place of lingual events using static palatography (discussed in Chapter 9). It has since become possible to extract high-speed data from ultrasound imaging (discussed in Chapter 8; see Miller and Finch, 2011). Newer methods, such as those discussed at the end of this chapter, will continue to add to our understanding of these complex sounds.

11.2.2   Other complex sounds

In contrast to the tight anatomical coupling that constrains lingual-lingual sounds, the speech articulators are often much more independent in other sounds with multiple constrictions. Common examples of these are lingual-labial sounds and oral-laryngeal sounds.

One of the most common examples of a *lingual-labial* sound is the labiovelar [w], which involves both labial and velar or uvular approximant constrictions. Other labiovelars such as [k͡p] occur in many West African languages. Labiovelars also commonly occur in the form of labialization (or more correctly, labiovelarization). *Labialization* in vowels can be realized as the rounded vs. unrounded or spread distinction (Figure 11.4; see Chapter 10), while *labiovelarization* (usually transcribed using a superscript "w") can cross-cut large groups of oral consonants, notably in Northwest Caucasian languages and in North American language families such as Salish and Athabaskan. Labiovelarization appears most commonly in combination with velar and uvular places of constriction, and least commonly with dental and alveolar places of articulation (Ruhlen, 1975).

Most *oral-laryngeal* sounds are relatively unconstrained by anatomical coupling (two notable exceptions to this being intrinsic fundamental frequency of vowels, discussed in Chapter 6, and the pharyngeals, which combine with laryngeals in many languages to make up a phonological class of *gutturals*). However, as with clicks, coordination of most oral-laryngeal sounds is tightly constrained by aerodynamic factors. In Chapter 6, we talked about the different articulatory events that go into producing ejectives, implosives, and pulmonic plosives. The timing of these events is crucial, as the buildup of necessary oral pressure is completely dependent on which closure (oral or laryngeal) is released first. In one rare class of sounds, the *glottalized resonants*, widespread in languages of the northwest coast of North America, there are no aerodynamic constraints on timing, so that the glottalization is free to occur before or after the oral constriction(s). This results in a high degree of

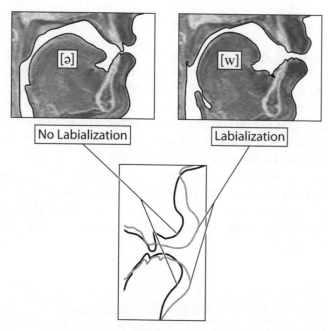

Figure 11.4 Non-labialized schwa (top) versus labialized [w] (bottom): right mid-sagittal cross-section (image by D. Derrick).

cross-linguistic variation in the oral-laryngeal coordination of glottalized resonants (Bird *et al.*, 2008).

11.3 Coarticulation

Now that we know how to put articulations together, we should be able to build a speech stream of any length, right? Well, almost. So far we've only talked about combining articulations within smaller-sized units of a language's inventory (i.e., segments or phonemes). Within these established units, one may assume that the organization of the component articulations is relatively stable. In fact, it has often been assumed that phonemes, or at least allophones, correspond to fixed motor plans. However, when segments or phonemes are combined into larger units, things become much more complicated.

The problem is this: when we transcribe speech, we write the characters all in a row, as if the sounds occur in a tidy sequence like pearls on a string. In real speech, however, articulations transition continuously from one to the next, with movements constantly overlapping, and sometimes conflicting. These various transitional processes fall under the rubric of coarticulation. We'll talk about two kinds of processes here: articulatory overlap and articulatory conflict.

11.3.1   Articulatory overlap

Generally speaking, *coarticulation* can be described as the *temporal overlap* of articulations belonging to neighboring sounds. That is, when two sounds come together, if any parts of the articulations that make up those sounds happen at the same time, there has been coarticulation. As you may imagine, under this definition, any two sounds that come together in natural speech must coarticulate to some degree. For a more detailed discussion of coarticulation, see Farnetani and Recasens (2010).

We discussed in Section 11.2 how some articulators are more tightly anatomically coupled than others. The simplest cases of coarticulation are ones where the articulators involved are not constrained by anatomical coupling. In such cases, the articulations happen at the same time, but do not interfere with each other.

Coarticulation at a distance?

The effects of coarticulation have been shown to occur across quite long distances. Cues to liquid sounds in English may be perceived up to two syllables away (West, 1999). What this means is that some parts of the tongue or lips are already moving into position for the liquid while other articulations are still being produced. This kind of long-distance coarticulation looks a lot like long-distance harmony.

Harmony refers to a range of phonological process whereby non-adjacent sounds affect one another in systematic ways. Some researchers (e.g., Gafos, 1999) have analyzed this as just a farther-away case of overlap. In this view, an articulator stays in a certain position over a long period of time, and if nothing else draws on that articulator, harmony can occur. Whether this is how some cases of harmony work, synchronically or historically, is a matter of some controversy, but the possible links to long-distance coarticulation are certainly tantalizing.

For example, if you speak a dialect of English with lip-rounding for the vowel /u/, when you say the words "soup" and "seep" in natural speech, you may notice that the lips are rounded for the /s/ in "soup," but not for the /s/ in "seep." Even when one says "stoop," where the /s/ and the rounded /u/ are separated by /t/, the lips may already be rounding during the /s/. To a listener who is aware that this rounding is part of the upcoming vowel and not of the /s/ itself, the rounding is ignored, so that the rounded version of /s/ sounds much like any other instance of /s/.

Similarly, nasal sounds in English have a well-known effect on a preceding vowel. Again, the issue here is timing – the opening of the VPP for the nasal consonant can happen well before the tongue constriction, overlapping in time with the preceding vowel.

11.3.2 Articulatory conflict

The cases of overlap described above are quite simple in that the articulators involved do not interfere much with one another. Because /s/, for example, has no lip or tongue dorsum constriction, its temporal overlap with /u/ in "soup" presents little difficulty. However, when adjacent speech sounds require anatomically coupled articulators to move in opposite directions, things get more interesting. This is good news for researchers, as we can learn much more about how coarticulation works when we see how it responds to this kind of *articulatory conflict*.

Many examples of articulatory conflict may be seen when vowels and consonants both draw on the same part of the tongue. For example, as discussed in Chapter 8, the tongue root is normally pulled quite far forward to produce the high vowel [i]. When this vowel is immediately preceded or followed by a pharyngeal constriction that requires the tongue root to be pulled back, a conflict occurs. When this happens, languages usually respond in one of three possible ways: *deletion, transition,* or *compromise.* Perhaps these are best explained through an example.

Imagine you're running to attend a concert of the A Band (your favorite accordion group!). You're almost there, and suddenly you get a text message telling you there's another must-attend concert of the B Band (your favorite banjo ensemble!) in a venue across the street, at exactly the same time. You have a problem: you cannot physically be in two different places at the same time. So, what do you do? Unless you want to just give up and go home, you pretty much have three choices: (a) *Deletion* – decide to choose one concert and skip (delete) the other one; (b) *Transition* – go to part of one concert, then leave and go (transition) to the other concert; or (c) *Compromise* – stand in the middle of the road between the two venues and try to get close enough to hear at least some of both concerts.

Returning to our tongue root example: (a) Deletion means eliminating one of the two targets – either the tongue root advancement for [i] or the tongue root backing for the pharyngeal; (b) Transition involves fronting the tongue root for the [i] vowel then pulling it back for the consonant; (c) Compromise would have the tongue move to a position somewhere between the two targets. Each solution occurs regularly in natural languages, and each has its obvious pros and cons.

So, how do speakers actually work out these conflicts? Do they plan it out ahead of time, or just figure it out as they go along? To recast the question in terms of our two types of theories: are our speech systems sensitive to context, allowing us to plan ahead and avoid the problems of coarticulation, or do our motor systems have built-in context-invariant mechanisms that can work out articulatory conflicts online?

11.3.3   Modeling coarticulation

First, to answer the above question, languages seem to employ multiple different strategies in resolving conflicts (Gick and Wilson, 2006). Not surprisingly, we'll find that we need both kinds of theory to handle this variety of different strategies. Let's look at how context-sensitive and context-invariant theories handle coarticulation.

Context-sensitive theories of coarticulation are often called "look-ahead" or "planning" theories. Guenther (1994) offers a more general version of a look-ahead theory in which a speaker looks ahead to later gestures in a sequence and optimizes the overlap of gestures with the goal of reducing the size and complexity of articulatory movements. Every context-sensitive theory depends on a memory buffer that holds the plan for producing upcoming utterances in a speech sequence. Cognitive psychologists have argued for speech planning down to the level of the phoneme (Dell, 1986; Levelt, 1989), while some speech researchers have found evidence that planning occurs at even lower levels, supporting the view that at least some aspects of coarticulation are indeed planned (Whalen, 1990).

Look-ahead in grasping . . . and flapping

If you are asked to pick a glass up and put it back down, you just grab it and put it down. If you are asked to pick a glass up and put it back upside-down, you may find that you twist your arm around first and grab it in an uncomfortable position so that when you flip it over your hand is in a more comfortable position. Rosenbaum and Jorgensen (1992) observed that people grasp objects in different ways at the beginning of a movement sequence so as to facilitate the end of the sequence, showing that people plan ahead to accommodate *end-state comfort*. This provides a useful tool for telling whether people are looking ahead and planning out movement sequences in advance.

Similar planning occurs in speech, though it can be tricky to observe. For example, in some dialects of English, /t/ and /d/ can be realized as flaps in certain environments. As discussed in Chapter 9, flaps are interesting in that they involve overshoot that moves parallel to the

(Continued)

opposing surface, rather than perpendicular to it. In an up-flap movement, the tongue starts below the alveolar ridge and moves above it;
in a down-flap movement, the tongue starts above the alveolar ridge
and moves below it. This means that you can end up with your tongue
tip in a very different position depending on which variant you choose.
Speakers will vary in whether they begin a sequence of flaps with the
tongue in a high or a low position, depending on which starting position will best accommodate end-state comfort (Derrick, 2011).

Context-invariant approaches can be especially powerful at handling
coarticulation, as they can deal with any conflict that arises using relatively
simple algorithms. These algorithms do not change depending on context
(they are, after all, context invariant!). Rather, they handle conflict by averaging out the goals of the competing articulations. For example, the Kelso
et al. (1986) model uses a weighted averaging to come up with the trajectory
of an articulator that's receiving multiple commands. In context-invariant
theories, the brain does not need to plan solutions to articulatory conflicts
because they are resolved on the fly.

Returning to our articulatory (tongue root) conflict above, it should now
be clear why both types of model can be useful. When we see a language
responding categorically to a conflict, as in (a) deletion and (b) transition,
this kind of solution fits well with a context-sensitive, look-ahead approach.
On the other hand, when a language shows evidence of (c) compromise
between two articulations, this looks much more like a context-invariant
solution.

Articulatory phonetics – and indeed any science – is only interesting
insofar as it tells us not just about what we can observe on the surface, but
also about the system that underlies our observations. To truly comprehend
how speech works, we must figure out not just the workings of the brain,
the ears or the mouth, not just the acoustics or kinematics of speech, nor
just the feed-forward mechanisms, the planning, or the sensory feedback
we experience. Rather, it's through continuing to build our models of speech
on a foundation of data in all of these areas that we can make progress
toward a better understanding of speech articulation.

11.4 Measuring the Whole Vocal Tract: Tomography

In order to see how different parts of the vocal tract work together, it's
useful to be able to image the whole vocal tract all at once. Various

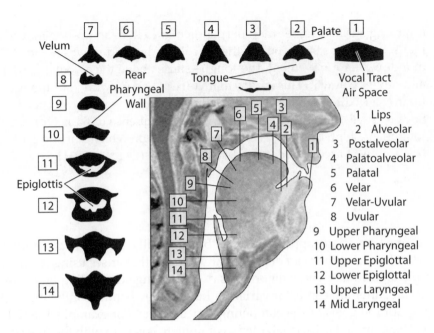

Figure 11.5 Vocal tract slices (in black), showing cross-sectional area of the vocal tract during production of schwa (image by D. Derrick).

tomographic methods can be used to do this. *Tomography* (*tomo-* Greek, "slice, section"), broadly speaking, refers to any technique that can image slices of an object. Often, when people use the term, they're specifically referring to the many ways these two-dimensional images of a structure can be put together to construct 3D, or *volumetric*, images. Cross-sectional slices like the ones shown in Figure 11.5, when stacked, can give an indication of how the 3D vocal tract would look.

Any measurement tool that can image a plane, including ultrasound, x-ray or MRI, can be used for tomography. Two tomographic methods that can give a very clear view of the whole vocal tract are computed tomography (CT) and structural MRI.

In *computed tomography* scans, 3D images are built out of x-rays taken around a rotational axis. The resulting images are very useful for distinguishing different tissues: bones show up the brightest because they are the most dense, muscles and fat are in between, and less dense fluid or air pockets (as in the lungs) are the darkest (see Figure 11.6). Although CT is not particularly good at imaging internal structure within similar kinds of tissue, CT differentiates cancerous tumors, blood, and bone very clearly, making it a popular tool for medical diagnosis. CT scans can provide images with extremely high spatial resolution that are well under a millimeter thick, but CT scans can take several minutes to produce as

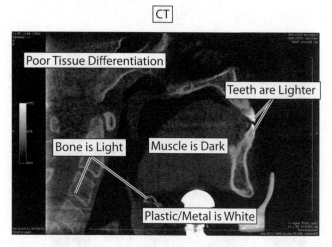

Figure 11.6 CT image of the vocal tract. The bright objects visible in the bottom-center and bottom-right are an ultrasound probe and a chinrest, respectively; this image was taken during an experiment that used simultaneous CT and ultrasound imaging: right midsagittal cross-section (image by D. Derrick).

they involve hundreds of x-ray images. Because of its poor temporal resolution, volumetric CT isn't normally used to measure the moving vocal tract.

A full-head CT irradiates a person with about 2 millisieverts (mSv) of ionizing radiation (Health Physics Society, 2010), an amount that poses some risk of causing cancer or other tissue damage. 2 mSv is the equivalent of more than half of the yearly 3–4 mSv of background radiation received from the sun and naturally radioactive ground materials, including radon (Oak Ridge National Laboratory, 2010). Between the low temporal resolution and the exposure to radiation, CT is a less popular research tool among articulatory phoneticians.

Structural MRI can also produce tomographic images of the whole vocal tract. Unlike CT, however, MRI does this by using high-powered magnets, regularly interrupted by radio frequencies, to align hydrogen atoms, as described in Chapter 2 (see Lauterbur, 1973). In this strong magnetic field, hydrogen atoms spin differently in different types of body tissue. The scanner interprets this information and converts it into images. Because the hydrogen atoms in soft tissue can move around relatively freely, MRI allows for much more highly detailed differentiation of soft tissue in the body than allowed by CT scan (see Figure 11.7). However, since hydrogen atoms are found in water, MRI does not detect bone well or teeth at all – with their lack of water, bones show up as dark gray, and teeth are black like air spaces.

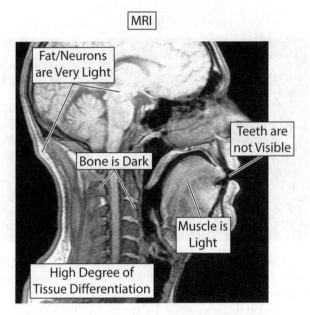

Figure 11.7 MRI image of the vocal tract: right midsagittal cross-section (image by D. Derrick).

MRI machines can trade off spatial and temporal resolution very effectively, making them very useful for scanning slower articulator motions. Every year, faster MRI machines and new techniques are developed that produce higher combined spatial and temporal resolution, and as a result we are rapidly approaching a time when we can use MRI to see the entire vocal tract moving in three dimensions during real-time speech. At present, though, only a single plane (usually the midsagittal) can be imaged fast enough to measure real-time speech, a technique known as *real-time MRI* (rtMRI). Researchers using rtMRI have achieved reasonably good-quality images at speeds approaching standard video (in a single plane), and methods for semi-automatic segmentation of these real-time images (Proctor *et al.*, 2010).

For those not willing to wait for improvements in rtMRI, it is also currently possible, though very tedious, to make a full volumetric MRI film of speech using iterated speech. In this technique, a participant is asked to repeat the same token in the same way over and over again, with slices taken in different locations during each repetition. The resulting images can then be used to construct a composite video showing a single instance of the utterance.

Despite its high cost and ongoing technical development, MRI is, and will remain for the foreseeable future, a valuable technology for articulatory phonetics research.

Exercises

Sufficient jargon

Define the following terms: context-sensitive models (look-ahead models), context-invariant models, pre-planned motor programs, motor primitives, motor programs, motor plans, articulatory gestures, mechanical perturbation, motor program level, motor system level, extrinsic timing, intrinsic timing, phase alignment, anatomically coupled, lingual-lingual sounds, liquids, light l [l], dark l [ɫ], rhotics, lingual ingressive, rarefy, lingual-labial, labialization, labiovelarization, oral-laryngeal, gutturals, glottalized resonants, coarticulation, temporal overlap, harmony, articulatory conflict, deletion, transition, compromise, end-state comfort, tomography, volumetric, computed tomography (CT), real-time MRI (rtMRI).

Short-answer questions

1   Describe two different mechanisms that could create the negative pressure behind the lips for a bilabial click.
2   It is usually the case that one is lying down for an MRI image. Describe two ways this position could affect the articulators in the image.
3   For each of the following measurement techniques, find and cite one speech research paper in which these techniques are used: CT and MRI. Follow the reference formatting used in the references section at the end of each chapter.

Practical assignment

For each chapter, this text has online assignments (at www.wiley.com/go/articulatoryphonetics) that either provide research data for analysis, or practical tools for understanding vocal tract anatomy. For Chapter 11, you will look at a set of MRI images of the same speaker producing different classes of sounds. You will measure differences between these groups and come to conclusions about the causes of those different patterns of articulation. The assignment and the related assignment images can be found in the online materials for this textbook under *Chapter 11*.

References

Abbs, J. H., and Gracco, V. L. (1984). Control of complex motor gestures: orofacial muscle responses to load perturbations of lip during speech. *Journal of Neurophysiology, 51*, 705–23.

Allott, R. (2003). Outline of a motor theory of natural language. *Cognitive Systems*, *6*, 93–101.

Bird, S., Caldecott, M., Campbell, F., Gick, B., and Shaw, P. (2008). Oral-laryngeal timing in glottalised resonants. *Journal of Phonetics*, *36*, 492–507.

Browman, C. P. and Goldstein, L. M. (1992). Articulatory phonology: an overview. *Phonetica*, *49*, 155–180.

Dell, G. S. (1986). A spreading-activation theory of retrieval in sentence production. *Psychological Review*, *93*, 283–321.

Derrick, D. (2011). Kinematic variations in flaps, taps and rhotics in English. PhD thesis. University of British Columbia.

Farnetani, E. and Recasens, D. (2010). Coarticulation and connected speech processes. In W. J. Hardcastle, J. Laver, and F. E. Gibbon (eds), *The Handbook of Phonetic Sciences* (2nd edition), Chichester, UK: Wiley-Blackwell, 316–352.

Fowler, C. A. (1980). Coarticulation and theories of extrinsic timing. *Journal of Phonetics*, *8*, 113–133.

Gafos, A. (1999). *The Articulatory Basis of Locality in Phonology*. New York: Garland.

Gick, B. and Wilson, I. (2006). Excrescent schwa and vowel laxing: cross-linguistic responses to conflicting articulatory targets. In L. Goldstein, D. H. Whalen, and C. T. Best (eds), *Laboratory Phonology 8*, Berlin: Mouton de Gruyter, 635–659.

Green, J. R., Moore, C. A., Higashikawa, M., and Steeve, R. W. (2000). The physiologic development of speech motor control: lip and jaw coordination. *Journal of Speech, Language, and Hearing Research*, *43*, 239–255.

Guenther, F. H. (1994). A neural network model of speech acquisition and motor equivalent speech production. *Biological Cybernetics*, *72*, 43–53.

Guenther, F. H. (2006). Cortical interactions underlying the production of speech sounds. *Journal of Communication Disorders*, *39*, 350–365.

Health Physics Society (2010). Radiation exposure from medical diagnostic imaging procedures: Health Physics Society factsheet (http://www.hps.org/documents/meddiagimaging.pdf)

Henke, W. (1966). Dynamic articulatory model of speech production using computer simulation. PhD thesis. MIT Massachusetts Institute of Technology.

Keele, S. W. (1968). Movement control in skilled motor performance. *Psychological Bulletin*, *70*, 387–403.

Keele, S. W. (1981). Behavioral analysis of movement. In V. Brooks (ed.), *Handbook of Physiology: Sec. 1: The nervous system, Vol. 2: Motor Control, Pt. 2*, Baltimore, MD: American Physiological Society, 1391–1414.

Kelso, J. A., Saltzman, E. L., and Tuller, B. (1986). The dynamical perspective on speech production: data and theory. *Journal of Phonetics*, *14*, 29–59.

Kelso, J. A. S., Tuller, B., Vatikiotis-Bateson, E., and Fowler, C. A. (1984). Functionally specific articulatory cooperation following jaw perturbations during speech: evidence for coordinative structures. *Journal of Experimental Psychology: Human Perception and Performance*, *10*, 812–832.

Lauterbur, P. C. (1973). Image formation by induced local interactions: examples of employing nuclear magnetic resonance. *Nature*, *242*(5394), 190–191.

Levelt, W. J. M. (1989). *Speaking*. Cambridge, MA: MIT Press.

Mielke, J., Baker, A., and Archangeli, D. (2010). Variability and homogeneity in American English /r/ allophony and /s/ retraction, in C. Fougeron, B. Kühnert,

M. d'Imperio, and N. Vallée (eds), *Laboratory Phonology 10 (Phonology and Phonetics 4–4)*. Berlin: de Gruyter Mouton, 699–730.

Miller, A. (2011). A kinematic study of mangetti dune !xung clicks. Unpublished manuscript. Ohio State University.

Miller, A. L., Brugman, H., Sands, B., Namaseb, L., Exter, M., and Collins, C. (2009). *Differences* in airstream and posterior place of articulation among N | uu clicks. *Journal of the International Phonetic Association, 39*, 129–161.

Miller, A. L. and Finch, K. B. (2011). Corrected high-frame rate anchored ultrasound with software alignment. *Journal of Speech, Language, and Hearing Research, 54*, 471–486.

Miller, J. (1996, June). 5 Element Codes Part 1. Ninjutsu – Ura & Omote. (http://www.ninjutsu.co.uk/uraomote/96/june.html#elem)

Munhall, K. G., Kawato, M., and Vatikiotis-Bateson, E. (2000). Coarticulation and physical models of speech production. In M. B. Broe and J. B. Pierrehumbert (eds), *Papers in Laboratory Phonology V: Acquisition and the Lexicon*. Cambridge, UK: Cambridge University Press, 9–28.

Mussa-Ivaldi, F. A., and Bizzi, E. (2000). Motor learning through the combination of primitives. *Philosophical Transactions of the Royal Society B: Biological Sciences, 355*(1404), 1755–1769.

Oak Ridge National Laboratory (2010). Table A.2. Comparison and description of various dose levels. (http://www.ornl.gov/sci/env_rpt/aser95/tb-a-2.pdf).

Öhman, S. (1967). Numerical model of coarticulation. *Journal of the Acoustical Society of America, 41*, 310–320.

Proctor, M. I., Bone, D., Katsamanis, N., and Narayanan, S. (2010). Rapid semi-automatic segmentation of real-time magnetic resonance images for parametric vocal tract analysis. In *Proceedings of Interspeech 2010*, 1576–1579.

Rosenbaum, D. A. and Jorgensen, M. J. (1992). Planning macroscopic aspects of manual control. *Human Movement Science, 11*, 61–69.

Ruhlen, M. (1975). *A Guide to the Languages of the World*. Stanford, CA: Stanford University.

Saltzman, E. and Byrd, D. (2000). Task-dynamics of gestural timing: phase windows and multifrequency rhythms. *Human Movement Science, 19*, 499–526.

Schmidt, R. A. (1975). A schema theory of discrete motor skill learning. *Psychological Review, 82*, 225–260.

Semjen, A. (1992). Plan decoding and response timing during execution of movement sequences. *Acta Psychologica, 79*, 255–273.

Shaffer, L. H. (1992). Motor programming and control. In G. E. Stelmach and J. Requin (eds), *Tutorials in Motor Behavior II*. Amsterdam: North-Holland, 181–194.

Sproat, R., and Fujimura, O. (1993). Allophonic variation in English /l/ and its implications for phonetic implementation. *Journal of Phonetics, 21*, 291–311.

Summers, J. J. and Anson, J. G. (2009). Current status of the motor program: revisited. *Human Movement Science, 28*, 566–577.

Throughman, K. A. and Shadmehr, R. (2000). Learning of action through adaptive combination of motor primitives. *Nature, 407*, 742–747.

Tiede, M. K., Boyce, S. E., Holland, C. K., and Choe, K. A. (2004). A new taxonomy of American English /r/ using MRI and ultrasound. *Journal of the Acoustical Society of America, 115*, 2633.

Turvey, M. T., Fitch, H. L., and Tuller, B. (1982). The Bernstein perspective: I. The problems of degrees of freedom and context-conditioned variability. In J. A. S. Kelso (ed.), *Human Motor Behavior: An Introduction*. Hillsdale, NJ: Lawrence Erlbaum Associates, 239–252.

West, P. (1999). Perception of distributed coarticulatory properties of English /l/ and /ɹ/. *Journal of Phonetics*, 27, 405–426.

Whalen, D. H. (1990). Coarticulation is largely planned. *Journal of Phonetics*, 18, 3–35.

Zhou, X., Espy-Wilson, C. Y., Boyce, S., Tiede, M., Holland, C., and Choe, A. (2008). A magnetic resonance imaging-based articulatory and acoustic study of "retroflex" and "bunched" American English /r/. *Journal of the Acoustical Society of America*, 123, 4466–4481.

Abbreviations Used in this Book

Abbreviation	Full name
ABD	Anterior belly of the digastric muscle
ATP	Adenosine triphosphate
ATR	Advanced tongue root
C1–C8	Cervical nerves
CN V	Trigeminal nerve
CN VII	Facial nerve
CN IX	Glossopharyngeal nerve
CN X	Vagus nerve
CN XI	Accessory nerve
CN XII	Hypoglossal nerve
CNS	Central nervous system
CT	Cricothyroid muscle
CT	Computed tomography
EEG	Electroencephalography
EGG	Electroglottography
EI	External intercostal muscles
EMA	Electromagnetic articulometer
EMG	Electromyography
EO	External oblique muscle
EPG	Electropalatography
ERPs	Event-related potentials
ERV	Expiratory reserve volume
f_0	Fundamental frequency

(Continued)

Articulatory Phonetics, First Edition. Bryan Gick, Ian Wilson, and Donald Derrick.
© 2013 Bryan Gick, Ian Wilson, and Donald Derrick. Published 2013 by Blackwell Publishing Ltd.

Abbreviation	Full name
fMRI	Functional Magnetic Resonance Imaging
FRC	Functional residual capacity
GG	Genioglossus muscle
GGa	Anterior genioglossus muscle
GGm	Middle genioglossus muscle
GGp	Posterior genioglossus muscle
HG	Hyoglossus muscle
IA	Interarytenoid muscle
IAo	Oblique interarytenoid muscle
IAt	Transverse interarytenoid muscle
IC	Inspiratory capacity
II	Internal intercostal muscle
III	Interchondral parts of the internal intercostal muscles
IL	Inferior longitudinal muscle
IO	Internal oblique muscle
IRV	Inspiratory reserve volume
L1–L5	Lumbar nerves
lats	Latissimus dorsi
LCA	Lateral cricoarytenoid muscle
LLS	Levator labii superioris
LLSAN	Levator labii superioris alaeque nasi
MEG	Magnetoencephalography
MRI	Magnetic resonance imaging
OO	Orbicularis oris muscle
OOi	Inferior part of the orbicularis oris muscle
OOm	Marginal part of the orbicularis oris muscle
OOp	Peripheral part of the orbicularis oris muscle
OOs	Superior part of the orbicularis oris muscle
OPI	Oropharyngeal isthmus
PBD	Posterior belly of the digastric muscle
PCA	Posterior cricoarytenoid muscle
PET	Positron emission tomography
PG	Palatoglossus
PGG	Transillumination/photoglottography
P_{IO}	Intra-oral air pressure
PNS	Peripheral nervous system
P_{SG}	Subglottal air pressure
RA	Rectus abdominis muscle
RTR	Retracted tongue root
RV	Residual volume
SCM	Sternocleidomastoid muscle
SG	Styloglossus muscle
SL	Superior longitudinal muscle
sMRI	Structural magnetic resonance imaging
SQUIDs	Superconducting quantum interference devices

Abbreviation	Full name
T1–T12	Thoracic nerves
TVA	Transversus abdominis
TA	Thyroarytenoid muscle
TLC	Total lung capacity
TMJ	Temporomandibular joint
TMS	Transcranial magnetic stimulation
TV	Tidal volume
VC	Vital capacity
VPI	Velopharyngeal insufficiency
VPP	Velopharyngeal port
ΔP	Delta (change in) air pressure

Muscles with Innervation, Origin, and Insertion

Articulatory Phonetics, First Edition. Bryan Gick, Ian Wilson, and Donald Derrick.
© 2013 Bryan Gick, Ian Wilson, and Donald Derrick. Published 2013 by Blackwell
Publishing Ltd.

Muscle	Abbreviation	Origin	Insertion	Innervation	Location	Main function
External intercostal	EI	Ribs 1–11	Ribs 2–12	C1–C12	Ribs	Inspiration
Interchondral part of the internal intercostal	III	Ribs 1–11	Ribs 2–12	C1–C12	Ribs	Inspiration
Internal intercostal (interosseous part)	II	Ribs 1–11	Ribs 2–12	C1–C12	Ribs	Expiration
Levator costalis		C7–T12 vertebrae	Ribs	C8–T11	Ribs	Inspiration
Serratus posterior superior		C7–T3 vertebrae	Ribs 2–5	C2–C5	Ribs	Inspiration
Serratus posterior inferior		T11–L3 vertebrae	T9–12	T11–L3	Ribs	Expiration
Sternocleidomastoid	SCM	Manubrium of sternum – to clavicle	Clavicle – to mastoid process	Accessory nerve (CN XI)	Neck	Tilts/rotates head, accessory in forced inspiration
Latissimus dorsi	lats	T6–T12 vertebrae	Humerus	C6–C8	Back	Expiration (forced)
Diaphragm		Upper lumbar vertebrae	Floor of the thoracic cavity	Phrenic nerve <- C3–C5	Abdomen	Inspiration
External obliques	EO	Lower 8 ribs just under rectus abdominis	Abdominal ligaments	T5–T12	Abdomen (2nd layer)	Expiration
Internal obliques	IO	Top of pelvic bone	Inguinal area	T7–L1	Abdomen (3rd layer)	Expiration

Muscle	Abbr.	Origin	Insertion	Innervation	Region	Action
Rectus abdominis	RA	Top of pelvic bone	Cartilages of ribs 5–7, xiphoid process	T6/7–T12	Abdomen (superficial)	Expiration
Transversus Abdominis	TVA	Crest of the pelvis and lower rib cage	Linea alba	T6/7–L1	Abdomen (deep)	Expiration
Cricothyroid	CT	Anterior and lateral part, cricoid cartilage	Inferior horn, thyroid cartilage	External laryngeal branch <- vagus nerve (CN X)	Larynx	Rotates thyroid against cricoid, stretching thyroarytenoid
Interarytenoid, Oblique (oblique interarytenoid)	IAo	Arytenoid cartilage	Arytenoid cartilage	Recurrent laryngeal branch <- vagus nerve (CN X)	Larynx	Adducts arytenoid cartilages, vocal folds
Interarytenoid, Transverse (transverse interarytenoid)	IAt	Arytenoid cartilage	Arytenoid cartilage	Recurrent laryngeal branch <- vagus nerve (CN X)	Larynx	Adducts arytenoid cartilages, vocal folds
Lateral Cricoarytenoid	LCA	Lateral part, cricoid cartilage	Arytenoid cartilage (muscular process)	Recurrent laryngeal branch <- vagus nerve (CN X)	Larynx	Adducts vocal folds, provides medial compression

(Continued)

Muscle	Abbreviation	Origin	Insertion	Innervation	Location	Main function
Posterior cricoarytenoid	PCA	Posterior part, cricoid cartilage	Arytenoid cartilage (muscular process)	Recurrent laryngeal branch <- vagus nerve (CN X)	Larynx	Abducts vocal folds
Thyroarytenoid	TA	Thyroid cartilage	Arytenoid cartilage (vocal process)	Recurrent laryngeal branch <- vagus nerve (CN X)	Larynx	Decreases fundamental frequency
Omohyoid		Upper border of scapula	Hyoid bone	C1–C3	Infrahyoid	Depresses hyoid bone
Sternohyoid		Manubrium of sternum	Hyoid bone	C1–C3	Infrahyoid	Depresses hyoid bone
Sternothyroid		Manubrium of the sternum	Hyoid bone	C1–C3	Infrahyoid	Depresses hyoid bone
Thyrohyoid		Thyroid cartilage	Hyoid bone	C1–C3	Infrahyoid	Depresses hyoid bone, raises larynx
Anterior belly of the digastric	ABD	Inner side, lower border of the jaw	Intermediate tendon, hyoid bone	Trigeminal (CN V)	Suprahyoid	Lowers jaw, raises hyoid
Posterior belly of the digastric	PBD	Mastoid process	Intermediate tendon, hyoid bone	Facial nerve (CN VII)	Suprahyoid	Lowers jaw, raises hyoid

Muscle	Origin	Insertion	Nerve	Region	Function
Stylohyoid	Styloid process	Greater horn, hyoid bone	Facial nerve (CN VII)	Suprahyoid	Raises and retracts hyoid
Inferior pharyngeal constrictor	Cricoid and thyroid cartilage	Pharyngeal raphe	Pharyngeal plexus <- vagus nerve (CN X)	Pharynx	Retracts larynx
Middle pharyngeal constrictor	Hyoid bone	Pharyngeal raphe	Pharyngeal plexus <- vagus nerve (CN X)	Pharynx	Retracts hyoid and tongue
Superior pharyngeal constrictor	Sphenoid bone, ligament linking sphenoid to lower jaw	Pharyngeal raphe	Pharyngeal plexus <- vagus nerve (CN X)	Pharynx	Helps close VPP
Salpingopharyngeus	Eustachian tube	Palatopharyngeus muscle	Pharyngeal plexus <- vagus nerve (CN X)	Pharynx	Raises larynx
Palatopharyngeus	Soft and hard palate	Thyroid cartilage	Vagus nerve (CN X) and accessory nerve (CN XI)	Pharynx	Raises larynx, lowers velum
Stylopharyngeus	Styloid process	Thyroid cartilage	Glossopharyngeal nerve (CN IX)	Pharynx	Elevates larynx, pulls pharynx walls laterally
Levator palati	Temporal bone and Eustachian tube	Soft palate	Vagus nerve (CN X)	Velum	Elevates soft palate
Musculus uvulae	Hard palate	Soft palate	Pharyngeal plexus <- Vagus nerve (CN X)	Velum	Stiffens velum

(Continued)

Muscle	Abbreviation	Origin	Insertion	Innervation	Location	Main function
Tensor palati		Sphenoid bone	Soft palate	Mandibular nerve <- trigeminal nerve (CN V)	Velum	Tenses soft palate
Masseter		Zygomatic arch	Ramus and angle of the mandible (external)	Mandibular nerve <- trigeminal nerve (CN V)	Jaw	Elevates mandible
Temporalis		Parietal bone	Coronoid process	Mandibular nerve <- trigeminal nerve (CN V)	Jaw	Elevates and retracts mandible
Pterygoid, lateral (lateral pterygoid)		Superior head: sphenoid bone. Inferior head: maxilla	Condyle of mandible	Mandibular nerve <- trigeminal nerve (CN V)	Jaw	Moves jaw side-to-side, protrudes jaw
Pterygoid, medial (medial pterygoid)		Deep head: sphenoid bone. Superficial head: palatine bone and maxilla	Ramus and angle of the mandible (internal)	Mandibular nerve <- trigeminal nerve (CN V)	Jaw	Elevates mandible
Geniohyoid		Mental spine of the mandible (mental symphysis)	Hyoid bone	Hypoglossal nerve (CN XII)	Jaw	Pulls hyoid up and forward, depresses jaw

Muscle	Abbr.	Origin	Insertion	Innervation	Type	Action
Genioglossus, anterior (anterior genioglossus)	GGa	Mental spine of the mandible (mental symphysis)	Body of tongue near tip	Hypoglossal nerve (CN XII)	Extrinsic tongue	Lowers and retracts tongue tip
Genioglossus, medial (medial genioglossus)	GGm	Mental spine of the mandible (mental symphysis)	Body of tongue near dorsum	Hypoglossal nerve (CN XII)	Extrinsic tongue	Lowers tongue body and aids in medial grooving
Genioglossus, posterior (posterior genioglossus)	GGp	Mental spine of the mandible (mental symphysis)	Body of tongue near root	Hypoglossal nerve (CN XII)	Extrinsic tongue	Advances tongue root
Hyoglossus	HG	Hyoid	Side of tongue, extending to tongue tip	Hypoglossal nerve (CN XII)	Extrinsic tongue	Depresses tongue
Mylohyoid		Mylohyoid line	Median raphe	Trigeminal nerve (CN V)	Extrinsic tongue	Elevates floor of the tongue, depresses mandible, raises hyoid
Palatoglossus	PG	Palatine aponeurosis	Tongue body	Vagus nerve (CN X)	Extrinsic tongue	Narrows OPI, pulls palate and tongue toward each other

(Continued)

Muscle	Abbreviation	Origin	Insertion	Innervation	Location	Main function
Styloglossus	SG	Styloid process	Tongue body and tip	Hypoglossal nerve (CN XII)	Extrinsic tongue	Retracts tongue, aids in tongue grooving
Inferior longitudinal	IL	Tongue root	Tongue tip	Hypoglossal nerve (CN XII)	Intrinsic tongue	Lower tongue tip/ body
Superior longitudinal	SL	Close to epiglottis, from lingual septum	Edges of the tongue	Hypoglossal nerve (CN XII)	Intrinsic tongue	Lifts and curls tongue tip
Transversus		Lingual septum	Sides of the tongue	Hypoglossal nerve (CN XII)	Intrinsic tongue	Compresses tongue medially
Verticalis		Superior surface border of the tongue	Inferior surface border of tongue	Hypoglossal nerve (CN XII)	Intrinsic tongue	Flattens and widens tongue
Buccinator		Maxilla and mandible	Orbicularis oris	Facial nerve (CN VII)	Face	Compresses cheeks against teeth
Depressor anguli oris		Mandible	Bottom of mouth	Facial nerve (CN VII)	Face	Depresses angle of mouth
Depressor labii inferioris		Oblique line of mandible	Lower lip and orbicularis oris	Facial nerve (CN VII)	Face	Depresses lower lip
Levator anguli oris		Maxilla	Top of mouth	Facial nerve (CN VII)	Face	Smile (sincere)
Levator labii superioris alaeque nasi	LLSAN	Maxilla	Nostril and upper lip	Facial nerve (CN VII)	Face	Elevates upper lip and wing of nose

Muscle	Abbreviation	Origin	Insertion	Innervation	Region	Action
Levator labii superioris	LLS	Lower orbit of the eyes	Upper lip	Facial nerve (CN VII)	Face	Elevates upper lip
Orbicularis oris, marginal superior	OOms	Maxilla and mandible	Skin around the lips	Facial nerve (CN VII)	Face	Purses lips
Orbicularis oris, peripheral superior	OOps	Maxilla and mandible	Skin around the lips	Facial nerve (CN VII)	Face	Protrudes lips
Orbicularis oris, marginal inferior	OOmi	Maxilla and mandible	Skin around the lips	Facial nerve (CN VII)	Face	Purses lips, pulls lower lip back for labiodentals
Orbicularis oris, peripheral inferior	OOpi	Maxilla and mandible	Skin around the lips	Facial nerve (CN VII)	Face	Protrudes lips, pulls lower lip back for labiodentals
Risorius		Near masseter muscle	Sides of mouth	Facial nerve (CN VII)	Face	Draws back angle of mouth (insincere smile)
Zygomaticus minor		Zygomatic bone	Upper lip	Facial nerve (CN VII)	Face	Elevates upper lip
Zygomaticus major		Zygomatic bone	Top of mouth	Facial nerve (CN VII)	Face	Draws angle of mouth upward and laterally (sincere smile)

Index

abduct, 75
actin, 38–40
action potential, 18–19, 38, 40–1
adduct, 75, 77
adenoid pad, 130, 134
Adenosine triphosphate (ATP), 40
advanced tongue root (ATR), 159
aero-tactile feedback, 5
agonist, 9
air pressure transducer, 67
airflow meter (pneumotachograph), 12,
    50, 66–7, 128
alaryngeal phonation, 107
alveoli, 51, 53
amygdalae, 26–7
anatomically coupled, 210, 218–19
angle, 146–7, 149, 151
angular gyrus, 22–3
anions, 18
ankyloglossia (tongue-tie), 178
antagonist, 9, 156, 177, 194
anterior, 8
anterior belly of the digastric (ABD),
    103–4, 151–2, 159
anterior genioglossus (GGa) muscle,
    153, 156, 158, 160, 170

aperiodic, 82
apical, 177
approximants, 167, 171–3, 179–80,
    196, 197, 211–2, 216
arcuate fasciculus, 23
articular facets, 54
articulations, 3
articulator disk, 147, 151
articulatory conflict, 217, 219–21
articulatory gestures, 208, 210, 220
aryepiglottic folds, 74, 77, 79, 90,
    109–12, 115, 120, 131, 138, 174,
    180
aryepiglottic muscles, 77, 111
aryepiglottic trill, 112
arytenoid cartilage, 72, 75, 77, 88,
    108–9
atlas, 53–4
atmospheric pressure, 48
attach phase, 40
audition, 4–5, 43
auditory cortex, 22–3
auditory feedback, 4–5, 157
axis, 53–4
axon, 16–19
axon terminal, 16–17

Articulatory Phonetics, First Edition. Bryan Gick, Ian Wilson, and Donald Derrick.
© 2013 Bryan Gick, Ian Wilson, and Donald Derrick. Published 2013 by Blackwell
Publishing Ltd.